THE POWER OF POSITIVE
CONFRONTATION

Books authored by Barbara Pachter

*When the Little Things Count . . . and They Always Count:
601 Essential Things Everyone in Business Needs to Know*

Books co-authored by Barbara Pachter

The Prentice Hall Complete Business Etiquette Handbook

Business Etiquette

*Minding Your Business Manners: Etiquette Tips for Presenting
Yourself Professionally in Every Business Situation*

*Climbing the Corporate Ladder:
What You Need to Know and Do to Be a Promotable Person*

THE POWER OF
POSITIVE
CONFRONTATION

The Skills You Need to Know to Handle
Conflicts at Work, at Home, and in Life

BARBARA PACHTER
with SUSAN MAGEE

MARLOWE & COMPANY • NEW YORK

Published by
Marlowe & Company
An Imprint of Avalon Publishing Group
161 William Street, 16th Floor
New York, NY 10038

The Power of Positive Confrontation: The Skills You Need to Know to Handle
Conflicts at Work, Home, and in Life
Copyright © 2000 by Barbara Pachter and Susan Magee

Don't Attack'em, WAC'em™ is a trademark of Pachter & Associates.

Library of Congress Catalog Card Number: 99-040096

cloth ISBN: 1-56924-679-3
paperback ISBN: 1-56924-608-4

Manufactured in the United States of America
Designed by Pauline Neuwirth, Neuwirth & Associates. Inc.
Distributed by Publishers Group West

This book is dedicated to the memory of my mother, Esther Pachter.

CONTENTS

Contents

Contents

ACKNOWLEDGMENTS

First and foremost I would like to thank my seminar participants and their employers, my clients. The participants worked hard. Their ideas, input, and stories were invaluable to this project. We learned together.

With gratitude and grateful acknowledgement, I would like also to thank the following people for their help and support: Ellen Greene, my agent, for her support, encouragement, and knowledge.

Matthew Lore, the world's most helpful editor, for the tremendous energy and talent he poured into this book. He is a true pleasure to work with.

Susan Magee—who always finds the right words.

Joyce Hoff, my hardworking, dedicated and loyal associate.

Joe Roy, a marketing and public relations whiz.

Dr. Bernard Hershenberg, a psychologist whose guidance has been invaluable.

And last but never least, my family. My son, Jacob, who is the light of my life. Martin Heiligman a loving and helpful partner. My father Victor Pachter and my sisters, Marsha Morrow and Linda Steinguard. Without their support this book may never have happened.

PREFACE

For more than 12 years I've been a business communications trainer specializing in communication and etiquette skills. Practically since the day I started, I've had participants make comments during my seminars, or come up to me at breaks or after workshop sessions, to share with me their experiences with a person with whom they were having difficulty. My seminar participants have come from all walks of life, and they have come from all levels of the corporate food chain—from senior VPs at Fortune 500 companies to administrative assistants in accounting firms. Again and again, these people have expressed an urgent need to talk about the conflicts and difficult situations in their lives, and asked for my help.

I can't tell you how often I've heard frustrations like these:

"My boss isn't fair . . . "

"My employees take advantage . . . "

"My next door neighbor is so inconsiderate . . . "

"My co-worker is driving me nuts . . . "

"I feel like a push-over . . . "

And after all of these stories, they would ask me the question: *"What can I do?"*

Some of the stories I've heard over the years have broken my heart. I've felt really bad for the people who sought me out, and at times I've even commiserated—I've been there myself. I think at one time or another we all have felt frustrated, tongue-tied, or fed up with someone else's behavior.

I listened with sympathy, but always, there was a part of me that wanted to reach out, give the person a shake, and say, "Why don't you do something about it?"

Over time, however, I made what I think is a significant discovery—*people don't say or do anything to the person bothering them mostly because they don't know what to say or do!*

I also noticed a negative communication pattern in many of the comments I've heard. Because people had difficulty talking to someone in an appropriate manner about a situation that was bothering them, they simply wouldn't talk with the other person. They'd complain about that person instead, to anyone who would give them a sympathetic ear, including me.

For some, this was the main reason they came to my seminar—to vent their emotions!

And yet, there were just as many people who, when faced with a bothersome situation, said or did something—only what they said or did, however well-intentioned, made the situation worse. They proudly told me their stories:

"I told him that if he wanted a bloody nose . . . " or

"I said, 'Who do you think you are, Miss High and Mighty!'" or

"I said, 'Gee, I'm so sorry to have to bother you with this . . . "

I cringed as I listened to many of these stories. I thought, "There's got to be a better way!" Many people believed that they were doing or saying the right thing, yet it was often clear to me, just hearing the stories, that they had not cleared things up with the other person. In fact, in most cases it sounded as though things had only gotten worse.

By not having the skills to confront another person in a positive way, the people I met often ended up making their world less pleasant and more stressful, both for themselves and for the other people in it—whether they intended to or not.

I soon realized that there was a tremendous need for people to learn how to express themselves effectively in difficult situations.

People need the skills to enable them to stand up for themselves. They need to learn how to confront positively instead of complaining or employing a host of other negative and self-destructive behaviors.

So I decided, once and for all, to meet that need.

This book is the result.

I strongly believe that knowing the skills of positive confrontation can make your life better. You will feel better about yourself. You will no longer behave like a wimp or a bully or use other bad behaviors you may have accidentally adopted along the way. You'll be able to deal with difficult people and situations directly and with confidence. No more "I wish I had said . . . " or "If only I had thought to . . ." or "It's no big deal . . . " (when you know it is a big deal). Best of all, positive confrontation will often lead to a positive resolution—rather than to more conflict.

I've shared with many of my seminar participants the stories I tell in this book—of confrontations good and bad, effective and not-so-effective. And I've taught them the strategies I teach here. They could not have been more enthusiastic about learning these skills. They have helped me fine-tune the ideas and the skills that are vital to a positive confrontation. Now almost every day I hear another success story about how a positive confrontation changed someone's life—or their relationship with another person—for the better.

I now have the pleasure of hearing people say:

"*I don't feel frustrated anymore . . .* " or

"*In the past I would have sulked or complained until the person got the hint, now I can just say something . . .* " or

"*Annoying things don't bother me as much because I know I can say something now . . .* "

If you're like most of us, you were never taught the skills in this book. They have already worked for thousands of people I have taught in my seminars and workshops. I believe they can work for you, too.

PART I

POSITIVE CONFRONTATION
What It Is and How It Can
Make Your Life Better

CHAPTER 1

CONFLICT, CONFLICT EVERYWHERE

Life is full of sticky situations, packed with difficult conversations, and loaded with confrontation. How do you handle these situations, conversations and confrontations? When someone's behavior is bothering you—be it a relative, co-worker or neighbor—what do you say to that person?

Maybe you don't say anything. If you don't, you're probably fed-up, worn-out, or just plain old sick and tired of not being able to tell someone close—or not-so-close—to you what's bothering you.

You're not alone if you feel this way.

Do you approach a problem with a friend or neighbor with good intentions but then "lose it"? Do you "clam up," "storm out," or just flat out "chicken out?"

Do you feel walked on, annoyed, bothered, taken advantage of, frustrated or upset by another person's behavior?

You guessed it! You're not alone if you have these feelings too. If you're reading this book, you may be like the men and women from all types of professions and from all walks of life that I've taught or have spoken with over the last ten years. These people feel the same way you do. Like you, they're tired of not being able to tell someone when something is bothering them. They're tired of avoiding difficult conversations. No one sets out in life to become a "clam," a "door slammer," or a "big chicken." But people adopt these negative behaviors anyway, all the time, and then they feel bad about themselves because of it.

Many people are honest enough with themselves to know they're not comfortable with confronting others. But they're stuck. What can they do about it?

Again, if you're like most of the people I've met and taught over the last decade, you probably could use some help in answering this question. These are smart, successful, well-adjusted, sometimes very highly paid, and well-liked people — and they don't know the answer either.

You may not be sure if you're having positive confrontations or not. Maybe you're simply curious about exactly what "positive confrontation" means. What, you may be wondering, is the power that can be harnessed through them? How can you make your life better?

Are You Holding Yourself Back?

Whether or not you know, you may have a way of handling, or not handling, conflict that has been holding you back. From what? From getting ahead at work. From having more satisfying relationships with friends and loved ones. From feeling empowered in a world that can often leave you feeling powerless.

You will see very clearly throughout this book, exactly how positive confrontation can improve your relationships, your self-esteem, your sense of well being, and even your career. It can empower you in your relationships with others. If you adopt and practice the skills I talk about in this book, it *will* empower you in dealing with others. Though I can't make any promises or give you any guarantees, I can tell you this: I get e-mails, faxes, letters, phone calls, and people who come up to me after my seminars — and they all say the same thing. They tell me that my approach to handling confrontation works for them.

That's why I'm certain it can work for you too.

The Big and Small Picture of Conflict

What exactly are the conflicts and the confrontations I'm address-ing here? Let's look at the big picture of conflict first. The world isn't all bad, but reading the paper or watching the evening news can sometimes make you worry. There are wars—cold and hot. There are racial tensions, crime, politicians taking pot shots, trouble in the schools. It's understandable that at times we feel drained of power or even just drained.

This book is not about whole-world global conflict. I can't help the entire world deal positively with conflict. I wish I could.

This book is about the smaller picture of conflict. It's smaller but still important—really, really important. The smaller picture is your life. It's mine. It's all of us as we go throughout our day and interact with others.

Difficult Communication . . . Difficult Conversation

In the bigger picture of conflict heads of state have trouble talk-ing to each other, getting their points across, being understood. This happens in the smaller picture too; except it happens with the per-son in the next cube, your roommate, your brother-in-law, or the teller at your bank.

Sometimes, in this smaller picture that is day-to-day living, we have a hard time talking to each other. We have a hard time express-ing ourselves appropriately to others. We don't know what to say. We don't know how the other person will react if we tell him or her how we really feel. There are many other reasons why we feel uncom-fortable having difficult conversations and dealing with conflict. Communicating successfully with others in uncomfortable situa-tions is especially difficult. We'll talk about why this is true in more detail in Chapter 3.

Let's concentrate for the moment on the effect of not being able to communicate successfully. The effect shows sometimes in little ways and sometimes in bigger ways. Look at road rage, cubicle clash-es, airline annoyance, roommate rumbles, boss baloney, friends in fights, and supermarket strife. Half the people you pass on a crowded street seem angry. The other half feels—at least some of the time—powerless. A silent frustration can take root in us. It grows. It keeps on growing.

It's the Same 12 Conflicts—Over and Over Again

Look at the list that shows some of the most common conflicts that people have. During each seminar I give, I ask the participants to write on an index card a situation with another person that is bothering them. After conducting hundreds of seminars it appears that the same conflicts happen over and over. These aren't the only conflict areas, but they are the most common ones.

TWELVE KINDS OF BEHAVIORS THAT DRIVE US NUTS:

1. **Space Spongers.** These are people who play their music too loud, leave messes for others to clean up, neighbors who let dogs in our yard, or co-workers who don't respect our property.

2. **Telephone Traitors.** When you deal with this person, you might have complaints like these: "I have to do all the calling." "She never calls me back." "He only calls when he wants something." "She leaves ten-minute messages on my voice mail."

3. **Bad Borrowers.** They return your car with no gas, CDs with scratches, or your office supplies go missing. And money—it doesn't get paid back.

4. **Constant Complainers.** Everyone knows one—the person who always has a problem or gripe that never gets resolved.

5. **Interloping Interrupters.** People don't like to be interrupted or not to be given an opportunity to join equally in a conversation.

6. **Callous Commenters.** Among other things, this can be the neighbor who makes nasty comments or the person

telling racist or sexist jokes. You don't like what this person says.

7. **Work Welchers.** Some people just don't do their fair share whether at home, work, or on the volunteer committee.

8. **Favoritism Frustration.** "What about me?" Your boss gives his pals the best projects or your mother-in-law gives better presents to her daughter's kids.

9. **Holiday Hogs.** Your spouse always wants to spend the holidays with his or her family. One of you wants to go to Hawaii for vacation; the other wants to hike the Appalachian trail.

10. **Request Refusers.** You ask your spouse to be on time for dinner. Your co-worker knows you need the report by 2 P.M. but doesn't deliver; your client will not give the tax information you've asked for. These are people who say they will grant your request but don't.

11. **Atrocious Askers.** You're asked to do something by your friend, boss, or loved one that you don't want to do or don't agree with.

12. **Interloping Loved Ones.** Some people want to tell you what they think—even if you don't want to hear it. Parents believe that their opinion/actions should be followed. Grandparents spoil the kids or don't listen to instructions from mom and dad.

These examples show us how ordinary, routine, and common human interactions and relationship issues become problems. Too often, what should be, and can be, easily resolved conflicts get messy, complicated and frustrating. You end up in a confrontation that turns aggressive or you don't have a confrontation at all. The problem gets ignored.

Your co-worker talks too loud and it's driving you crazy. A man steals your parking space at the mall. Your sister-in-law makes a comment you find offensive. Your boss criticizes you but not your other teammates . . . These may be run-of-the-mill communications problems—but they come up again and again for people everywhere, all the time. These are the behaviors in others that we too often ignore, overlook or overact to for a simple reason: *We don't know what else to do.*

People think not having a confrontation is easier than having a confrontation. It's not. It's just that it's not easy to know what to say or how to say it—in a way that's both Polite and Powerful—if no one ever taught you.

So what I'm talking about are the ordinary conflicts that arise all the time, for everyone—at work, at home, in line at the bank, at the dry cleaner's, with your neighbors, your in-laws, or your kid's teacher. Difficult communication affects all areas of your life. I will use examples throughout this book that illustrate conflicts at work, at home, and just about everywhere else. The names and faces change. The details vary. All of the examples I use here and throughout this book are real. They've been told to me by participants of my workshops or come directly from my own experience. I do protect people's privacy, but I don't have to make anything up. I have more examples told to me by real people than I could ever use, proving to me again and again how badly people need the skills I talk about in this book.

The Communication Problem Is the Same . . .

The faces and unpleasant situations that I hear about may change, but the underlying communication problem is often the same: *We have a hard time talking to each other.* If we can't talk to each other constructively, we can't have positive confrontations and we can't resolve problems. The effect of living without conflict resolution is that we don't feel good about the other person or ourselves. The effect can often be cumulative. It can sneak up on you, this feeling of powerlessness or anger. One difficult conversation you don't have leads to another you don't have. One difficult conversation that ends in shouting leads to another that ends in shouting. You feel taken advantage of, sick and tired, or mad. Or maybe you feel a little out of control. Feeling powerless, mad, or out of control is not a fun or healthy way to go through life.

The problem we have with successfully resolving many kinds of day-to-day difficulties is the same and so is the solution—which you will learn about in this book. You can use this solution if you have a hard time speaking up or if you speak up too harshly, quickly, or aggressively. In Parts II and III of this book, I present the solution as a series of communication skills and techniques for communication that you can easily learn and adopt.

It's up to you to choose to use the skills and techniques to positively resolve the conflicts you may have in your life. I hope you will choose to adopt them, to make them a part of the way you operate out there in the wide world. You'll be glad if you do because these are life enhancing skills that in all likelihood no one ever taught you. This isn't saying anything bad about you if you don't know them. Very few people ever learn how to have difficult conversations comfortably. They don't teach you how to have a positive confrontation in high school or college. Fewer of us go on to figure it out on our own.

What I Can't Help You With

Before I go any further I must stop and clarify something—I'm not going to teach you skills to deal with extreme or abusive situations. Sadly, a woman approached me after a seminar and asked me how she should handle her husband who was physically abusive to her. Though my heart went out to her, I told her positive confrontation was not a solution for her current situation. She needed professional help and I urged her to get it.

I don't know what kind of conversation to tell you to have if you meet someone on a dark street who makes you nervous. You should probably avoid a conversation and just get yourself to a safe place. While I do address how to deal with rude strangers, for the most part, I'm talking about those day-to-day conflicts that crop up, drive you crazy, and never seem to get better—not dangerous situations. As you will discover by the end of this book, addressing rude strangers may not be the necessity you thought it was when you started reading this book. You'll see.

How I Can Help You Solve the Problem of Not Being Able to Talk to People in Difficult Situations:

I just told you what I can't do. Here's what I *can* do:

- Help you if you're having a hard time talking honestly to another person about something that's bothering you.
- Show you how to handle conflict better through "Polite and Powerful" behavior—you'll learn what it looks like, sounds like and acts like.
- Improve your life in what will seem like a small way at first. Then it will ripple. It will reach and spread, touching more and more corners of your world in a positive way.

"Oh, This Isn't for Me"

Oh, maybe it is! I don't care who you are, how much money you make, or don't make. I don't care about your gender, your race, or your religion or what your hobbies are. Everyone, absolutely everyone, has conflict in his or her life. At some point, eventually you will find yourself in a confrontation. The big question is this: How will you handle it?

Many people think, believe, even flat out insist that they're approaching conflict the right way. You might think that you're an assertive person, but you may be wrong. Look at the following, a letter to Ann Landers, and see for yourself. I hear this kind of story all the time.

> "Dear Ann Landers: A few years ago I was in the elevator of a New York department store, and the woman in front of me kept swinging her head from side to side. Her hair hit me in the face every time. I finally tapped her on the shoulder and said, `The next time your hair hits me in the face, you will not need a haircut for a very long time . . . ' Your readers might like to try my approach." (Sept. 18, 1998).

This woman believed that she was acting appropriately. She believed she was sticking up for herself, taking a stand, speaking up. But she blew it. She was not Polite. She was rude. She was not Powerful. She was aggressive. And to Ann Landers's credit, she didn't recommend this approach. I'll give the woman who wrote this letter the benefit of the doubt. She probably had no idea she was behaving inappropriately. I can give her the benefit of doubt because if I've learned anything over the last ten years it's that people really don't know *how* they're behaving in difficult situations and confrontations. They don't understand how they appear to others and what effect their behavior can have on other people.

This is why, even if you think you behave well during conflict, I challenge you to read this book. Then tell me if you're handling yourself and your difficult conversations in the best way possible!

It's Not Brain Surgery—But Brain Surgeons Need It Too

Okay, not everyone is so easily convinced that the power of positive confrontation is all that powerful. A man who attended one of my seminars sponsored by a professional association said, quite sarcastically, "Well this sure isn't brain surgery."

"No, of course not," I said. "But that doesn't mean it can't change your life in a positive and lasting way." Then a surprising thing happened. A woman in the audience stood up and said, "I am a brain surgeon and I didn't know any of this. I've been frustrated because my supervisor has been asking me to work weekends all the time. He's not asking anyone else. I'm here because I keep saying to myself, 'I have to say something, but I don't know what to say or how to say it.' "

Positive confrontation skills benefit everyone—brain surgeons have trouble handling conflict on the job and at home. So do sales people, homemakers, airline pilots, administrative assistants, husbands, PTA presidents, Cub Scout leaders, wives, and significant others.

These skills are applicable to every area of your life. Anyone who has a problem telling co-workers, friends, family and significant others their concerns—politely and powerfully—will benefit. It's also for any-one who has ever left a restaurant, movie theatre, or grocery store thinking, when that jerk butted ahead of me, "I should have said, 'Hey, jerk! Whaddya think you're doing?' "

And this book is for anyone who thinks that telling a jerk off is a positive action. It's for anyone that may think that sticking up for yourself means putting another person down. As you'll soon discov-er, what we think is acceptable or appropriate behavior may actual-ly be rude and unacceptable behavior.

So What Exactly Is Polite and Powerful Behavior?

Speaking of rude . . . Polite and Powerful *isn't*. Here's what it is:

It's a description for the way you handle yourself during a positive confrontation. It's more than saying "please" and "thank you."

It's more than having the guts to march up to someone and express yourself.

What Does *Assertiveness* Mean?

No one really knows. You can look it up in the dictionary, but I ask people all the time to describe the behavior that would charac-terize "assertive." Usually what I hear is silence.

Ask ten people what it means to be "assertive" and you will get a shrug or you will get ten different answers. This is why "assertive-ness" is not my favorite word for this kind of discussion. The woman who wrote to Ann Landers thought she was being assertive. People think of themselves as assertive and meanwhile other people think of them as passive or aggressive. This is why "assertiveness" can get confusing. That's why I call the behavior I talk about in this book Polite and Powerful. It's a more precise description for the behavior used in a positive confrontation.

Polite and Powerful is a combination of skills that combines what most people think of as *assertiveness* training with *etiquette* training. Ten years ago, I began teaching both of these skill areas. More and more I saw that many of the same issues I addressed in my assertiveness classes—becoming a powerful person—were cropping up in my etiquette classes—becoming a polite person—and vice versa. Many of the questions overlapped. Many of the skills overlapped. It was clear—the joining of Polite and Powerful behavior provided a practical skill area so many people need.

Minding More Than Your Manners

Business and social etiquette is more than learning about table manners, such as which water glass is yours at a business lunch or a wedding reception. In reality, that's only a small, small part of any modern etiquette training. (Your water glass, by the way, is on the right).

Another critical, but lesser-known, aspect of etiquette, whether in the boardroom or your living room, is understanding how to get along with others. It teaches you how to make the best impression on others, including your boss, book group, customers, great-aunt, and your neighbor.

Trust me when I tell you this—a lot of people ignorant of etiquette skills don't get promoted—no matter how smart or technocapable they are. People with poor etiquette skills are not made president of their civic association. They are not asked to head important department projects or help out at the church bake sale and then they grumble about it.

"Etiquette" is all about treating others the right way. The "right way" means with tact in both your words and actions. It's what you say and how you say it. It's treating people with kindness. This is the polite part of positive confrontation.

Etiquette Meets Assertiveness

In my classes, I help people understand that they have a right to be heard and to speak up. But you have to act on this belief and you have to act correctly—that means politely and powerfully. You need to have good control over both your verbal and non-verbal skills if you're going to appear as a powerful person to someone else. Again, the combination of etiquette training and assertiveness training gets people to tune into how they may be appearing to others. It helps them understand how their verbal and non-verbal communication is either helping or harming an already difficult situation. We send silent messages out to others, all day long, day after day, often without knowing what we're sending.

If you're just polite, it may not be enough to handle a difficult situation. You may come off as wimpy. If you're just powerful, that won't work either. Without the polite behavior it's often just aggression. You need both for positive confrontation.

I Had No Idea I Did That!

Once people tune in, many are in for a big surprise! Oh I can tell you stories that would make your straight hair curl. You will say, "No way did someone do that . . ." But the fact is, people do unbelievable things every day. Things you would think, no one would do that— like clip their fingernails in the weekly marketing meeting, or throw a chair at a wall of a crowded conference room in anger. You may not do anything like that, but we all have bad habits.

I suggested to a client that he videotape himself. He did and was shocked to discover that every other word out of his mouth was "Okay." He heard how bad he sounded. No wonder he wasn't asked to give more of the department's key presentations. *Before* he listened to the tape, he thought his boss "had it in for him" by not giving him the plum assignments. Afterwards, he understood that he was probably the one holding himself back in this area.

Like this man, you'll learn how to identify and break the habits that have been holding you back from increased success at work and satisfaction in your relationships. You'll learn about the specific dos and don'ts of positive confrontation using verbal and nonverbal communication skills and techniques. And you'll learn about the benefits of positive confrontation throughout this book.

The Benefits of Positive Confrontation

Speaking of the benefits of positive confrontation . . . there are many. But explaining the benefits—the increased self-esteem and lower stress level for starters—that Polite and Powerful people experience, is a little like explaining the benefits of exercise. You know why it would be good for you; you just may not know how to go about doing it or you may be having trouble getting started. I'm not just saying that Polite and Powerful can change your life in a positive and lasting way. I can prove it. I can prove it in the way I handle myself in tough situations. I can prove it by the filing cabinets I have stuffed with comments I have received from participants of my seminars.

People describe to me the relief they feel at having finally confronted someone about something that may have been bothering them. Others say that they no longer feel taken advantage of by people at work or that they are able to quickly resolve misunderstandings with friends. As a result, people feel happier at work and in their personal lives. Most of the time you will feel the benefits in little ways—an improved relationship with an in-law or co-worker here or a less stressful day at work there—the little ways add up. You are a less stressed and a more in-control person.

The benefits of positive confrontation can change your life. Learning how to be Polite and Powerful might not cure all of your problems, but if you have a problem with positive confrontation and telling other people how their behavior is affecting you, this book can help you reduce the stress this problem has been causing in your life.

Trust me on this too: It's much better to be an ex-wimp than an active wimp. You will discover creative space in your brain you did not know you had. And you didn't know you had it because complaining or a host of other non-positive behaviors was sucking up that creative energy. Not being Polite and Powerful can wear you out mentally. It can drain you physically. Two more reasons—enhanced emotional well-being and better health—to give positive confrontation a try.

Where Do We Go from Here?

After a brief confession from me, an exploration into who you are as a confronter and how you got the way you are, we head right into the land of positive confrontation. Step-by-step and brick-by-brick we'll build the skills you need so that you too can become a Polite and Powerful person. I have seen it proven time and time again—when people have the right skills and the right tools, an approach rooted in being Polite and Powerful works.

With practice, it's surprisingly easy to learn and apply the behavior and skills of Polite and Powerful behavior that will lead you to positive confrontation. I've created a simple model called WAC'em which you'll hear about in much greater detail soon. WAC'em will help overcome what is often the biggest obstacle to confrontation—figuring out exactly what's bothering you and what you want to say to, or ask from, the other person—all in a way that's positive. In other words, getting your words together for a difficult conversation or confrontation won't be a problem anymore.

This sounds like a cinch. And in time, it will become easy for you. But in the beginning you'll see that it's actually trickier than you thought—this process of figuring out what's really bothering you and what you really want from the other person. Understanding and being able to successfully vocalize what you want will be one of your biggest challenges when facing a confrontation or difficult conversation. A positive confrontation depends upon understanding your own position and knowing what you want from the other person. It's not simple at first. But WAC'em will help you prepare for confrontations and difficult conversations in a step-by-step, brick-by-brick manner. Later, handling the sticky situations and having the conversations that now make you wince will become much simpler. You'll see.

Along the road of this book, I will encourage you to do four things:

1. Gain awareness of how you present yourself, including your confrontational style.
2. Limit the assumptions you make about the behavior of other people.

3. Have a confrontation when necessary—and be Polite and Powerful when you do.
4. Learn how to reduce conflict in your life.

Avoiding Conflict

Are you surprised by number four above? Isn't the point of this book to have positive confrontations? Yes, it is—when it's necessary and appropriate. But Polite and Powerful people know how to present themselves in a way that invites less conflict. Also, Polite and Powerful people learn when "letting something go" is the better, healthier alternative to confrontation.

Practice, Practice, Practice

You will have to practice. Learning new skills takes time. I don't want you to put this book down and tackle a big one tomorrow. In other words, no telling your boss you don't think he's fair, or your significant other that you don't want to get married. Start slow. Build your confidence. In time, you will have a whole new way of operating in the world—a way that's more effective and positive. Over time, Polite and Powerful behavior will come naturally to you. You'll feel better about yourself. You'll feel better about your relationships with other people. You may not always get what you want from the other person—but I promise you that if you practice and work at having positive confrontations for a time—you will at least know where you honestly stand. And you can be certain that you'll be the one standing tall.

For now, feel good knowing that you're on your way.

THE CONFRONTATIONAL ROAD LESS TRAVELED IS PAVED BY BULLIES AND WIMPS

As I told you in the last chapter, I've met more people than I can count who have a hard time resolving day-to-day conflicts positively. But my knowledge of this communication problem doesn't come simply from teaching Polite and Powerful skills to others. My knowledge is also first-hand. At one time in my life, there was no one in the world who needed this book more than I did.

This leads me to a confession: I used to be a wimp. A big one. I'm not kidding—huge.

This surprises most of the people who attend my seminars—seminars about how to confront other people in a positive way.

Think about it: How else would I know this subject so well? How else could I be this enthusiastic about this communication issue?

Back to the huge wimp: The professionals I teach look at me and say, "You! No way. You don't look like a wimp." It's true, I don't. I'm tall and I stand tall. I talk to huge crowds and look at ease. I have command of my words and of my gestures. I can walk across a stage without feeling like I might fall or faint. And after years of teaching hundreds of seminars, you can bet my voice reaches the last row of just about any room.

Yet, there I was. Queen of the wimps.

Once Upon a Time . . .

When I was a kid, I was incredibly shy. Being tall wasn't the greatest feature to have then. Now, I love it, but then . . . There I was, feeling like a skinny tree, all elbows and knees. It was the era of "children should be seen and not heard," and I think that was especially true for little girls. We were encouraged to play nicely and be ladies—we still are. A woman told me that the coach of her daughter's basketball team told the players during a game to get out there and "play like ladies." How, her daughter wanted to know, was she supposed to shoot baskets and be a lady?

Little boys got—and still get—messages too. Many encouraged them to be tough: "Don't get mad, get even." Of course, crying for most boys was out of the question. Tears meant "he's a wimp."

Kids get messages from their parents about how to handle conflict and other people. You went to school, church, Little League, Girl Scouts and you got messages in these places too, messages about how you were expected to behave. Many of those messages were good, but some of them may not have been so wonderful: *It's okay to yell when you're unhappy. It's okay not to talk to someone if you're upset with him.*

Childhood Messages Can Chase You into Adulthood

Again, some of these messages were good, but others may be causing you problems to this day. Messages about how to handle yourself in difficult situations don't just get in. These messages get in and stay in. Over time your self-confidence chips away, or you have trouble in relationships, or it's easier to get new friends than deal with the old ones. For me, it was classic wimp syndrome—I fantasized about speaking up but I couldn't bring myself to do it.

Naturally being a wimp followed me out of adolescence and into the world of adulthood. What better place to discover exactly the width and depth of your wimpiness than in your professional life? Many years ago, when I was first starting out in the corporate world, I worked for a largely male-dominated aerospace company. I can tell you tales of how

I was slighted or treated rudely by people at work—everyone from a big boss to the woman in the company parking lot who screamed at me for taking what she considered "her spot." But I'm not going to tell them all, just one. The one that changed everything for me:

Once during a meeting with one of the company's directors, a powerful man told me, "Why don't you stay home and have babies like a good gal."

Well!

Lucky for me I had the good luck of working for a director named Ann Davis. She was one of two high-level women in the entire company. She was confident and self-assured—two things I wasn't then. She became my mentor. So after the director said this demeaning statement to me I ran, top speed, into Ann's office crying.

She asked me, "Why didn't you just tell him you were offended by his comment?"

"You mean I can tell him that?" I asked.

I look back now and think, "Duh, Barbara!" But then I honestly didn't know that I had a right to do this until Ann told me that I did. What I did instead of telling that director he offended me was complain. And did I ever complain! I complained to Ann and my sisters and my neighbor . . . In fact, that was my standard operating procedure. If someone treated me unfairly, poorly, or rudely, I used to complain to my girlfriends about that person's behavior—I'd complain to my hairdresser or the stranger sitting next to me on the plane. I wasn't picky. I just needed an ear. I could talk for hours and hours about it. I could wear your ear out and still want to complain more.

But I never said a word to the person bugging me. Never. Not one word. And by not confronting, I felt bad about myself.

Speaking of Crummy Self-Esteem

Speaking of feeling bad about yourself . . .

Let's get it over with—the self-esteem part of any discussion about confronting others. Here's what I learned about self-esteem . . . We can all suffer from bad self-esteem at times, some of us more than others. Yes, it feels bad. Yes, it probably holds us back at times. I certainly recognize that it's a reason why many of us don't confront positively. But it's not the *only* reason.

The preoccupation with bad "self-esteem" is not necessarily helpful. As I was trying to cure my own wimpiness, I read books. They helped to a degree. But I found many of them frustrating. Mostly these books talked to me about why I had gotten the wimpy way that I was—poor self-esteem. I knew that I had poor self-esteem! I wasn't a complete wimp, or hopeless in every situation in my life, but yes, I needed help with my self-esteem. Why else was I reading the book in the first place? I wasn't looking for someone to psychoanalyze me. I was looking for a step-by-step guide on how to assert myself positively.

There was no guide. But slowly over time, with patience and practice, I did learn how to confront others in a more positive way and my self-esteem in this area improved dramatically. I looked to Ann, my mentor, for continued guidance. Sometimes, just watching her in action was inspiration. I saw how she remained calm, no matter what the other person said or did. In tense situations, her body language was strong but not overwhelming. Her word choice always seemed Polite yet Powerful.

I realized that in order to fulfill my career goals, I was going to have to become a Polite and Powerful person too. I understood the cost of not being a Polite and Powerful person. When I was a photojournalist, I had applied for an editor's job. I was told that I would be contacted for an interview. They forgot to interview me. At the time, I accepted that.

I let them forget me!

A New Formula for Success

I knew that kind of behavior on my part had to stop. I was never going to get anywhere if I continued to let people forget to interview me. I was going to have to become a person without fear of sticking up for herself. And I was going to have to become a person who could do this without alienating other people. Not alienating others matters. I don't care what your gender is, what era you're living in, or what technical skills or special talents you may have, I don't think you can just assert yourself any way you want, walk away and still have people respect you. You have to deal with other people—even people who are bugging you—in a respectful manner. If you want to rise to the top of your profession, start your own business, or run your neighborhood association, you must learn how to do this. You must learn how to get along with other people.

I'm sure you know someone who is highly successful and not well-liked. In fact, the successful person may be the hot-tempered CEO of your company who, when he walks into a department, makes people freeze in fear. In my opinion, this is just the Powerful without the Polite. I don't care how successful this person may be in business. To me, respect carved out of fear means you're not a successful person in your relationships and in life in general. I believe that you can be both Polite and Powerful and still have people like and respect you. I believe that having good relationships with others is the more positive way to go through life. Otherwise, I don't think success is worth it. I would never want to be the kind of person who entered a room and instilled fear in others. Respect—yes. Fear—no.

Back in my wimpy days, my goal may not have been becoming the CEO of a Fortune 500 company, but still, I had career goals that were important to me. And I had a lot to learn. But learn I did. With Ann's help, I was able to tell that director I worked with that I didn't like his comments about a woman's duty to stay at home and be a "good gal." The next go-around for an editor's job I made sure I was interviewed.

As my confrontations became more positive, I started having some positive outcomes. Once when I brought it to a manager's attention that he kept cutting me off in meetings, he apologized and listened to me in the future. Eventually, he liked my ideas and he promoted me.

Speaking of Good Self-Esteem . . .

I started feeling better about myself because I liked the way I handled myself. I started handling myself better in my relationships. This was an important change for me. I was a single mom with a son. I wanted to set a good example for my son on how to handle himself in life's sticky situations. Kids can smell a hypocrite from a mile off. You have to live what you preach.

I didn't want to end up in another relationship, like in my first marriage, where I had a hard time expressing my true and honest feelings.

I also didn't want to stew over what I perceived as slights anymore. Like the time my cousin came to visit me for the weekend. As soon as she came to my house, she said, "Yuck, you got another dog. He's so big and ugly!"

Well, I'm a dog person. My dog is a well-loved member of my family. I was offended by my cousin's comment about him and I wanted to say something to her. But what? I was stuck. You know how that feels I'm sure—indignant and tongue-tied at the same time. It's so frustrating! At first, I didn't say anything. I needed to get my thoughts together. Later, though, I realized I couldn't, and didn't want to, let her comment go without saying something about it. It was affecting my ability to enjoy her visit. So I finally got my guts up and confronted her. She couldn't have apologized faster and we had a great time after that.

The old wimpy me would have held my silent grudge. That grudge would have festered. After she left I would have set fire to the carpet—that's how fast I would have run to the telephone. I would have been complaining to my sisters and friends about what a jerk she was before her car was off my block. But because I had spoken up, I was free of this behavior. Wow, did that feel good.

In littler ways and then bigger ones, my life got better—my stress level went down as my confidence went up. So when I tell you I know that the skills you'll acquire will help you learn how to resolve conflict and have difficult conversations, I know firsthand that they will help. I know firsthand how much better it feels being Polite and Powerful. It's a new kind of freedom.

I want you to be free too.

Looking Back Now . . .

If I had known how to confront positively years ago it would have helped me in my first marriage—it probably would have ended sooner, because that was for the best. I'm certain it would have helped during my divorce (talk about difficult conversations!) It would have helped me deal with rude people in the grocery store or a college professor who gave me a hard time.

Polite and Powerful provides you with tools for all areas of your life. It would have helped me reduce the overall level of stress in my life. You'll learn, as I have, how to look at your behavior to discover if you may be a source of conflict for someone else.

What Messages Did You Get?

Remember the messages I received to be "a good girl"? You got messages too. Take a few minutes and think about what they were. Think of how these messages may continue to influence you in your interactions with others, especially in difficult situations.

Messages I Got That Helped Me Become A Wimp or Bully:

The next chapter will help you identify the confrontational style you have, most likely, unknowingly adopted. Understanding who you are is the first step in saying, "I don't want to yell at people anymore," or "I'm tired of ignoring problems" or "I want to handle myself better."

You don't have to let old messages influence you anymore. You can break free. You've already started.

CHAPTER 3

CONFRONTERS: THE BULLY, THE WIMP, THE BIG MOUTH IN ACTION

You know who I was as a confronter—a wimp. Now it's time to ask yourself: Who are you as a confronter? Who are you when you're dealing with co-workers, family, and friends in sticky situations?

You can't say you don't know who you are as a confronter or that you're no particular kind of confronter. You *are* someone as a confronter. Everyone is.

I know this is hard. No one wants to admit, "I scream my head off in confrontations," or "I avoid difficult conversations like the plague." Admitting to these behaviors is admitting that your behavior is unattractive or self-defeating to others. I hated to think of myself as a wimp.

But if you avoid people during difficult situations, yell at them, or employ other kinds of destructive behaviors, it means you've fallen into a negative confrontational pattern. More people than you could ever count, right this minute, everywhere in offices and homes and grocery stores, all over the world, are having negative confrontations. No one wants to be the bully or the wimp—yet it's a pattern we've fallen into, a habit that becomes a part of who we are. It's human nature to keep doing what we do, even bad things that we wish we could stop doing.

Even when we realize our behavior is bad, negative, or driving the people around us crazy, unless we have a better behavior to replace it with, we continue to act in ways that are negative for ourselves and others.

So, Who Are You?

Most people don't know who they are as a confronter. You probably haven't given it much thought before. Start thinking about it now. Try to remember the last confrontation you had with a friend or co-worker. How did it go? Did you raise your voice? Did you give them the silent treatment instead of speaking up? Did you cry or pound your fist? Did you get your point across? Were you able to be honest about how you really felt? Did you give the other person a chance to speak honestly to you?

Being honest during a confrontation can be extremely difficult. There are many reasons why we hold back from telling another person the truth about how we feel. We worry that we'll hurt his feelings. We worry that she won't like us anymore. There are other reasons besides these two why we hold back or lose our tempers during confrontations. We'll explore these reasons in more detail shortly.

As you read through this chapter, I want you to remember that no matter what behavior you've been employing in confrontations, you can be honest *and* also choose your words carefully. You *can* treat the other person with respect. You *can* handle your body language in a way that makes you look powerful—if you know the skills to enable you to do so.

But what if you don't know these skills?

Then, of course, handling yourself well is going to be harder, if not impossible.

So we often don't handle ourselves well. This is why instead of having the conversation with the person who is bugging you, you do or say nothing, or you do or say something you regret.

The last time you wanted to tell somebody something honestly and didn't open your mouth, did you think, "It's no big deal?" or

"Maybe next time?" or "He's just a jerk?" Maybe it wasn't a big deal. Maybe there will be a next time. Maybe the guy was a jerk. Maybe. Maybe not. Yet another benefit to understanding the art of positive confrontation is that it can enable you to think, "it's no big deal," and actually mean it. With practice and patience with yourself, you'll get there. I promise you can. If the Queen of the Wimps— me—can get there, you can too. For now, concentrate on being honest with yourself about your confrontational style. If you're ignoring a friend or relative's bothersome behavior and saying to yourself "it's no big deal" when in your heart, deep down, you know it matters to you—you've got a problem. If you're yelling your head off during meetings and saying to yourself, "I wish I hadn't done that again," you've got a problem there too.

"I'll Get'em Next Time!"

If, when confronted by another person's bothersome behavior you froze up instead of spoke up, were you full of regret? Did you say to yourself, "I'll say something next time?"

Is there a next time?

Probably not.

Or if you lost your cool with the person, did you think, "The next time, I'll handle myself better." Did you handle yourself better the next time?

Probably not.

Usually you won't say something the next time or be calm the next time unless you change what you've been doing. But how do you change what you're not doing or what you're doing?

You're not alone. A lot of people make vows about how they'll behave during the next sticky situation, the next difficult conversation or confrontation. But aren't you tired of making vows that you break? You get all pumped up with confidence and excitement and then you open your mouth and nothing comes out or the wrong thing comes out.

Welcome to the planet of the wimps and bullies.

Before You Can Be Honest with Others . . .

It isn't always easy being honest with others and it isn't always easy being honest with yourself. Developing self-awareness, however, depends upon your willingness to be honest with yourself. It's often not fun. Especially in the beginning, when you're uncovering your behavioral blunders, it can seem downright unpleasant. Yes, it's tempting to ignore the glitches in your otherwise not-so-bad behavior. It's tempting to say to yourself, "I have friends! People like me! I'm doing fine."

Yes, I'm sure people like you and you have friends and much of your life is good. You probably are an honest person in all the other areas of your life, but that doesn't mean your confrontational style is a positive and honest one. It's essential that you figure out who you are as a confronter. You need to become more aware of what pattern of behavior you may have. You need to discover if you're honest with others or not. Only then can you can modify, improve, and if necessary, get a whole new confrontational style. This process of self-discovery is worth it because your life and your relationships can get even better than they are now. I'm not kidding—positive confrontation will improve your life in so many ways.

Self-Assessment Quizzes Can Help

I used to feel bad after taking self-assessment quizzes. It seemed that suddenly I had a whole new problem to worry about. Then I realized that the only way to change is to start with self-knowledge. Change is not really possible without it. So, even if you're tempted to skip over this part, please don't. Take this short quiz. It's important!

WHEN INTERACTING WITH OTHERS:

	True	False	Not Sure
1. I ignore other people's behavior even if it is bothering me.	❑	❑	❑
2. I tell other people about someone's behavior and its effect on me without talking about it directly with that person.	❑	❑	❑
3. I will often say, "I'm sorry" to things that aren't my fault.	❑	❑	❑
4. If I have a problem with a friend, I will stop calling him or her until he or she gets the hint that I'm upset.	❑	❑	❑
5. I believe that other people are usually the cause of the problem.	❑	❑	❑
6. I can't help it; I yell when I'm upset.	❑	❑	❑
7. I have said to myself, "He or she should know that it's not okay to say or do that to me."	❑	❑	❑
8. It is important that I always win or get my way.	❑	❑	❑
9. I have hit walls or thrown things when upset.	❑	❑	❑
10. I worry that if I tell someone what's bothering me, it will hurt their feelings or they won't like me anymore.	❑	❑	❑
11. I think that there are a lot of rude, insensitive, and selfish people out there in the world.	❑	❑	❑
12. If I confront someone, I will make it seem like it's my fault so that I won't hurt their feelings.	❑	❑	❑

As I'm sure you've figured out by now, if you answered "true" to even a few of these questions, you've fallen into a negative confronting pattern. If you answered "not sure," chances are you may have a negative confronting pattern.

If you can't answer these questions definitively, your awareness of your own behavior is something you need to work on. For a few days, pay attention to how you handle conflict at work, on the highway, or in a line at the movies. Do you say something if you find someone else's behavior rude or annoying? If so, what words do you use? If you ignored someone else's bothersome behavior, do you know why? Paying attention to these kind of things will help you develop an awareness of your confrontational style.

What Holds You Back from Confronting?

As you develop an awareness of your confrontational style, be aware also of the most common reasons why people don't confront. These five reasons crop up again and again. Read on to discover if you see yourself in any of these patterns.

Five Reasons Why You May Not Be Confronting

Here are the most common reasons I've discovered why people aren't confronting others:

1. You think, "the other person *must* know that his or her behavior is inappropriate or bothersome." There is no jar deep enough to hold all of the nickels I get for this one: "Shouldn't he already know that what he is doing is upsetting to me?" or "How come I have to tell her? She should know." Well guess what? People don't always know.

This story is hard to believe for some of us women, but about a year ago, a man in one of my classes was horrified to discover how much the women he worked with resented being called "hon." His father and grandfather always said it and it became his habit too. He thought he was being friendly.

People make very quick assumptions, usually negative ones, about the motivations of others. Usually too quick and too negative. What you think is inappropriate may be fine for the other person. And what's acceptable or common knowledge for one person, may not be for another. Like Kate's boss. He would criticize her, but never compliment her. She said to me, "Why do I have to say anything to him? Why do I have to ask for good feedback? He should know this."

I said, "Maybe he doesn't know. Maybe he thinks it's only appropriate to talk to you when there's a problem." This works in the opposite way too. There is the supervisor who has difficulty telling employees what they are doing is wrong. He thinks, "They should know why I'm upset with them." But why should they? People can't read other people's minds.

I met a woman with two younger sisters. Their parents had been hurt in an accident and required constant help. She was handling all the details of their care. She resented it. Finally, after stewing for several weeks, she confronted her sisters. "Why aren't you helping me?" she demanded. "It's not fair."

Her sisters were shocked. "We thought you wanted to be the one to handle it and be in charge—you always have in the past. You're the big sister."

They were only too happy to help.

Here's another story: Two colleagues were upset at their college interns for taking long lunches. They had been annoyed and assumed the interns were abusing the system. In fact, one of the men had to cut his own lunch short to have telephone coverage at his office because he knew his intern would not be back when she was supposed to be. After my seminar, they decided to confront them. The two co-workers met beforehand and figured out what to say to the interns. When they finally said something to them, it turned out that they discovered that the interns didn't know about the lunch schedule! No one ever told them.

2. I don't want to hurt the other person's feelings. This holds people back from confronting people they know well, acquaintances, and even people they don't know. You might not believe the number of people who tell me they can't get off the phone with telemarketers. It's not because they want the product, it's because they have a hard time saying no.

With people we do know, we want to preserve the relationship at all costs. We worry that if we say something confrontational it will jeopardize the relationship.

"If you don't have anything nice to say, don't say anything at all." Just about everyone grows up with this advice. It's bad advice. Don't misunderstand. I teach business etiquette; I would never tell you to be rude. But are you always going to say "nice things"? Of course not. The Polite and Powerful spin to this saying is: "Say what you mean, mean what you say, but don't say it meanly."

Confronting seems to go against the nurturing role to which so many women have been conditioned. Many women have been raised to be the peacemakers. Women need to ask themselves how many times they have said to a girlfriend, "Are you mad at me?" or "Don't be mad at me," to realize that perhaps they use this reason for not confronting.

This is an issue for men too. Andrew is an attorney who likes his secretary as a person, but he doesn't like all the mistakes she makes on his documents. He admitted to me that he was afraid that if he confronted her about her mistakes, he would hurt her feelings and she would start to cry. Maybe she would cry and get upset with him if he said something. But what are the consequences of his silence? He admitted that he was "cool to her" when she made mistakes. Is that better? I don't think so. I encouraged him to be honest with his secretary. Maybe she would improve her performance or seek additional word processing experience.

3. You mean I'm allowed to tell someone I don't like his or her behavior?

People don't know they have this right. This was me many years ago. I didn't understand that I could tell someone my concerns about their bothersome behavior or annoying comments. I hear it all the time now, "Can I really tell someone I don't like when she does that?"

"Yes," I tell them. "Yes, yes, yes."

Denise won't tell her boss that another colleague got recognition for the same job they both worked on. "He's the boss," she said. "It's not my place to tell him about this."

But, I pointed out to her, it is her place. Who else is going to give her the recognition?

Jack has this problem too. A friend of his has been driving him crazy. "He wants me to join an incentive sales program. I don't want to join. He keeps asking and I keep saying no."

I said to Jack, "Why don't you tell him that you'd like him to stop asking."

"Oh," Jack said. "I guess I never thought about it."

"Well," I told him. "Think about it now."

A woman told me that she's tired of her aunt calling her to give her unsolicited opinions. "You mean I'm allowed to tell my aunt I don't always want to hear her opinion?" Yes, I told this woman, if you do it Politely and Powerfully—absolutely.

4. I'm afraid of what might happen. Again, we must be mindful of the risks of being honest. Even if you have a positive confrontation and are able to be honest, that doesn't guarantee you will like the outcome. Depending on the nature of the relationship, the confrontation could be seen as a power struggle. It may in fact, be a risk. You may not have the power or any leverage and so you may not get what you're asking for.

This risk often occurs in work-related relationships. If your conflict is with someone higher up in the food chain than yourself, what will be the consequences of having a confrontation? You could confront your boss on something, but it is your boss so sometimes, no matter what, it will be his or her way. Because you're the underling, the higher-up may not appreciate or want your honesty. Could you lose your job even if you handle yourself Politely and Powerfully? Though I can tell you it doesn't happen a lot, it does happen. It's possible that your boss may hold your honesty against you. Just because someone says, "No tell me, I really want to know what you think," doesn't mean they really want to know what you think. In Chapter 9, we'll talk more about how to weigh the risk versus the possible gains of confronting someone higher up than yourself. For now, understand that yes, there can be risks associated with being honest with your boss.

There can be risks in personal relationships too. You may worry that if you confront a friend or loved one, he or she will become upset with you and that would negatively impact the relationship.

Here's a story I've heard a few times in one form or another: An unhappy man goes to his neighbor's leasing agent or landlord about a problem with his neighbor instead of to the man directly. I asked him why. He said, "I'm concerned about how he'll react."

Meanwhile the neighbor in question is wondering why his neighbor didn't come to him and talk about his problem. I don't blame him. He may not have known he was bugging his neighbor. Why not give him the benefit of the doubt?

I hear this one a lot too: A man doesn't like having to pay for everything when he takes his girlfriend out. He's afraid she'll dump him if he speaks up. But, if he's annoyed, that won't go away either. His repressed feelings will leak out one way or the other. Unless he can be honest, the relationship will probably suffer.

And then there are strangers. Maybe it's smart to be afraid of what might happen if you're confronting a stranger. Since you don't know the person, you don't know how they may respond. This holds people back from speaking up. I tell people, "Use your judgment," but often because they're afraid of the reaction they will get, they don't say anything when they should.

A woman's company was flying her into town so she could attend my seminar. She told me she didn't want to tell the man next to her on the plane that his earphones were too loud. "Why?" I asked.

"I didn't know him," she said. "I didn't know how he'd react."

How would he react? On the plane? With all those people around? Nine times out of ten, the person turns the music down. She could have spoken up.

She was in the right class!

5. I'm afraid of becoming aggressive. People think that if they get upset or angry they will automatically explode, so they deny that they're upset and they don't confront.

People confuse anger and aggression. Anger and aggression are *not* the same. Anger is the emotion. Aggression is the behavior. Emotions aren't good or bad, they just are what they are. It's what you do or don't do as a result of feeling them that can be good or bad. You can learn to express your anger Politely and Powerfully.

Tamica can't confront her employee after she's discussed inappropriate things—more than once—in their department's meeting. "I'm afraid I'm going to start yelling and have a hard time stopping," she said. But what if Tamica keeps holding back? She's bound to explode sooner or later and then what will be the consequences to her relationship with the employee? Probably, the relationship will suffer.

A father who won't confront his son about his late night hours has the same problem. He won't speak up because he doesn't trust himself to keep his temper in check if his son talks back. He's tired of fighting with him. But, strong feelings don't go away. Chances are, he'll blow up one day anyway. Wouldn't it be better if he could have a calm conversation with his son before that happens? I think so!

Three Non-Confronters in Action

You may not confront because of one of the reasons above, but you do, in fact, do something. To give you an idea of what you may be doing when you're not confronting, I've profiled three common types of non-confronters in terms of their behavior.

THE COMPLAINER

Our first non-confronter is a complainer. Complainer is a nice way of saying "wimp." As you already know, this used to be me.

This person doesn't confront the person who is saying or doing something bothersome. They need to complain in order to get relief from their bad feelings. And does this person complain—to friends, families, co-workers, anyone who will listen will suffice. Unfortunately, the relief a complainer feels is often short-lived.

Betsy's manager makes fun of her in front of other people. She won't say anything to him, but goes home and cries on the telephone with her sister. Then her husband gets home and she talks about it for the rest of the night. Does this stop her manager from making fun of her? No—he doesn't know how she feels so he's not going to stop.

A man complains to his wife about his friend who stands him up—again—at the racquetball court. But does he tell his friend? No!

Complainers waste an enormous amount of energy.

THE AVOIDER

Avoiders waste creative energy too. They are wimps who will do just about anything not to have a confrontation with people who may be bothering them. They say, "It's not that big of an issue," when it is an issue. "Why rock the boat?" Often they don't just avoid having a confrontation; they avoid the other person as well. It's easier than hurting someone's feelings.

I met a woman who used to take a morning walk with her neighbor. But the neighbor was constantly complaining about her husband, boss, noise pollution, and how she couldn't get decent oranges at the produce stand. You name it—she complained about it.

The woman didn't want to hear all this negative talk. This was her only time of day to relax. She told me she didn't want to hurt her neighbor's feelings so she just found excuses not to walk with her. It didn't occur to her that the excuse-making was obvious and that the neighbor's feelings were hurt anyway.

This woman became an avoider. Avoiders make up excuses: "I can't make it . . . because . . . well you see . . ."

The woman who told me this story is an avoider too: "A relative who lives with me watches how I do things, like fixing a sandwich, and tells me how she does it, implying that I am doing it incorrectly. It really upsets me—but I don't want to hurt her feelings. I find myself sneaking into the kitchen to avoid her comments."

How can it not bother you to have your every move watched? People shouldn't have to sneak around in their own houses.

One manager in the financial services industry revealed that his counterpart "calls me to brag about her new deal. She goes on and on. I'm happy for her and I don't want to hurt her feelings by saying something, but it really wastes my time. I try to avoid her calls."

I encouraged him to stop avoiding and start talking to her— Politely and Powerfully.

A pharmaceutical sales representative got angry with one of his doctors and could not confront him. He kept saying, "Next time, I'll say something . . ." But he couldn't bring himself to do it. Unfortunately, he couldn't let his negative feelings go. He just stopped calling on the doctor. As a result, he and his company lost business. This kind of behavior is not going to advance anyone's professional image or career.

The ultimate avoider is the Arab woman in one of my overseas classes who said, "I don't confront my friends; I just keep getting new ones."

THE PRETENDER

Denial. Denial. Denial. Pretenders accept things, which if they were honest, they wouldn't. "There is no problem, none whatsoever, things couldn't be better." Unlike the avoider, the pretender can't even admit he or she has difficult feelings. Sadly, these are also people whose health suffers, often chronically. I met a woman who was "encouraged" by upper management to take an overseas assignment with the international division of her company. She really didn't want to leave the United States but couldn't admit that because she was afraid it would hurt her career. She told everyone, even herself that she had no problem with it—until her hair started falling out. Her doctor told her it was stress. She finally had to speak to her boss because when your hair is falling out of your head, it gives you incentive to stop pretending.

Parents I know will not confront their son about his disruptive behavior. He smokes cigarettes, cuts class, and hangs out with a kid who has been arrested. They say he's going through a phase. Maybe they don't want to deal with his real problems. Whatever their reasons for not speaking up, pretending that problems don't exist does not make them go away. They often get worse and worse over time. I wonder what will happen to this boy in the future—is he headed for bigger trouble? Unless his parents can stop pretending his behavior is acceptable, he may be.

The Price Non-Confronters Pay

Complainers, avoiders, and pretenders have other things in common besides their wimpiness. They have high stress levels, low self-esteem, and what about the person's bothersome behavior causing the stress? It continues, of course. Why should it stop? These non-confronters can complain, avoid and pretend all they like, except their problems with others don't evaporate. This form of behavior lends itself to feelings of powerlessness. What a crummy way to go through life!

■

People Who Do Confront—But Incorrectly

Then there are the people who do confront, only they don't do it positively. They often are bewildered by the outcome. They often end up feeling even worse. There are three common reasons why this can happen during a confrontation:

THREE REASONS WHY CONFRONTATIONS CAN BECOME NEGATIVE

1. I repress my feelings and then "blow up." Feelings don't go away. A woman took a continuing education class. She liked the woman who sat next to her—until she became an annoying gum clicker. Finally, the woman couldn't take it anymore. She blew up at the clicker. "Don't you know how *bleep, bleep* annoying that is!" The clicker was embarrassed. She immediately swallowed her gum and the next class sat far away from the woman.

What would have happened if the woman had approached the clicker in a more Polite and Powerful fashion? Maybe they would still like each other and sit next to each other!

The woman who yelled at the gum clicker learned—the hard way—that feelings stay inside you. They gather emotional heat and take on lots of energy. If you're still facing the situation, or something else bothersome happens with the same person—bang! It's easy to at some point to explode either on the issue or anything else that may crop up.

2. That jerk had it coming! Some people are convinced that the world is packed with jerks. Many people were taught "Don't get mad, get even!" This give-him-a-taste-of-his-own-medicine is not an excuse for your bad behavior—ever. It can also bring out aggression in the other person.

I heard this story: "I caught my future mother-in-law listening in to a very personal conversation I was having with her daughter. I screamed 'Bitch,' and stormed out of the house. I thought she deserved it at the time. But we're married now, and my relationship with my mother-in-law has never really been the same since that night. I said I was sorry, but I think she still holds it against me. She doesn't talk to me as much. She doesn't go out of her way to get me into conversations."

It's not surprising. People will often hold it against you if you scream at them. Though it doesn't always happen, if you blow a fuse, you can incur permanent damage to a relationship.

3. I thought I was being assertive. You may think you were "assertive" but if you used angry gestures, self-discounting or bad language, you thought wrong. You may not have meant to become aggressive or passive, but you did. Why? Because it's easy to become aggressive without meaning to. Later on, I'll give you tons of details and dos and don'ts for your verbal and non-verbal signals—and this is why.

I was behind a man in the express line at the grocery store. There was a man in front of him who had a full cart. The man said, "Hey you! What are you trying to pull! Get in another line."

The man who get yelled at was clearly embarrassed. He said he didn't know he was in the wrong line. The man who yelled at him looked like a big bully.

The Price These Bungling Confronters Pay

You may mean well. You may think you're being assertive. You may think the other person had it coming, but that's no excuse for becoming aggressive. These kinds of people can also have low self-esteem and feel out of control. They often achieve the opposite result—they invite more conflict into their lives instead of resolving it. Again, not a pleasant or positive way to be in your dealings with others.

Four Negative Confronters in Action

Negative confronters have some common behavioral profiles too. Here are four of them to watch out for:

THE BULLY

Unfortunately, the kid who crushed your lunch box has grown up, is still a bully, and is now in the working world or living next door. You may think of this person as the person no one messes with.

This is the person who says, "She had it coming!" This person must get his or her way and will often become aggressive if, and when, challenged. He or she is frustrated and doesn't know how to express it other than through aggressive behavior. He or she wants to win. End of discussion.

Some of the actions in the following examples are hard to believe, but bullies will amaze you. Like the professor who gets upset when there are typos in his documents. He doesn't say "Can you please fix this document," to his secretary. He just jams papers under her chin. You can bet she fixes them fast, but does she like her boss? I think it's safe to assume that she doesn't.

Also hard to believe is the boss who cursed out an employee and threw a chair at him because he was not kept informed on an important project.

And the pharmaceutical sales representative who *had* to see the doctor. He refused to take no for answer. He walked right into the examining room while there was a patient in the room! As a result, he was instructed never to come back to that office again.

THE SHOUTER

Shouters are a subset of the full-blown bully. This person is not happy about what is going on. And the only way he or she knows how to express his or her displeasure is by shouting, then shouting some more.

An administrative assistant told me this tale: "I was told to get new business cards for the telemarketing group. The regional director told me to change their titles to 'telemarketers' instead of 'inside sales representatives.' One of the senior telemarketers didn't like the new title. He started screaming at me. He screams all the time."

Sometimes there are shouters-by-accident. These are people who approach a conflict with the best of intentions but their behavior doesn't match their intentions. People get upset and they lose control. And then they shout and shout some more. Later, they usually feel bad about losing it.

THE SELF-DISCOUNTER

This is the person who by his verbal or non-verbal communication negates what he is saying. She will say during a confrontation, "Gee, sorry. Well, you know how sensitive I am . . ." or "This is probably just my problem but . . ." or " "I think kinda, maybe, sort of, what's bothering me could be . . ." Or, they say, "I'm offended by the comment," and the offending person can't hear them because he or she has her head down and voice lowered.

You got your guts up to confront but you negated your position, blamed yourself, or didn't get your point across. You're back in the land of the wimps.

THE DISPLACER

This is the person who suffers in silence—for a while—then bam! They ignore the real issue and reach the boiling point and blow a lid about another issue. True feelings leak out one way or another, sometimes to areas of conflict that are safer. Alan, for example, said he cannot confront his wife about financial issues because he is afraid of their bitter arguments.

Instead, he snaps at her for other, little things, like leaving dirty dishes in the sink. He gets irritated beyond what the offense calls for. As a result, she gets irritated at him for snapping at her. She's confused about his behavior. They end up fighting over issues in their relationship that aren't really substantial and meaningful. Meanwhile, the real problem often goes ignored.

As you can see, relationships suffer under the weight of displacement, sometimes seriously. It happened to two roommates who got along great until one of the women started having her boyfriend over all the time. The other roommate felt her privacy was being violated. But she didn't say anything. Then one day she discovered the woman had taken her CD without returning it. They got into a terrible, door-slamming, loud fight. Of course, the fight had very little to do, if anything, with the CD.

Needless to say, one woman packed her bags and moved out.

Both women were upset and hurt. They didn't talk for two years!
My nickel jar overflows on this kind of story too.

So Who Are You?

The point of these profiles is not so you cast yourself as this or that type. It's just to help you become more aware of some all-too common negative behaviors. You may also have recognized yourself in more than one profile. That's very common. There are cross-overs and overlaps. For example, avoiders sometimes become displacers. (See chart on facing page.)

Hopefully by now you're getting a clearer picture of who you are as a confronter. Maybe you don't like it. Many participants in my seminars look glum at this point. If you're feeling glum, don't. There's help.

Now You Have a Choice

Beyond all the reasons you may have for not confronting or for confronting negatively is this: You didn't know there was another way. You didn't realize you were making mistakes.

You didn't know about Polite and Powerful because no one ever taught you—until now.

Once you learn the tools to confront positively—including WAC'em, the eleven simple steps, the dos and don'ts of verbal and non-verbal signals—then how you confront becomes a choice. You can choose to have positive confrontations. You can choose not to let any of the reasons or behaviors described here rule you any longer. No more avoiding, shouting, blaming, being quiet, pounding your fist. No more feeling crummy for being a bully, a complainer or a shouter.

And as you'll soon discover, not only do you have choices, the choice you make has consequences. Sometimes HUGE consequences.

Behavioral Profiles

Reasons for not confronting or confronting negatively	NON-CONFRONTERS			NEGATIVE CONFRONTERS			
	Complainer	Avoider	Pretender	Bully	Shouter	Self-Discounter	Displacer
DON'T CONFRONT							
1. The other person must know that his or her behavior is inappropriate.	✓	✓					
2. I don't want to hurt the other person's feelings.	✓	✓					
3. I can tell someone I don't like his or her behavior?	✓	✓					
4. I'm afraid of what might happen.	✓	✓	✓				
5. I'm afraid of becoming aggressive.	✓	✓					✓
CONFRONT NEGATIVELY							
1. I repress . . . and then blow up.				✓	✓		✓
2. He had it coming.				✓	✓		
3. I thought I was assertive.					✓	✓	

CHAPTER 4

THE CHOICES AND CONSEQUENCES OF CONFRONTATIONAL BEHAVIOR

You now know the reasons why you may not be confronting or why you may not be doing it well. You now have a better understanding of who you are as a confronter. This awareness is a positive step. But you also need to understand the consequences of confronting or not confronting others.

Once you understand how your relationships, self-esteem, and professional image—whether you serve on the PTA or are a CEO (or both!)— can suffer when you don't have a positive confrontation, you will have a big incentive to learn and use Polite and Powerful behavior during a confrontation. You will want to try out these skills. It will be hard for you to go back.

Before they learn about positive confrontation most people simply don't think about the choices and consequences of confrontational behavior. They don't even understand that they even have or are making a choice. But Polite and Powerful behavior is a choice. There are other choices. I illustrate them below.

■

The Conflict

Here's a simple, but common enough kind of conflict that has to do with sharing space. It can occur both in your neighborhood or at your office—someone is playing his or her music too loudly. When I use this example in my seminars, someone always comments, "I've had this problem too."

Suppose your co-worker, Alex, is playing his radio too loudly in the next cube. It's distracting and you're having trouble getting your work done. You can choose to respond in one of three ways:

You Choose to Be a Complainer, Avoider or Pretender

Classic passive behavior. You don't know what to say and even if you did, you're afraid that if you say something Alex might get mad at you. So you complain about Alex to your co-workers, saying "That Alex is so selfish," to anyone who will listen. Or you avoid the situation or pretend it's not bothering you by going to the conference room to do your work, often missing important phone calls.

I like to define passive this way: Complainers, avoiders and pretenders let their lives be taken over by another person's behavior, and that's like getting a table at your favorite restaurant and letting the waiter eat your dinner.

When someone is doing or saying something to you that you don't like and you choose not to say or do anything you are passive. This is what avoiders and pretenders do. Complainers will talk about the person's behavior but never to the person doing it.

Ultimately what your passive behavior is saying is that you value other people's feelings and rights more than your own.

Here are the consequences that you bring upon yourself by not asking Alex to turn his radio down:

Nothing changes. Alex's radio plays on at the same volume. Why would it change? He doesn't know that he's bothering you because you haven't told him. Your ability to work is still impaired.

You feel bad about yourself. Of course you do; you're a wimp! You may want very badly to be able to confront him directly. You may promise yourself to "do it tomorrow," but this tomorrow's sun never comes up. You may try to pretend that the situation isn't bothering you, or that it's mature of you not to let things bother you. But this pretending only makes you feel worse. It will quietly and swiftly erode your self-esteem.

Your relationship with that person usually suffers. A woman in one of my seminars once described how she felt about an annoying co-worker: "Even hearing Karla's voice from across the office made the blood freeze in my veins." It's not that significant if you only have to see Karla once a year, but what do you do when "Karla" is a person you have to see everyday? What if Karla is your boss, teammate, or neighbor? The woman can't wish her away. She is going to have to deal with Karla sooner or later.

The purgatory of passivity is resentment. It will form the way a puddle does, drop by drop. Before the first song even stops playing, you may be annoyed. Then as the drops accumulate, the puddle of resentment is suddenly a stream of resentment. In order to relieve the stress of having this resentment build, you may start complaining or bad-mouthing Alex: "How dare he do that to me?"

Relationships drown in resentment.

Or, you may start to avoid Alex. This is a kind of purgatory too. I have met many people who admit that they will go out of buildings, around corners, up extra flights of stairs, walk or drive miles out of their way—all because taking the direct route could mean running into (and having to deal with) that person. But there aren't enough stairs in the world that will climb you up and out of yourself.

Others may think of you in a negative way. Whiner. Wimp. These are just a few negative names others may attach to you. You might be the most technically able person to lead your company's next big project, but if you've been labeled a wimp, the higher-ups assessing you may worry that you won't be able to get the job done or handle a conflict that may arise.

Exceptions—When Passive May Be the Best Choice

I am not suggesting that, at times, choosing not to do or say something may be the right, most positive choice you can make. You may choose not to confront for many valid reasons: it's not the right time or place, it's not the politically savvy thing to do, you will never see the person again. Or it may simply be a personality quirk. Consider these scenarios:

- Your friend is always late. It drives you crazy, but you've been friends for years. You come to accept this about her. It's one of her quirks. Why do you accept it? Because she accepts your quirks.
- Your co-worker has been in a terrible mood all day. She snaps at you every time you ask her a question. But you know that her mother has been very ill and the burden of care is falling upon her shoulders. Even though the "snapping" is bothersome, you realize her bothersome behavior is only temporary and out of character. You decide to say nothing.
- You're having a miserable, crummy, and rotten day. And now your roommate is leaving dishes in the sink. But you realize that you'll probably feel better the next day. You decide not to confront her about the dishes while you're feeling this on edge.
- You work with a programmer who is legendary for both his brilliant computer skills and his temper. One day he blows up at you for an honest mistake you've made. He's shouting at you. He's pounding his fists. Though his behavior is upsetting, you decide he will only become more out of control if you try to confront him about it. You decide to speak with him at a later time.

But Keep in Mind . . .

As you learned in the last chapter, passive behavior isn't always qualified by an unwillingness to act. You may, in fact, be confronting someone but you may be doing it passively, like the self-discounter. You finally get up your courage to confront but then you lose your effectiveness by making mistakes in your verbal or nonverbal communication.

Jean decides to say something to Alex, although she doesn't want to hurt his feelings. She sticks her head over his cube and says, "I know I'm such a pain and you're going to think that I'm a pest, but your music is so distracting. I'm sorry, I am having such a hard time concentrating . . ."

Why should Jean put herself down just because Alex's music is bothering her? She shouldn't, but she was so afraid of hurting his feelings that she chose to demean herself and her own position instead. This is self-defeating behavior and it happens all the time.

Consider what happened to Rick, a clinical researcher for a drug company.

Rick was getting more and more upset with his boss because he was being given a lot of extra work without being compensated for it. So Rick decided to ask his boss for a raise. "I told him I had been working really long hours. He agreed. I told him I was handling responsibility beyond what I was initially hired for. He agreed. He told me I was a hard worker and he sure did appreciate me. Then he asked me how the project was going. I was in his office for a half an hour and when I came out I realized that we had talked about everything except my raise. I really never asked him for it. I guess I was waiting for him to bring it up, but he didn't."

You Choose to Be a Bully, a Shouter or a Displacer

That Alex is a jerk! How could he not know that it's too loud? You get madder and madder thinking about how inconsiderate he is. You get so mad that you jump up, hang over his cube, and shout at him, "Turn that *@^$ radio off right now or I'll come over there and unplug it myself."

If we asked someone "Why do you shout at other people?" He or she might say, "I had to do something." "I can't help it," or "It's just how I am."

But when you confront someone and yell, scream, curse, put down, berate, and/or insult, you are not simply reacting or simply following your nature. You are choosing to bring an avalanche of negative consequences right down on top of yourself:

The behavior may or may not stop. Alex may turn the radio off. Then again, he might think that you're the jerk and he may leave the radio on to annoy you even more. You might succeed in intimidating Alex and he will lower his radio, but remember, when attacked, people attack back. Alex may later decide to "get you back" in other ways.

Your relationship suffers. Alex doesn't like to get yelled at. No one does! It is difficult to have a successful work or personal relationship with someone who shouts at you. In fact this kind of behavior often destroys relationships.

You feel bad about yourself. This is the confusing one. You may have a momentary high after shouting at Alex. In fact, your self-esteem may surge. This "good" feeling is what often gives people the belief that aggressive behavior is okay. But trust me, it doesn't last. You have lost control of yourself and sooner or later you will realize this.

Others may have a negative impression of you. You might be considered a hothead, someone who "needs to be handled." Your co-workers or friends may view you as someone who has no self-control. Alex may even be afraid of you. Again, you may be the most technically capable person to get the promotion, but you might not get it because of your confrontational style.

Exception—When Aggressive Behavior May Be the Right Choice

Of course, there are times when you may choose to be aggressive and this may be a positive choice, especially if you are under threat. Here's a situation in which a woman chose to act aggressively. She had no regrets:

A photographer friend of mine was hired to shoot a church pageant. She had permission to be there and permission to photograph the event. The man sitting behind her either did not know that fact, or chose to ignore it. When she turned around to take a picture, he grabbed her camera straps and started choking her with them. He told her she was not allowed to take pictures inside the church. He wouldn't let her go. She grabbed his tie, pulled hard, and said, "Get your hands off me—now!"

He may not have meant to choke her, but he was choking her. He did drop his hands as a result of her grabbing his tie. In this kind of situation, her aggression was appropriate.

Confusing an "Aggressive" with a "Positive" Confrontation

Both aggression and Polite and Powerful behavior respond to another person's bothersome behavior. This is what confuses many people. Because they have done something, they believe they have acted appropriately.

Darlene described to me what she considered her own positive confrontational behavior. A woman on the same committee had pointed her finger and spoke rudely to her: "I grabbed her finger and held it. I told her, 'Who do you think you are? Don't you dare ever point at me again!' "

Darlene thought, because she had taken action that she had behaved in a positive manner. She didn't. She behaved rudely herself by grabbing her finger and shouting back. She was aggressive.

This is a common misconception for people who don't know the Polite and Powerful alternative. These are the people who think that they have only two options—to confront aggressively or not to confront at all. They believe that because they have defended themselves, or spoken up, it was a positive action. Taking action is only one part of positive confrontation. It's *how* that action is taken that is also important.

An Unfair Label

Keep in mind, too, that when you have a positive confrontation, someone may unfairly label you as "aggressive." Maybe the other person didn't know how to handle a Polite and Powerful person. Maybe someone will be unused to, or unfamiliar with, this kind of behavior from you (maybe you used to be a confrontational weakling).

You Choose to Be Polite and Powerful

Alex probably doesn't realize that his music is bothering you. You get up, walk around to his desk and ask him if you can talk with him for a moment. You calmly explain that the radio is distracting you. You are not able to get your work done. You tell him you would appreciate it if he could lower it.

Polite and Powerful Behavior Defined

I would like to now give you a simple explanation of what Polite and Powerful behavior is in action. Let's forget about the terms passive, assertive, and aggressive because as you can see, there's a lot of confusion about what qualifies to some people as assertive and to others as passive and so on. You'll see why Polite and Powerful makes so much sense.

Polite and Powerful behavior in action means:

- You know what's bothering you;
- You know what it is you want from the other person;
- You understand your own position *and* you understand the other person's point of view;
- You make a conscious choice to say something directly, respectfully, and powerfully; and
- You use polite language when you speak.

The consequences of making this choice are:

The bothersome behavior often stops. Alex will probably lower his radio. Why not? Most people are not jerks who "are out to get you." When treated with respect, most people will treat you the same way.

There are no guarantees that you will get what you want, but it gives you the best chance for getting what you want, or equally important, for working out an alternative solution.

Your relationship with that person can usually be maintained and can often get better. When you're able to work through your difficulties with others, your relationships at work and in your personal life are likely to improve because they will be more honest. When you confront Politely and Powerfully, you can stop secretly resenting that person. You don't have to ignore or avoid people. You can stop complaining and pretending, too. Again, there are no guarantees, but Polite and Powerful is your best chance for maintaining the relationship.

You feel good about yourself. Of course you do! You've done something that has been respectful to yourself and to the other person. You're not letting your negative feelings rule your life. You are in control.

Others have a positive view of you. Here's a surprise—even Alex may appreciate that you have let him know that his behavior was bothering you. He may be impressed by your directness and willingness to speak up on your own behalf! (He certainly wouldn't have a good opinion of you if he finds out you're bad-mouthing him around the office). Polite and Powerful people are able to work well with all types of people and that's a quality promotable people share.

The Benefits of Polite and Powerful At a Glance

The chart below sums up the benefits/consequences of each of the confrontational choices you make:

	PASSIVE	AGGRESSIVE	POLITE AND POWERFUL
Bothersome Behavior	Continues	Stops/Continues	Often Stops
Relationship	Suffers	Suffers	Maintain/May Improve
Self-Esteem	Down	Up then Down	Up
Your Image	Suffers	Suffers	Can Improve

It's hard to believe after seeing this chart that anyone would choose to damage their professional and personal relationships, to let their self-esteem run dry, and to encourage others to think poorly of them. But every day, by not practicing Polite and Powerful behavior, that's exactly what millions of people do!

Many people who attend my seminars are often stunned with this discovery. I routinely hear statements like, "I just didn't realize this before," or "I didn't understand that I was letting my friendships suffer because I'm not able to tell people how I really feel."

When you have a certain way of operating in the world, including how you decide to confront or not confront, it becomes an unexamined habit. You aren't aware of how it affects you and others around you.

But once you do see and understand your own behavior you can change your life for the better. I have seen it proven over and over again that with a new awareness, even if it seems hard at first, comes the ability to make a positive change in your life. Polite and Powerful behavior is the gateway to positive confrontation.

Once they realize how their relationships, self-esteem, and professional image have been suffering, it's especially difficult for people who want to be successful in business and in their personal lives to return to their old passive or aggressive behaviors.

Be Honest: Think of the last time you had or wanted to have a confrontation. Which choice did you make? What were the consequences of that choice in your professional or personal life? Would you handle yourself differently now?

Polite and Powerful Is No Guarantee That You Will Get What You Want

Most people find they get what they want or at least some degree of satisfaction when they confront Politely and Powerfully. I wish I could guarantee you these results too, but I can't.

A confrontation involves at least two people. You don't control the other person; you can only control yourself. You don't know how the other person will react. You can make predictions but it's only a guess. But this I can guarantee: No matter what the outcome, when you confront Politely and Powerfully you feel good about yourself and you often know where you stand with that person. Later on we'll look at a specific situation where the person acted Politely and Powerfully and boy, did she get a surprise!

Of course, you don't have to confront or to even choose Polite and Powerful, but now it's an option you didn't have before.

CHAPTER 5

THE JERK TEST

Okay—you've decided that Polite and Powerful *is* for you. You're going to learn the skills of Polite and Powerful. You're going to speak up once and for all. No more jerks are going to get the best of you!

But before you do decide to speak up, I ask you to pause and take the jerk test first. This is important. Let's talk about jerks for a minute.

I think "jerk" is a great word.

It's strong—yet not so strong that it's offensive. It's equal-opportunity and gender-neutral. Men are jerks. Women are jerks. Anyone, in fact, can be a jerk. But how many people are, in fact, jerks?

Probably not as many as we think. There are lots of reasons why people behave they way they do. Being a jerk is only one of them. Some of the others may be culture, gender, personal experience, individual expectations/priorities, age, nonverbal communication, religion . . . I could keep going.

We are lightning fast to make negative assumptions about the behaviors of others. Often it's because we don't understand what's driving the person who is driving us crazy. What's informing them, influencing them? Ironically, we, in our too-quick judgment, become jerks too. Once you do understand what motivates the other person, you still may not like the person's behavior, and that's fine. It doesn't, however, necessarily mean the other person is a jerk (and you're not either).

If you approach a confrontation thinking "Wow! What a jerk!" you may be setting yourself up for a negative experience. If we've decided that someone is a jerk, that means we feel he or she has treated us badly, unfairly, unjustly—feelings we don't like. You can easily end up in the land of aggression when you're upset. But if you approach a confrontation thinking, "Maybe this person is a jerk. Maybe not. I'll find out what I'm dealing with first," you are far more likely to have a positive experience.

Is it easy giving someone the benefit of the doubt? Not always. Our first impression often sticks, especially when we're upset. But it's worth it to find out if the person really is a jerk or not—you may save yourself from a negative confrontation. In fact, you may discover there's no confrontation to be had.

Take the Jerk Test

Here are six questions you should stop and ask yourself, before assuming that someone is a jerk.

1. Does the other person really understand the effect of his or her nonverbal communication?

People express themselves verbally *and* nonverbally. They may have every intention of being Polite and Powerful but their body language may be conveying another message—and they don't know it.

Here's the tricky part. People will believe your nonverbals before they believe your verbals. The suspected "jerk" may not realize their nonverbal messages are confusing. They don't always match the intent of the words. A network engineer thought that a woman in his group did not take him seriously at meetings. "She always laughs at me or giggles," he said, "like my opinion doesn't count." He was quite upset with her.

After learning the skills of positive confrontation, he was able to confront her—without losing his temper. To his amazement, she was in amazement upon hearing about her behavior. She had no idea that she was laughing or giggling. She had no intention of discounting him. She thanked him for confronting her about it. Who else, she had to wonder, had she unknowingly offended?

Maybe this seems silly. Who doesn't know when they're laughing or giggling? But trust my experience on this one. I have taught and coached thousands of people about verbal and nonverbal signals. I can tell you, really and truly, people often don't know they're giggling, snapping gum, crossing their arms, over-smiling, chewing pencils, frowning; you name it, people do it—unaware of their own behavior, all the time. Like the woman who told me she didn't point her finger while she was pointing her finger at me!

You may have this problem too. As we discuss in Chapter 8, consistent verbal and nonverbal behavior is very important to positive confrontation.

2. What is the other person's culture?

In the United States, our village is global; our outlook is not. I know—I teach international etiquette. This is an area that leads to so much misunderstanding, it's incredible. Whether you do business internationally or never leave your state, you *will* be interacting with individuals with different cultural backgrounds and communicating with individuals who are speaking English as a second language (ESL). I used to teach ESL. It's difficult. Words are important—with them we express our ideas and voice our thoughts. But when someone speaks ESL their vocabulary can be limited. They may not be able to fully get their thoughts across. We can also have a hard time listening to ESL speakers as their pronunciation of English may be awkward or their speech slow. So not only do we have a hard time literally understanding each other because of language barriers, but also the opportunity for conflict, given a lack of cultural awareness on all sides, is rich and ripe.

Here's a simple definition of culture that explains why it engenders so much conflict: The beliefs, attitudes, ideas, and values that *one* group of people has in common. What is important in *one* culture may be of no consequence in another. What's offensive in one, may be quite acceptable in another.

Most people, regardless of their culture, have a tendency to judge what is different as wrong. When I ask a group of Americans: "What side of the street do the British drive on? Most will answer: "The wrong side!" If I ask a group of Brits, they will say the same thing.

It's not the wrong side; it's the other side.

An American sales representative had lunch brought in for himself and his Indian customer. The meal had meat in it. The customer, as are many Indians, was a vegetarian and was offended. Why didn't he bring in a vegetarian meal, he wondered? How could he not know I don't eat meat? The customer stopped seeing the representative. The representative had no idea what happened. Each quickly assumed the other was a jerk.

Nonverbal communication, such as eye contacts, gestures, body language can also cause lots of international misunderstandings. For a more in-depth look at both domestic and international etiquette issues that will help you avoid, or not become the source of, conflict with others see Chapter 16.

3. Did the person really mean harm?

Most people do not mean to harm others. Most people do not set out to hurt others. But many people do become preoccupied and do not pay attention to what they may be saying or doing or how their actions can have an impact on others. The Ann Landers column from Chapter 1 is a good illustration. The hair-flipping woman probably didn't know she was a hair flipper. The hair flip, the mustache twirl, are things people often do unconsciously. They don't realize that what they're doing annoys others and can convey a negative message.

Think about it—why would anyone flip her hair into someone else's face *on purpose*? It doesn't make sense. You would have to be beyond a jerk to do that.

Years ago, as I was getting onto the highway, a man from another car laid on his horn and called me something a lot worse than a jerk. *I had no idea I had cut him off.* I believed I had the right of way. He was so convinced I was worse than a jerk. I was out to get him. I wasn't. I made a mistake.

4. Is it the person or the policy?

Many times we get upset with someone, but in reality, and this is especially true in a business context, that person may be following the company's or organization's procedures. We may not know it or like it but it's not the other person's fault.

A claims adjuster complained that people in his office sent him needless e-mails. "Why," he wanted to know, "are people wasting my time? I don't care who is in the office when. Why do I need to know everyone's vacation plans?" As he was complaining to his supervisor, he found out that some departments in his company had policies that *everyone* was to be told when the person would be out of the office! Since he was in one of the departments with this rule, "Why," his supervisor wanted to know, "didn't you know that?"

A woman wanted to work from home when her child was ill. She was upset when her boss told her she had to use her sick time. When she asked her about it later, her boss told her that she was following company policy. It was a policy that she didn't agree with and that could be changed in the future, but until then, she had to stick to the guidelines.

5. Did the person know how to use the technology?

Remember when the copier was the most complicated thing you had to deal with at work? When the worst thing someone could do was leave the paper tray empty? Then came voice mail, e-mail, fax, call waiting, cell phones, laptops, modems, networks—and it all came fast. New technology has appeared on our desks and in our homes so quickly that many of us are still trying to figure out how to turn on our computers. A lot of us are still trying to figure out how to incorporate it into our work lives. The new technology gives us ways to do things better, faster, and cheaper. It's also given us a whole new source of conflict in the workplace.

People do all sort of strange and rude things when communicating with new technology, usually unintentionally. Still, it can look bad. Many people don't know that they are going to look like a jerk if they use their cell phone in a crowded restaurant. Scores of people don't know that people don't want ten-minute messages left on their voice mail systems. People hate that, they think jerk!

Because this is such a hot button area for conflict, we explore techno-etiquette and all aspects of etiquette in more depth in Chapter 15 as well. For now, know that it is often a source of conflict.

6. Does the person have the same or enough information?

We assume that a person knows as much about a situation as we do. They don't always know because we haven't told them, it was an

THE POWER OF POSITIVE CONFRONTATION

oversight, or they have the wrong information. Shakespeare made a living out of circumstances like this.

A group of four male friends always spend New Year's together: "Three of us have been in touch to make our plans. The fourth guy is not in touch with us during the year as much because he has an all-consuming job. We can't make plans without him. I have called him and he hasn't returned my calls. If we leave him out, he will be upset. But if we wait, we won't be able to get a reservation."

I asked him, if when leaving a message, did he give his friend the reason for the call? He said, "Well . . . No, I just asked him to call me back."

After realizing this, he decided to leave a different message for his friend:

"Tom, we're trying to make New Year's plans but we can't do it without you. We don't want to leave you out so please call Jeff by Friday so we can make a deposit at the restaurant. OK?"

Tom wasn't being a jerk, he didn't realize the urgency. He called back—by Friday.

To Let It Go or Not Let It Go?

Once you realize that the person you think is a jerk may not be a jerk at all, you're in a better position either to let it go or to have a positive confrontation. You are more likely to be Polite and Powerful if you're not working on a negative assumption.

But What if the Person *Is* a Jerk?

Hopefully, you see that jerks are not as plentiful as you may have thought. Yet they do exist. If you do come in contact with a jerk, what can you do?

First, let me tell you what you shouldn't do:

- **Do unto others**. This is how road rage escalates into violence, "You cut me off, I cut you off." This makes you a jerk back.

- **Behave rudely.** I heard about a couple who had just started dating. They were cut off in their car by an aggressive driver. The man drove ahead of them, rolled down his window and spit out the window. It landed on the aggressive driver's windshield. He had good aim, but the following week, he didn't have a date. His new girlfriend was turned off by his rude behavior and broke up with him. It may not have been her only reason, but it certainly contributed to the overall image of this man she was forming—an image she didn't like.
- **Resort to old behaviors.** If the jerk is really bothering you and you have to see this person regularly, don't complain about the jerk. Don't avoid the jerk or pretend the jerk doesn't bother you. Don't shout, bully, or displace either.

What You Can Do if You Meet a Jerk

- You can choose to ignore the jerk. Is it worth it? If the person is a total stranger, then why bother? Chances are you'll never see him or her again. (You'll see why this option becomes easier to choose further down the road.)
- You can choose to act Politely and Powerfully.

Taking Polite and Powerful action might be your best option, especially if the person is someone you have to see on a regular basis. Why let a jerk get on your nerves repeatedly? Why should a jerk stress you out? You can deal with jerks—as long as you do it Politely and Powerfully.

I hope that by now, you understand why Polite and Powerful is the positive way to approach confrontation. It's the choice with all the benefits: lower stress, better relationships, and improved self-esteem. At this point most people tell me they are firmly committed to learning all the skills that make up Polite and Powerful behavior.

So here we go. WAC'em is next.

PART II

THE NUTS, BOLTS, AND SCREWS OF POSITIVE CONFRONTATION

CHAPTER 6

DON'T ATTACK 'EM, WAC 'EM

In the first part of this book, we focused on helping you figure out who you are as a confronter. We discussed why you will want to try Polite and Powerful behavior instead. As you now know, it's a more effective, less stressful, and more positive way of dealing with life's day-to-day conflict.

So let's suppose that you've been having a problem with another person. You're not sure what to say or how to handle it. But you do know that you're tired of complaining, avoiding, pretending, or shouting. You're tired of not being able to tell people what you want from them. You've taken the jerk test.

It's time to confront the other person.

Except now you have an advantage. Now you understand that you have a better choice than your old behavior and you're choosing it. That's great! But exactly how do you do it? How do you have a positive confrontation?

As I've said, confrontation, even a positive one, falls into the category of difficult communication/difficult conversation. For most of us, it's the hardest type of conversation there is. As you know by now, this is true because most people haven't been taught what to say and how to say it in a way that's both Polite and Powerful. Once you know what you're going to say and how to say it, your most difficult obstacle to confrontation is removed.

WAC'em

Positive confrontation begins here, with WAC'em. Your first step to this better way of dealing with day-to-day conflicts and life's difficult conversations is to learn this simple model. WAC'em is an acronym. Each letter stands for a key step in getting your words for a difficult conversation together.

W = What. What's really bothering you. Define the problem.

A = Ask. What do you want to ask the other person to do or change? Define what would solve the problem for you.

C = Check-In. You've asked the other person to change something about his or behavior. What does he or she think about it? You need to check-in and find out.

Don't Attack'em, WAC'em

Don't attack people. WAC them instead. You'll get much better results.

You know that if you're an attacking displacer, shouter, bully, complainer, or avoider, you can make yourself look bad; you'll feel bad; the behavior that's bothering you will probably continue. But if you WAC the other person with your well thought out words, words that are both Polite and Powerful, you have a much better chance of feeling good about yourself, of projecting a positive image out into the world and of getting the other person's bothersome behavior to stop.

WAC'em is simple, yes, but it has been field tested on men and women from all walks of life, income levels, educational levels—it works! WAC'em will help you figure out what's *really* bothering you and what you *really* want from the other person.

Keep in mind that it may be simple, yet putting it into practice isn't as easy as it sounds. Most people have no idea how challenging it is to get their words together for a difficult conversation until they sit down and try. That's why it's really important that you figure out what you want to say *before* you say something. It helps ensure that when you do say something, what you say will come out Polite and Powerfully—not passively or aggressively. It's easy to choke on your words, get nervous, get upset, or even cry when you're in a situation you're not prepared for.

So prepare using WAC'em. Each letter of WAC'em stands for a crucial element of a positive confrontation. Using each letter to guide and remind you, you will be able to figure out your words. I'll look at each letter separately and then at the end of this chapter, we'll put it all together.

The W:
What's *Really* Bothering You?

Answering this question will help you clarify your thoughts. But you need to be very specific when you decide on your W. If your confrontation is with your co-worker in the next cube or your brother, what is it about the person's behavior or comments that you are having difficulty with?

Break it down: What exactly is the person doing or saying? Describe it. Here's some advice on defining your W:

1. **Be specific**. Don't generalize. Avoid words like always and never. Instead, link the behavior with a specific situation: Yesterday, Sean arrived twenty minutes late to my meeting. Betty was supposed to pay the parking ticket by Tuesday. Dan comes home and puts his papers on top of the television and doesn't hang his clothes in the closet.

2. **Don't label the person's behavior**. He's selfish or she's inconsiderate are examples of labels. Think instead, What is the specific behavior that's bothering me?

3. **Don't get into how you feel yet**. For now, just concentrate on the other person, not the effect the other person's behavior had on you.

Getting the W Right

Figuring out your W is not always easy for the participants of my seminars. Here are two examples of people who thought figuring out their W was easy. They were wrong!

Example I

"I am so sick of my co-worker talking to her new boyfriend on the phone. It drives me crazy. One day she was on for two straight hours. My W is that she is acting like a love-sick idiot."

Where this W went wrong: In this case, the W—What's bothering me?—was personal rather than specific. She didn't stick to the behavior. She made a judgment instead. If she goes into her confrontation packing this W, the other person can turn around and say, "Who are you to tell me I'm love-sick? You're just jealous."

The W should have been something like: "When you have extended personal conversations on the phone, it's distracting."

Example II

"When I give presentations to the sales department, the department manager always talks, laughs, and jokes with others. My W is that I want to tell him that his behavior is always rude, unprofessional, and a poor example to set in front of the workforce."

This person also got sidetracked by labeling the manager's behavior. Plus, he generalized, which is not going to set the tone for a positive confrontation. The W is found in the behavior, "Yesterday during my budget presentation, I heard you telling jokes to Tom." Always go back to the person's behavior. That's where you'll find the W.

The Trouble with Labels

Let's talk a bit more about this tendency we have to label others. If your brother is borrowing your car and not returning it with any gas in it, this may seem like a no-brainer. The W—What's bothering you—is that your brother is selfish or inconsiderate. He may even qualify as a jerk in this situation. You think, no problem, that's my W: My brother is selfish.

Only, it is a problem. You've negatively labeled his behavior. You haven't described what he's done that has bothered you and in fact, he may have a different interpretation about his behavior.

If you were to confront him and say, "You're selfish," he can turn around and say, "No, I'm not. Just last month, I mowed your lawn," or give any number of reasons and excuses to explain away his behavior and prove you wrong. This is how good old-fashioned family arguments begin.

In this case, the W should very specifically describe what your brother has done: He returned your car with no gas in it.

I Can't Fix "Unfair"

I've asked hundreds of participants when they come up to me at my seminars and complain about someone, "What exactly is bothering you?" They have difficulty verbalizing their concerns. They will often use huge generalizations to describe the other person's behavior. I hear adjectives like "difficult," "lousy," or "unfair." These words, or labels, tell me nothing. They all can have lots of different meanings to different people and they're usually negative.

One person told me, "My boss is a lousy manager. He just gives me attitude when he seems unhappy with me." Another said: "My teammate is not pulling her weight." Yet another said, "My boss is unfair."

I responded that I couldn't help them fix "lousy" and "unfair" or any of the other generalizations. By having to figure out the W, though, they'd be encouraged to be specific and clarify what they mean. So the comment about the 'unfair' boss became: "My boss signed up my three co-workers for the computer class but he didn't register me."

That is clear! The seminar participant can confront his boss about that, if he chooses to do so.

Notice—and this is very important—the W is non-accusatory.

You're simply describing the person's behavior—without judging it. You have a right to comment on another person's behavior if it affects you. You don't have a right to verbally attack the other person.

Suppose you're upset with your sister-in-law because she hasn't hosted her share of holiday dinners. Listen to the difference:

"Blanche, you never host holiday dinners."

versus:

"Blanche, we've had holiday dinners at my house for the last two years."

If you were Blanche, how would hearing the first statement make you feel? Probably defensive, ambushed, embarrassed. Maybe Blanche honestly thought you liked having holiday dinners at your house. If you accuse her, Blanche instantly becomes uncomfortable. This W does not set the stage for a positive confrontation.

The second W statement, on the other hand, does. You're describing the situation that's bothering you. You're not accusing, you're stating a fact as you see it. You're much more likely to get Blanche engaged in a positive confrontation.

More examples of getting more specific about your Ws:

"You always make me drive."

versus:

"For the past few weekends when we've gone out, I've done all the driving."

"I should have known you can't keep your mouth shut."

versus

"I heard from Ethel that you told her Tom and I are seeing a marriage counselor."

When you're working on your W, don't generalize. Don't bring up past grievances. Stick to the specific, immediate problem. Keep your W specific, but simple.

Why Does This Behavior Bother You?

Not only do you need to define the specific behavior that's bothering you. You need to clarify why it bothers you. What effect does that person's behavior have on you? This is also important information for the other person to have.

Back to Blanche:

"We've had holiday dinners at my house for the last two years." (Describes what's bothering you)
"As a result, the majority of the preparation and clean-up has been my responsibility." (The effect it has on you).

Another example:

"For the past few weekends when we've gone out, I've done all the driving." (Describes what's bothering you.)
"I'm not able to drink." (The effect it has on you.)

Give It Up If It's Not Your Issue

Sometimes, when you start thinking about how the behavior affects you, you may discover it has no effect on you. If it doesn't affect you, then it's not really your issue. And if it's not your issue, why do you want to confront the person?

A woman once complained that her sister-in-law never cooked for her brother. I asked her if he was sick and unable to cook for himself. She said no. I said, "Well then, what effect does this have on you?" She paused and then said, "None," she said. "I guess it's not my concern."

Bingo!

Alice complained that her boyfriend never did anything. Again, this is not a W anyone can work with. When I asked her, "What exactly is bothering you about your boyfriend's behavior?" she said, "He sits around and reads all the time."

Then I asked, "What effect does this have on you?"

"Well, I was packing for our trip and he was just reading."

"Do you pack for him?" I asked.

"No."

"Does he pack for himself?"

"Yes," she said, "but he waits until the last minute."

Again, I asked, "What effect does this have on you?

"None," she admitted. "I guess, I just do it differently."

There may be lots of other issues between this couple. But this one, at least, has been resolved.

If You Still Can't Give it Up . . .

There may be times when you will choose to say something to a person, even if his or her behavior has no direct effect on you—except that you believe the behavior is unfair or unjust. This could be when a co-worker leaves early whenever the boss is out of the office. It drives you crazy because you think it's not fair. Your neighbor repeatedly parks in your condo's handicapped parking spot. Why the heck can't she park somewhere else?

In this kind of situation, you may want to say something because you believe an injustice is being done. I'll discuss this in further detail in Chapter 12.

If It Is Your Issue, Make Sure the *Why* Is Honest

As I said in an earlier part of this book, honesty isn't always easy. But it's usually better to be honest. If you make up an excuse about why you're upset, even if it's to spare the other person's feelings, you can create another problem. The other person can respond to the excuse.

If you told Blanche: "I feel like I can't do as good a job as I want," you open the door for Blanche to say: "You've done a wonderful job! Don't worry about it."

This isn't what you want to hear from Blanche. You want her to respond to your real concern—not get sidetracked by an excuse.

This is why getting your W's right—and honest—is so important.

Expressing Emotion

Sometimes the effect of another person's behavior is how it made you feel. I encourage you to express those feelings when it's appropriate.

Depending upon your relationship with the person you may want to say:

"I don't like it when you call me lazy." (Less emotion expressed)

or

"When you call me lazy, it hurts my feelings." (More emotion expressed)

"You didn't call when you said you would." (Less emotion expressed)

or

"When you don't call me when you say you're going to, I get scared." (More emotion expressed)

Expressing Emotions in Business

If you have a personal relationship with the person you're WAC'ing, it's often appropriate to tell the person how his or behavior made you feel — often if a person understands that you've been upset, that's enough for them to change his or her behavior. But, if it's a business situation that isn't highly personal or a person you're not especially close to, you may want to keep your W very simple — here's what's bothering me — and leave your feelings out of it.

If you do decide to share your feelings, don't make excuses for them, just be honest about them. This is especially true in business situations. I tell people if something is really bothering you and it's a business situation, you do have a right to tell the person bothering you how it makes you feel — just keep it simple. No excuses! Do not give a lot of history: "Boss, when you criticize my work in front of other people, it embarrasses me. My father used to do this to me when I was a kid . . ."

It's perfectly acceptable to say: "When you criticize my work in front of other people, it embarrasses me." You are describing the effect his behavior is having on you.

Say What You Mean but Say It Politely and Powerfully

If you catch more flies with honey, think of tact as honey. You are far more likely to get what you want out of a confrontation by being tactful. What you say can set the whole tone for your confrontation. Your wording really matters. Here are some important guidelines for choosing and using polite but powerful language:

1. **Write your W down**. What's bothering you? Put it on paper. This will help clarify the issues for you. This is especially important in the beginning as you're getting your WAC'em feet wet. When you get upset, you may exaggerate or get defensive. Writing your thoughts slows you down; it will help you focus on the person's bothersome behavior and to avoid labeling. You can stop and change the words. You can edit yourself. Remember, this writing exercise is for your benefit only. You're not going to read it to the other person. In fact, you don't want to because we often write more formally than we speak. Later, we'll discuss when it's appropriate to WAC someone in writing.

2. **Avoid blaming, accusatory "You" statements**. Compare the following statements:

> "You *never* tell me things."
>
> versus
>
> "I need the information."

"I" statements are usually assertive statements. "You" statements are often aggressive statements. "You" statements encourage blame and generalizations. "I" statements will encourage you to keep the emphasis on your self. Remember, "You" statements can put people on the defensive. Notice the difference in how each of the following sounds:

> "You are always saying mean things." (Offensive)
>
> versus

"I'm offended by the comment." (Polite and Powerful)

"You're getting too emotional." (Offensive)

versus

"I'd like to sit down and discuss this calmly." (Polite and Powerful)

"You" statements are often accompanied by negative words. Negative words put people on the defensive:

"You **neglected** your chores."
"You **messed up** my hair color."
"You **failed to** meet the deadline."

What do these statements do? They blame. Avoid negative words like: *Failed, forgot, neglected, wrong, didn't*. These are words that put people on the defensive. Try phrasing like this instead:

"I need your help putting the kids to bed."
"This color needs to be redone."
"Deadlines need to be met."

The more positive phrasing above will help you set a tone, an atmosphere in which the other person can listen to your point of view. People hear "you failed," "you did it wrong," and immediately close up and get ready for battle. "I" statements combined with positive phrasing keeps the communication channel open.

3. **Avoid harsh adjectives and descriptive words when describing the other person's behavior**. Though you want to figure out what's bothering you, you don't want to use the word "bother," as in "You really bother me." Avoid other harsh words, like "disgusting," "lazy," "selfish," "revolting," and "annoying." These have the same effect as negative words—they put the other person on the defensive. If that happens, the chances of having a positive confrontation aren't so good.

4. **Avoid exaggerating or generalizing with "always," "never," and "seldom."** These words are not conducive to open communication. The other person feels attacked. Instead of engaging in a dialogue, you

put yourself in a position of having to defend the generalization you just made. This is not a positive way to start your WAC'em wording.

When "You" Statements Are Necessary

Sometimes a "you" statement can, when it's descriptive rather than accusatory, be what you'll want to say. Sometimes, you will need to use "you" to describe the other person's behavior. There's often no other way to do it. Just make sure it doesn't turn into a negative statement.

"Yesterday, when you arrived thirty minutes late to my meeting . . ."
"Last night, you said 'I don't want to go . . .' "

Softening Statements

When you prepare your WAC'em wording, it's often useful to begin your W—what's bothering me—with a statement that will help put the other person at ease. These are called softening statements. They can soften, or ease, the tension of a difficult conversation by showing the other person that you're giving him or her the benefit of the doubt. These statements can make it easier for the other person to listen to your W. Some examples of effective softening statements include:

"I'm sure you don't mean any harm by this . . ."
"I bet you don't realize this . . ."
"I can see this was an oversight and . . ."
"John, I'm sure you meant no harm, but when you call me hon, I'm offended.

Getting Your W Right

As you can see, figuring out your W can sometimes be tricky. But it gets easier over time. After some practice, you will be able to zoom in on your W very quickly just by asking yourself: What's bothering me? Don't rush it though in the beginning. Keep writing your W's down until it becomes second nature. It's essential that you get your W right. Remember these points:

- Be specific. Describe the other person's behavior, don't judge it.
- Don't label or generalize—no "selfish," no "inconsiderate," no "always," or "nevers."
- Understand the effect the person's behavior has on you.
- Use positive wording to express your W, including "I" statements.
- Don't use negative or harsh words, like bother, annoy, stupid, etc.
- Use a softening statement to put the other person at ease, when appropriate.

The A:
What Do You Want to Ask the Other Person to Do?

Once you have your W figured out, it's time to move on to your A—What do you want to *ask* the other person to do? How can he or she correct the situation that's bothering or annoying to you? This is our second letter of WAC'em.

You shouldn't just tell someone your W, what's bothering you, and then walk away: "When you let your dog run without a leash, he does his business in my yard." You can't assume the other person will "get" what's bothering you. This is why you must have your A clearly defined before you go into a confrontation or have the difficult conversation. After delivering your W, you must go on to explain what you want the person to do about it. In this case what you want to ask for may be, "I would like you to keep your dog out of my yard."

You must define your A beforehand. I've had people who've admitted to me that in their excitement to confront positively, they've forgotten or neglected to prepare their A. If you confront someone without knowing the A, you will let the other person have control over the conversation. Worse still, there can often be no resolution.

What You Want To *Ask* For Needs To Be Specific

Like your wording for the W, you must be specific about your A. If you're not specific in what you ask the other person to do, you may not get what you want. You may get what the person thinks you want or what the person wants to do or give.

Defining what you want to ask the other person to do can be a surprisingly difficult step. Sometimes, it's even harder than defining the W. We often complain about a person's behavior, but we don't always know what we want in its place. Clarifying what you want will help you know what to ask for. There isn't a wrong or right. You must decide what you want or what's important to you.

Let's look at an example:

The boss who didn't sign his employee up for the training that others were going to get is a good one. The A in this case is "I'd like the training too." But remember to be as specific as possible. An even better A in this case is: "I would appreciate it if you could sign me up for the computer training in July."

If you don't say your A, which is, "I'd like to be signed up for the next training?" your Boss may offer another resolution. He can say, "Sorry, you can go to the marketing conference." But what if you want this specific training? The training, not the marketing conference, is important to your career development. Your A must be specific. The training class may be full and you won't be able to take it, but this represents your best chance of getting what you want.

When In Doubt Wait

If you don't know what it is you want to ask for, don't confront yet. A marketing director for a publishing company hadn't yet thought through her A and this is what happened: "I was talking to my boss and my employee came and stood at the door. It really distracted and bothered me."

She confronted her employee. Her W was: "When you stand at my door when I'm talking to someone, it distracts me." But she never told her employee what she wanted. Sometimes people can infer the meaning and figure it out. But sometimes they don't.

She never gave the A, which should have been something like, "I'd prefer it if you would not stand there. Please leave me a note or message that you need to speak to me."

Because she didn't give her A, her employee stood in the hallway instead of the doorway!

Another example:

> Your roommate plays his stereo loudly when he comes home from a night out. Your W:
>
> "I can't sleep when you play your music late at night. I have to get up early for work."
>
> But what's late at night? You might think it's ten o'clock. But your roommate thinks it's midnight.
>
> Your A might be: "I would appreciate it if you wouldn't play your stereo after 10 P.M."

Write Your A Down on Paper

You will get the same benefit out of writing down your A as you do from writing down your W—it will help clarify your thoughts.

To get started, begin your sentences with: "I would prefer . . ." or "I want . . ." or "I would like . . ." Even a simple "Please" is a fine start. Like softening statements, these kinds of openings will help create an atmosphere in which the other person can listen to you.

Deciding Upon How Direct You Should Be

Depending upon your relationship with the person or the seriousness of the situation, you choose to be very direct or less so.

When you're very direct, you're very specific about the outcome you want: "I want," or "I have to have . . ." This is often used with subordinates.

You can be a little less direct by expressing your preference: "I would like," or "I would prefer . . ."

Or, the least direct, is to soften your statements with a question. It can be a softer assertive statement. "Could you not play your stereo after 11 P.M.?" or "Is it possible . . . ?" You may want to use this approach if you're talking up the ladder.

Hierarchy of Directness:

I want. I have to have. (Most direct)
I would like. I would prefer. (Less direct)
Could you? Is it possible? (Least direct)

Position versus Want

The A forces you to become clear about what you want from the other person. Though we often use "position" and "want" as interchangeable words, it's really the intent behind them that we need to be concerned with. A *want* states your desired outcome. A *position* on the other hand, is much stronger and has much more significance. A position has a consequence to it. Don't go from *wants* to *positions* carelessly or lightly. You're limiting the amount of give and take and the ability to work out a mutual solution. Don't state a position unless you're prepared to follow through.

For example, maybe you have repeatedly asked your roommate not to play his music loudly at night. Finally, you take a position:

"I would appreciate it if you wouldn't play your stereo after 10 P.M."
(Want)

versus

"I would appreciate it if you wouldn't play your stereo after 10 P.M.

If you're not able to do this, I'm going to have to move out."
(Position)

"Please visit Mom in the nursing home every week." (Want)
versus
"I really want you to visit Mom in the nursing home every week. If
you can't, I'll need to move her closer to us." (Position)

Ask For What is Possible

When you ask for what you want, it must be in the person's power
or ability to give it to you. You ask your co-worker to get to your
meeting on time. But he's required to be at another meeting that
ends just as yours is beginning. He can't possibly be on time.

You're at the airport ticket counter. Your flight has been can-
celled. You tell the agent: "I must be on the next plane." Well, if the
next flight is already full, you can't get on it. You're setting yourself
up for a bigger conflict.

One man in my class commented on his friend that who was sac-
rificing his health by using steroids in pursuit of world weight lifting
records. His A was to ask him to stop it. I told him he could express
his concern, but it wasn't within his power to make someone stop
using steroids.

Like defining your W, zeroing in on your A will get easier with
time and practice. You will probably get to the point where you
don't have to write it down. You will be able to ask yourself: What
do I want to ask the other person to do? and figure it out on the
spot.

The C
Check-In with the Other Person

Our last letter of WAC'em is the C. You'll be happy to know this
one is simple and easy. But we need this last step because just as it
takes two to swing dance, it takes two to have a confrontation. You've

said both your W and your A in a clear, direct manner—**What's** bothering you and what you've **Asked** the person to do. Now you need to connect with the other person. The C, which stands for **Check-In,** allows that to happen.

The C is often a question that requires a response from the other person. It's important to know that the other person has heard you and you need to hear the other person's thoughts or opinions.

The other person may have good ideas, too.

Your C can be as simple as asking the other person, "Okay?" Some other phrases might include:

"Is that okay?"
"What do you think?"
"Can that happen?"

Now that you've WAC'ed the person, he or she may have a number of different responses—even some that you're not counting on. This we discuss in Chapter 9.

Putting It All Together

As I mentioned earlier, interrupting is a common bother, both in the workplace and at home. Using this as our example, let's go through the W, A, and C using this as your conflict.

The W—What's Bothering You

W: "It's hard for me to hear your point when I haven't had an opportunity to finish mine."

or

W: "I've noticed that I am unable to finish what I'm saying before I'm interrupted. I don't feel listened to."

The A—What Do You Want to Ask the Person to Do?

A: I respect what you have to say and if you ask me a question, I want you to let me finish what I am saying without interrupting.

or

A: I will give you a signal to let you know that I'm finished talking.

The C—Your Check-In to See If What You've Asked for Can Happen

C: Okay?

or

C: Can you do that?

Remember the twelve most common conflicts that we discussed in Chapter One? Here are WAC'em words for these conflict areas that my participants have created. These are actual WAC'em words that people have created for their real-life situations. These are not meant to be solutions for your situations. They illustrate how others have applied WAC'em to their situations. This isn't meant to save you the work!

WAC'em Words for Life's Common Conflicts

Situation: The occupant of the next cube spends vast amounts of time organizing his social life on the phone. It's very distracting (and his social life is more interesting than mine is!)

WAC'em Wording: "Since we sit so close together and there isn't much privacy, I can hear most/all of your conversations and they are very distracting. I would appreciate it if you could lower your voice when you are on the phone. Okay?"

Situation: I want to spend Christmas with my family; my spouse wants to spend it with his/hers.

WAC'em Wording: "We've been spending Christmas with your family every year and I get homesick. Can we alternate holidays?" (Here, a separate C is not necessary, it's implied in your A)

Situation: When it rains my neighbor's sump pump drains into the street and the water freezes in front of my driveway and mailbox.

WAC'em Wording: "You may be unaware that the water from your sump pump run-off freezes in front of my driveway and mailbox. It's dangerous. Please have the water run into a safer area. Okay?"

Situation: My neighbor's dogs run loose and do their business on my lawn. It really gets on my nerves!

WAC'em Wording: "I don't know if you are aware of this, but your dogs run into my yard and do their business there. I don't like cleaning up after them. Please take precautions so it doesn't happen again. Okay?"

Situation: I have a friend who calls and only complains about her life. I'm sick of having only negative conversations.

WAC'em Wording: "Sally, the last couple of months when we talk you've been very negative about things in your life. It's difficult to listen to and it brings me down. You have good things in your life and I would appreciate talking about those things too. Will you try this please?"

Situation: A friend always calls during the day and leaves a message that says: "Hi. How is it going? Give me a call back." It drives me crazy because she knows that I am not there during the day. It's a long distance call that I have to return.

WAC'em Wording: "You call during the day when I'm working. It's a strain on my budget to call you back and be the one to pay for the call. I'd like to share the phone expenses more equally. Let's alternate the calls. Can we do that?"

Situation: My wife listens to my business messages on the answering machine, and does not save them, and forgets to tell me about them for several days, if at all.

WAC'em Wording: "Sweetie, when I don't get my messages, it makes me look unprofessional and irresponsible. I really need to get them. To take the burden off of you, I want to use an answering service. What do you think?"

Situation: My husband did not call and he was late.

WAC'em Wording: "When I wake up in the middle of the night and I don't know where you are, God-awful thoughts go through my head. Can you please call from now on if you are going to be late?"

Situation: A close and dear friend for years is heavily involved in an incentive business and wants me to join and I have absolutely no interest. She keeps asking. She doesn't get the hint.

WAC'em Wording: "We've discussed me joining your business and I've said numerous times that I'm not interested. It's starting to interfere with our friendship. I would appreciate if we could stop talking about it. Is that all right with you?"

Situation: A counterpart tells our manager everything that is said in our meetings, including things that could be damaging to one or more of the representatives.

WAC'em Wording: "Joe, maybe you are not aware that there is a code of honor among the sales representatives. If you have a problem or any issue, I'd like you to address it with me before you go to my manager. Can you do that?"

Situation: A co-worker that I had to work closely with was calling me names to other co-workers.

WAC'em Wording: "It's been brought to my attention that negative comments were made about me to our teammates. I would prefer if you have any personal or professional comments about me that you come directly to me. Can you do that?"

Situation: A customer puts his hand on my knee both in his office and business social situations.

WAC'em Wording: "It really makes me uncomfortable when you touch my knee. And I want you to stop." (There's no C because there is no need for a discussion. It's unacceptable behavior).

Situation: A co-worker makes racial comments about people and thinks that he's being funny. He hasn't picked up on hints that I don't like it.

WAC'em Wording: "I'm offended by your jokes. I don't think they are funny and would appreciate it if you would not tell them around me. Okay?"

Situation: One of my sales representatives complains to our customers about her personal life. The customers have told me that it makes them feel uncomfortable.

WAC'em Wording: "Some of our customers have told me that it makes them uncomfortable when you talk about your personal life. Please keep this type of conversation to a minimum. I'm counting on you for this."

Situation: My husband disciplines our six-year-old son and spanks him harder than I feel necessary. He thinks that he has to instill fear to get respect. He says: "That's how I was raised."

WAC'em Wording: "I am concerned about how our son is disciplined. I don't believe fear is necessary in order to discipline him and I worry about his mental health later. I want us to come up with an alternate punishment. Okay?"

Situation: My co-worker routinely makes appointments for which he is either late or doesn't show up at all.

WAC'em Wording: "When we have an appointment I set aside time for you. And when you don't come or are late, it messes up my schedule. In the future please be on time or let me know if you are going to be late so I can reschedule."

Working with WAC'em

WAC'em is not a rigid model. You'll find as you WAC people instead of attack them, it gets easier to quickly zero in on your W's and A's. There may be times when you just use individual parts of this. And sometimes that is all that is necessary.

Just Using the "W"

Sometimes just stating that something is bothering you—without attacking the person—is all that is needed. Sometimes just being able to express your displeasure is sufficient to get your point across.

And it's vitally important in building your self-esteem.

"I worry when I don't get a phone call from you." This may be all you need to say. You don't need to ask for anything. The other person understands what's bothering you and what it takes to fix the situation.

Just Using the "A"

Sometimes just stating what you want without attacking the person is all you need to do. "Please ask me before you borrow my

CDs." You don't need to go into a whole explanation. In this case, the W may be obvious.

Just using the A can help with on-the-spot issues. Quickly ask yourself, "What do I want to ask for?" Examples:

- If someone is not arriving on time to your meetings, the W is pretty clear. What do you want that person to do in the future? "I need you to be at the meeting by 10:05 at the latest."
- If you are not being told the priorities of your assignments, what do you want your boss to do? "Boss, when I get an assignment from you, I also need to be given its priority."
- Patricia is a high-level senior researcher in manufacturing. She held a meeting in the United States with her European counterparts, who did not take her seriously. She had asked a patent attorney to address the group. While he was talking he referred to her as "honey." One of the Europeans laughed. She had to do something immediately. There was no time for WAC'em. She simply and calmly said her A: "Tom, I don't want to be called honey."

Not Using WAC'em

The examples I have used in this chapter may sound simple. But for all of us who encounter situations like these day after day, they're not. We tend to think our own problems are truly exceptional. Sometimes they are. But I hear the same kind of stories every week. In fact, most of the time, we all have variations on the same conflicts.

And sometimes, these stories can be extreme.

A woman in a seminar told me that her co-worker kept complaining to her that their boss gave her—the co-worker—more work than the other employees in the department.

Yet, she didn't confront the boss. She got so frustrated she quit and left the company. She left a good job and a good company because she didn't know how to confront the boss!

This woman was afraid to say something. What she was afraid of,

I'm not sure. Since the dire consequence occurred anyway, which was losing her job, what would she have lost if she had WAC'ed her boss? Nothing. And she might have gained a lot. Many bosses are just waiting for you to say something.

Use Your WAC'em Card

On the dust jacket of this book is your very own WAC'em card. While you're getting experience in having positive confrontations, carry it with you. It will help. It will remind you to figure out:

W = **What's** bothering me?
A = What do I want to **Ask** the person to do or change?
C = I must **Check-in** with the other person.

One data processor told me that he carries it in his wallet and when he has an immediate situation, he'll go to the men's room and study the card and get his thoughts together.

A director of human resources told me she used it before she confronted her secretary and it helped her.

You probably won't need to carry it around for a long time. The more you practice WAC'em, the better you are going to get at it.

Welcome to WAC'em and the power of positive confrontation!

CHAPTER 7

ELIMINATE
YOUR VERBAL VICES

WAC'em helps you get your words together so you can have a difficult conversation with confidence and success. I discussed many aspects of your verbal skills in the last chapter. We talked about how to put a positive spin on your WAC'em words by avoiding "You" statements, negative and harsh words, and by using softening statements.

But your verbal skills are so critical to a positive confrontation — we can't stop yet. Your use of language is a large part of the Polite and Powerful verbal package. Don't roll your eyes and brace yourself for a crash refresher on grammar — but I am going to remind you to pay attention not only to what you're saying, your ideas and thoughts that you want to express, but *how* you're saying them. What language are you using when you speak? Is it Polite? Is it Powerful?

How you word your thoughts or ideas will affect how they are received. How you say those words that will affect how they're received too. You don't want your language skills getting in the way when you're having a tough conversation with someone.

Self-Discounting Language

The use of self-discounting language is a big problem area for those new to the world of powerful confrontation!

Self-discounting words or phrases can diminish your positive words and squash your intent to be powerful. If you discount your words, it's easy for the other person to do so too.

People use self-discounting language and then can't understand why others don't take them seriously. I keep a secret tally of the number of self-discounting words and phrases my participants use during the seminar when they ask their questions or make their comments. The last time I did this, I stopped at twenty. And that was before the first break!

If you use self-discounting language, this is a habit you need to break. If you don't break it, you will never be able to truly harness the power of positive confrontation. Here are the problem areas of self-discounting language to watch out for.

Wishy-Washy Words

These are self-discounting words and phrases like: "I think," "I hope," "Maybe," "Kinda," "Sort of," "Perhaps." The illustration I use in my seminars is, "I hope that perhaps this will be valuable information for you."

What? Do I or do I not think this is valuable information? Yes I do! Instead, the better way to say this without self-discounting language is: "I know you'll find this information valuable."

One participant (who was a smart and high-level manager) said: "I don't know if I'm wording this right and it's just my opinion . . ." (I don't know either.)

I have heard sales representatives say to potential customers:

"So, I guess I'll get moving on this . . ." (Will you or won't you?)

"I'm hoping that if you look at the total package . . ." (I'm hoping too!)

Now compare the statements when the self-discounting language is used and then corrected:

SELF-DISCOUNTING	POLITE AND POWERFUL
"So, I guess I'll get moving on this . . ."	"I'm going to get started on this today."
"I'm hoping that if you look at the total package . . . "	"Look at the total package. You'll see how it can reduce your costs . . ."
"Perhaps we can find a solution to your problem."	"I'm confident we can find a solution to your concern."
"I'm thinking we should start here."	"Let's start here."
"I was hoping that perhaps you could re-fax the material."	"Please re-fax the material."
"We were kind of in a way somewhat embarrassed."	"We were embarrassed."
"Maybe we should go to another place."	"I'd like to try another restaurant."

A salesperson tried to sell me a new telephone answering service and she said: "It's kind of convenient to have your phone answered while you're out." "My thought was, "is it convenient or not?" Either way, I didn't want to do business with someone that indecisive.

"I Think" versus "I Know"

The excessive use of "I think" is another tentative and self-discounting way of speaking. If you really know something, don't say, "I think . . ."

I said to my son one day when he asked to go to a friend's house to play, "I think it's okay." He responded: "Mom, do you think so or do you know so?"

I said, "I know so."

Why didn't I just say so? I do now.

■

"I'm Sorry I Can't Apologize"

People also say, "I'm sorry," when they have nothing to be sorry for—a similar habit to the "I think" example, above.

A pharmaceutical sales representative said to a doctor: "I'm sorry to bother you today. I see you are very busy."

She didn't even realize she had said this until the doctor asked her why she thought she was bothering him. And he even added: "Don't you have valuable information for me?" And she wondered why she didn't get a lot of time with the doctors.

Don't say, "I'm sorry," unless you meet the following criteria:

a. You mean it;
b. It's your responsibility and you have something to be sorry for. If you spill something, you trip someone, etc. be sorry.

Self-Discounting WAC'em Starts

Don't open a WAC'em discussion by making an apology or using tentative language. You're being polite—but polite doesn't mean you discount your W or your A.

Starts You Don't Want to Start WAC'em With . . .

WHAT YOU SAY . . .	THE OTHER PERSON IS PROBABLY THINKING . . .
"I hate to bring this up . . ."	So why are you bringing it up?
"I know this has been a bad time for you . . ."	It sure is, so don't make it worse.
"Maybe you'll think I'm being too emotional . . ."	Uh-oh, she's getting emotional.
"I'm having a problem with you . . ."	Get in line.
"I don't want to hurt your feelings BUT . . ."	I don't want you to hurt them either.

WHAT YOU SAY . . .	THE OTHER PERSON IS PROBABLY THINKING . . .
"I may be wrong . . ."	You're right; you are wrong!
"I'm not sure about this . . ."	Neither am I.
This is probably a dumb idea . . ."	It probably is.

Weak Endings for Strong Statements

I have seen this over and over—people in my classes will explain something or come up with a great Polite and Powerful statement that's crystal clear. A beauty of a W and a C. Then they blow it by adding "I don't know" or a tentative question that undermines his or her opinion or statement.

"I Don't Know" (But You Do!)

Women are famous for using this self-defeating, self-discounting phrase. A woman in my class offered a very eloquent opinion about an issue we were discussing. It was clear that she knew what she was talking about. Yet before she finished speaking, she paused and said, "Well, I don't know . . ." Yet she did know because what she had just said was valid and made terrific sense! And she didn't even know she had done this until I told her. She was shocked!

I spoke to a group of female physicians about this tendency. An experienced professional added that she didn't use "I don't know," but she realized that she added something else to the end of her sentences. When giving instructions to interns she would explain a complicated procedure and then end the discussion with, "Oh, gee, but what do I know!" (Her interns were probably thinking, "Well hopefully a lot, since you're in charge!)

When she said this, it's as if she said, "I don't trust my own opinion or knowledge."

Why do women in particular have this habit? There are probably many reasons—many of which have to do with gender roles and the like. Nevertheless, let's not get distracted by the reasons at this point. What you need to do right now is recognize the habit and stop doing it.

Self-Discounting Tag Questions

People deny they do this, but they do this one too. They say a good, strong Polite and Powerful statement and then stick a tentative question onto the end of it. This is like putting a tail on a dog that's already wagging one This is yet another self-defeating verbal mistake. Doing so illustrates your uncertainty and tentativeness.

"We'll go there, won't we?"
"This is fair to both of us. Isn't it?"

Why say: "That new Italian restaurant is great. Do you think you might like it?" if you really want to go?

Why not say: "That new Italian restaurant is great. I'd like you to come with me."

But Isn't the C in WAC'em Often a Question?

Yes, but here's the difference:

"Mandy, when you leave uneaten food in the lunchroom refrigerator for long periods of time, it smells up the whole room. Will you start cleaning your food out every two or three days?"

In this case, your A and the C are the same sentence and the Polite and Powerful statement is a question. Mandy will have to give you a yes or no. You need to know if she's going to cooperate or not.

Now if you had said: "Mandy, when you leave uneaten food in the lunchroom refrigerator for long periods of time, it smells up the whole room. It would be great if you could clean it out—maybe every other day or something like that. What do you think? I don't know."

Well if you don't know, Mandy probably doesn't either.

You're telling the other person that you're unsure of your own ideas or simply setting yourself up to not get what you want.

Or, you may frustrate the other person:

"We will go there, won't we?"

"No."

"But I have to go there!"

"Then why ask me if we're going if you've already made up your mind?"

"Well . . . you know . . . I don't know! Let's just go."

Other Verbal Problems

Self-discounting language isn't the only verbal problem that causes people problems during confrontations. There are a host of others to watch out for:

Curse Words

I was brought into a company to coach the senior manager who cursed during his weekly meeting. The secretaries knew not to answer their telephones during this forty-five-minute meeting because his loud use of these words could be overheard!

Cursing at someone is not appropriate in the work place or anywhere else for that matter. Yet people do it. They get frustrated. They don't know how to express themselves so they reach for the nearest word that's convenient, easy-to-use and that everyone understands. *&$% — it's out of their mouth and in the room. This person looks bad. If you curse, you do too. I'm not a goody-two-shoes, believe me. I just know how bad it is for your professional and personal image.

People have not been promoted and they have been fired for cursing at work. As far as your personal life goes — I don't know anyone who enjoys being cussed out. Do you?

Use of Filler Words

Filling belongs on the inside of a cream puff, not in a Polite and Powerful person's WAC'em wording. Excessive use of filler words is noticeable. Do this and you will sound bad. Sometimes you will sound terrible. Have you ever listened to a presentation or a speech given by a person who repeatedly says, "Um," "Like," "Okay," "All right," "You know," "Do you know what I mean?"

This use of filler words sounds awful! It's often painful to listen to him or her. You're dying for that cane to pull him or her off the stage.

The use of an occasional "Okay" or "All right" is okay and all right. It's a problem when people overuse them. Then they become a distraction and people start paying more attention to the filler words than the content of what you are saying to them.

This is the manager who calls a customer and leaves a voice mail message, but there are so many "ums" in the message that the potential customer wonders whether he should use him.

This is the university tour guide who kept repeating "And whatnot . . ." At the end of the tour when he asked for questions, a young girl in the tour turned, and asked her mother very loudly, "What's a 'whatnot?' " He was embarrassed.

People are often very surprised to learn that they use these words too. You can tune into the tone and volume of your voice with this simple trick: Every time you leave a voice mail message, use the feature that will let you replay it. Listen to yourself. Are you overusing fillers? Re-record your message if necessary. This is such an easy way to evaluate yourself. Take advantage of it.

One woman said to me after evaluating herself, "No wonder people don't listen to me. All they can do is count how many times I said, 'like.' I sounded really bad!"

"You" Instead of "I"

We discussed this in the last chapter. I'm bringing it up again because it's one of the biggest reasons why people are perceived as aggressive instead of Polite and Powerful. And they don't even realize the difference. They don't realize how much better their comments will be taken if they use "I" statement instead of "you" statements. Unless you must use "you" to describe the other's person's behavior, as in, "You were two hours past your curfew . . ." stick to the "I."

Say the following aloud and listen to the difference:

"You"	"I"
"You're wrong."	"I disagree."
"You're not explaining it right."	"I'm not understanding."
"You're always late."	"I need you to be on time."
"You talked back to me."	"I need to have your respect in front of the team."
"You didn't tell me."	"I didn't know."
"You're in my seat."	"I also have 6C."

Wow, what a difference! Check yourself. Make sure you're using "I" not "You" statements.

"You" will be glad you did.

Avoid Sexist Language

Both men and women call females "girls." They're women. They should be referred to as such by both genders. People ask what's the big deal? If you're the "girl," it can be.

I've heard stories . . . like the woman who was temping in a publishing company. The publisher—the top person in this division—told her: "Be a good girl and make a cup of coffee."

She was outraged!

Some people use the world "ladies." Ladies is better than "girls," but generally the preferred term is women.

Other names not to call people: Sweetie, Bud, Dear, Sugar, and Big Guy.

Grammar Gremlins and Diction Don'ts

I've coached people and have had to tell them that their grammar makes them sound less intelligent than they are. It's true. It does.

If your grammar is bad or careless, try your best to clean it up. There are many great books available for quick basic skill brushups (I know a lot of people who use them). There are also courses at community colleges and adult learning centers.

The reason I encourage you to brush up is evident in the next example.

You say as your W to your supervisor, "I'm worried about the deadline because sales *ain't* getting me the numbers on time." Well, you may be correct that the sales department isn't getting you the numbers on time. Unfortunately, you have just tarnished your message and your credibility with that one improper word. That "ain't" taints—you and your message.

Lots of people make mistakes in how they use language and grammar. Lots of people know better, but as we now know, we all walk around with bad habits that need to be broken. If you use "ain't," break this habit as fast as you can. I have a friend who used to snap a rubber band on her wrist to remind herself not to say something—in her case, "Youse guys." I think it's a good trick that can help you catch yourself making a mistake.

You also need to watch out for:

Double Negatives

Double negatives may require a double rubber band. "I don't got none," is a double negative and a grammatical nightmare besides. The correct way to say this is:

"I don't have any," or "I do not have the numbers from sales," or "I have none of the above."

Diction Vixens

Diction, as in the examples above, has to do with your word choice. And it's also your delivery of those words. Delivery counts. We make assumptions about people based on their delivery. One man in my class complained that he didn't feel listened to by others. After listening to him, I felt I knew why. His diction wasn't proper. He looked like such a nice and capable man—except he had this drawback—he mutilated words.

Many people have told me that their assumptions about people who do not use good diction are negative. Maybe this isn't fair. I can't fix the unfairness of the situation. However, I can help you fix your diction.

Another Confession

Not only was I that huge wimp, but I was a word jumbler.

When I was starting my career (I was in Kansas at the time), I was sent for speech coaching. The woman coaching me was big, blonde, and a chain smoker. This was a time when you could still smoke in the office buildings and before I was Polite and Powerful. She scared me. She said to start talking and I started giving her one of my speeches.

I only spoke for about five minutes. Through the cloud of smoke, I saw her shaking her head, as if I were one sorry sack of a speech reader.

Finally, she stops me, squints her eyes and says, "You're from the East Coast, aren't you Barbara?"

I was afraid to ask how she knew. She said "You look great, but you say 'gotta' and 'gonna.' You need to stop that. You jumble your words together and you sound terrible."

Though she wounded my pride at the time, she was right. It

sounds terrible during a speech or presentation to hear "gonna" and "gotta."

Try it right now. Say the following aloud and compare how each *sounds*:

"I'm gonna tell you about Polite and Powerful behavior. You've gotta have these skills."

versus

"I am going to tell you about Polite and Powerful behavior. You have to have these skills."

Other Word Jumblers to Watch out For

SAY . . .	INSTEAD OF . . .
Did you eat?	Jeet?
Sandwich	Samwich
Them/Those/There	Dem/Dose/Dare
Did you?	Didja?
Don't know	Dunno
Whaddya	What do you
Have to	Hafta

Vernacular Vexations

Everybody else says it, "*So whads da big deal?*"

Every part of the country and every major city has its little verbal idiosyncrasies. In the Philadelphia area, where I'm from, people say "Youse can come over," instead of "You can come over."

This aspect of your diction may seem small, but these are the kinds of things that can undermine the effectiveness of your WAC'em words—and your image in general. Remember, the hometown folks might not notice—but what if you have to leave and speak to people in other cities? They will notice. (Sometimes they'll even think you're strange!)

Tune into your town's talk. Are there little things you may have picked up and incorporated into your speech without even knowing?

Big Words Because They're Big

I had a professor in college who used to charge us a dime every time we used what he considered an unnecessarily "big" or "ten cent" word. I thought he was a bit of a kook until I got out into the working world and encountered the "big word droppers." I'm not saying that you don't want to have a powerful vocabulary; you do. However, using big words during a difficult conversation can be confusing or insulting. Keep it simple.

Using words to try to make yourself appear smart is not smart. You don't need to get your confidence for a confrontation this way—your skills and practice will. You may end up using a word the other person isn't familiar with. This will make him or her either confused, feel put down or both. This isn't polite and it isn't powerful. The most important thing is to be yourself (with good grammar and diction).

Why Use:	When You Can Say:
Penultimate	Next to the last
Nascent	Beginning
Reiterate	Repeat
Abscond	Take off

Another piece of advice: If you're not sure how to pronounce a word, skip it.

One more: If you're not sure what it means, skip that one too.

Use Polite Language—Always

You may think, "Of course this Barbara Pachter is a politeness pusher; she teaches this stuff!" That's true, but one of the reasons I sincerely enjoy my job, even enough to write about it, is because I have often seen how the little things, like saying, "I appreciate your thinking of me," "No thank you. Maybe another time," and even "Good morning," can change the way other people respond to you. Really.

Dori used to work for a five-star hotel chain which required even their behind-the-scenes employees to use such verbiage as "Good morning/Good afternoon/Good evening" instead of "Hello." Instead of "Yes, or "Sure I can do that," she said, "Certainly."

After leaving her job there, she continued with her polite verbiage. She became a secretary. One day one of the vice-presidents, a pretty big honcho, was passing by her desk. He stopped and said. "Excuse me, but are you the one who always says, 'Good morning' and 'my pleasure' when I call for Richard?"

She said that she was. He told her how much he enjoyed talking with her and how impressed he was by her telephone skills!

Try it. You will be amazed at the results you get.

On Your Own

Now that you understand how important your verbal skills are, not only for a positive confrontation, but for projecting an overall positive image, you have some incentive for discovering your own bad verbal habits, grammar gremlins, and diction vixens.

Take each of the verbal categories we've discussed in this chapter and focus on each one for a few days. Take this self-assessment. Ask yourself, am I:

1. Using wishy washy words (kind of, sort of, maybe)?
2. Saying, "I think," when "I know?"
3. Apologizing for no reason?

4. Compromising a strong statement by adding a weak ending to it?
5. Saying, "I don't know," when you do know?
6. Cursing?
7. Filling my sentences with distracting words like, "Um," "Okay," and "Like?"
8. Employing "You" statements when "I" statements are more effective?
9. Using sexist language?
10. Using good grammar?
11. Pronouncing my words carefully? (If you answer "I dunno," you may want to know!)
12. Using vernacular that some people might not understand?
13. Throwing out big words because they're big?

Tune in to yourself. Hear what you're saying to others. When you catch yourself making a mistake, write it down. Keep a log. Awareness goes a long, long way in breaking bad verbal habits. Once you break a habit, move on to the next area. In a few weeks you'll be surprised at your own progress.

CHAPTER 8

VITAL NONVERBALS

You've learned how important your verbals are for contributing to the success of your WAC'em wording. But often what you *don't* say will impact the outcome of your confrontation and difficult conversation too. In other words, your nonverbals are also at work affecting the way the other person is receiving your WAC'em wording.

Have you ever seen or heard someone:

- Agree to do something while shaking his or her head no at the same time?
- Smile while telling another person something negative?
- Give a presentation where he rocks back and forth on his heels repeatedly?
- Say he wants to meet someone and then stands with his arms crossed all night?

These points illustrate what happens when your nonverbal communication doesn't match your verbal communication. When they don't match, you've got problems, especially during a confrontation. I illustrate this in my seminars by saying, "I am really pleased to be here," yet I am crossing my arms, looking down and frowning at the same time. I don't look like I'm happy to be anywhere near this group—and they see it.

Many people have no clue how they're presenting themselves in terms of their nonverbal behavior. Nonverbal behaviors become habits. We do things that others might consider rude or gross without realizing it. We do things that make us appear timid or silly without realizing it. You might think you're behaving Politely and Powerfully, but you may not be. You may only be delivering your verbal message correctly. Strong WAC'em wording is not enough for a successful confrontation. In order to have a positive confrontation, your verbals and non-verbals must both be Polite and Powerful.

Nonverbal communication is comprised of your body language, your voice, and even your visual appearance. So we'll look at all the areas of each that can have a positive or negative effect on confrontations.

Who Are You As a Nonverbal Communicator?

Try to get an idea of where you may be in terms of understanding the signals or messages you're sending to others. In many of my classes, the participants take a self-assessment on their non-verbal skills. It's amazing how high people rate themselves. I tell the group: "This is your self-assessment. *Other people may see you differently!* You need to know if that gap exists."

Of course everyone thinks I'm talking about the person next to them.

There are people who resist me like crazy. It's hard for them to believe that they may be rude or passive in their behavior without knowing it. Like the man who pounded his fist and told me he was positive that he was assertive and in command of his nonverbal signals. And then there was the woman who was practicing her WAC'em phrasing and talked so loudly I had to back away.

To these folks and to you I say, *"Don't tell me you don't do these things until you get feedback from other people that you don't do these things."*

We All Make Mistakes

Even I'm not immune to making mistakes and I teach these skills practically every day of my life. I believe I know what I'm doing with my body language when I'm up in front of a group. Yet I found out that when I was pregnant I had been standing up in front of large groups of people scratching my big tummy. I had no idea I was doing it until some of the participants told me! I appreciated that feedback!

Take the following assessment and see how you rate yourself:

	YES	NO	DON'T KNOW
1. I look people in the eye when speaking to them.	❏	❏	❏
2. My facial expression is consistent with what I am saying.	❏	❏	❏
3. I do not point my finger at others when I speak.	❏	❏	❏
4. I speak loudly enough for others to hear.	❏	❏	❏
5. I do not giggle at the end of my sentences.	❏	❏	❏
6. When talking with others, I do not play with my hair, tie, mustache, or jewelry or crack my knuckles or play with change in my pockets.	❏	❏	❏
7. I don't slouch, sway, or lean when standing.	❏	❏	❏
8. I know the proper distance to stand when speaking with others.	❏	❏	❏
9. I'm aware of what gestures I'm using.	❏	❏	❏
10. I show that I am listening to others.	❏	❏	❏

Again, the idea behind this self-assessment is not to make you feel good or bad about yourself. Just as you tuned in to your confrontational style, I simply want you to become aware of how you might be presenting yourself nonverbally to others. You project an image of yourself; others perceive that image. You have no control over how others perceive you, but you can control what you project to other people. This is a hard concept for people to accept. I promise you that if your nonverbal skills are poor, they are probably holding you back in many aspects of your life, including positive confrontation.

Think of it this way. Suppose your WAC'em is for a problem with your neighbor:

W = You may not be aware that Spot comes into my yard and relieves himself on my property. I don't like having to clean up after him. (What's bothering you.)

A = I would appreciate it if you would make sure Spot doesn't come into my yard. (What you want to ask the other person to do.)

C = Okay? (Check-in to see if they can or will do what you've asked.)

This is Polite and Powerful language. But what if while you are saying the words, your head is bent and you're looking at your shoes? Or you're shaking your fist and raising your voice?

Your words were Polite and Powerful but the rest of you wasn't and it can influence how you're perceived. Here's a surprising piece of information: Research shows that people will believe your nonverbal messages before they believe your words.

On-Your-Own Assignment

Have yourself videotaped annually—either with your own video camera or at a work training session. Role-play a work situation with a friend or pretend you're giving a presentation. Go back over the self-assessment quiz above to see how you're doing on your communication skills.

The Little Things Add Up

I tell people that the little things: how you stand, your eye contact, your choice of gestures, etc.—are little things until they're all together. Once together they create an impression of you—sometimes a big one. And that impression can either work for you or against you. *You want it to work for you.* You want to be perceived as a Polite and Powerful person.

Top Ten Annoying Things People do with their Body

1. Point finger at others
2. Stick out tongue/licking lips when speaking
3. Wring their hands
4. Sway
5. Use very stern facial expression
6. Use too broad or no gestures at all/hands on hips
7. Pound fist
8. Tap foot when seated
9. Look at floor when speaking
10. Play with change in pocket

Body Language Basics

"I had an eye-opening experience on my body language. I was sitting and talking with my mother in her living room. She brought up an uncomfortable subject. I pulled my knees into my chest, grabbed a pillow, and held it in front of my chest and then put on my sunglasses. I did all this without realizing it. My mother then asked, 'Are you uncomfortable?' Only then did I notice that I rolled myself into a ball and was trying to hide. We both laughed at how obvious the body language was."—Seminar Participant

---

It's especially critical to pay attention to your body language when you're in an uncomfortable situation. Are you telling people you're uncomfortable by how you stand? A man was at a cocktail party. His body was saying, "I don't want to be here," by slouching and standing in a corner and not looking pleased. A friend went up to him and said, "Why are you letting everyone know you are miserable being here and you should be avoided like the plague?"

Stance/Posture

How do you stand? Are you open to the person you are communicating with or WACing? Are your feet together? Are your fists on your hips? Are you shifting and conveying nervousness? Are you like tons of women who cross their legs and rest on an ankle?

The way you stand, especially while having a difficult conversation, reveals a lot about you. Is it conveying the image of a confident, Polite and Powerful person—or not.

Here's how Polite and Powerful people stand when talking comfortably or confronting others: Feet parallel, approximately four to six inches apart. Distribute your weight evenly on both feet. Keep your shoulders back, but not way back as if you were in boot camp. Hold your chin up, but not way up. And unless you're gesturing, your hands are down at your side.

Meet Mary Meek

Women have a tendency to cross their legs and rest on one ankle and then fidget with their hands. It conveys nervousness. It's hard to be taken seriously with your WAC'em if you don't look like a serious person.

A few years ago, there was a picture in *Newsweek* (September 2, 1996) of Kathleen Kennedy Townsend, the Lt. Governor of Maryland, with Ted Kennedy, her brother, Joseph, and cousin, Patrick. I ask people who she is—and the responses I get back are not flattering: the babysitter, girlfriend, etc.

Why? She is clutching her hands, not standing up straight with weight on one foot, and looking away from the camera. She is also wearing a short sleeve suit that is not as powerful as a long sleeved suit. Based on her posture, she conveys a negative impression.

During my seminar breaks, I will often ask a woman to look at her feet. She is often surprised to find that her legs are crossed.

Meet the John Wayne Wannabe

Men tend to stand like "John Wayne" with their feet very far apart and their hands on their hips. In this stance, they are taking up a lot of space which can be perceived as aggressive.

Or they can stand passively with their feet together and hands in their pockets and they sway back and forth while they play with the change in their pocket. But that is distracting and detracting behavior. No one will believe that you really believe you are an assertive, powerful person.

Gestures

Gestures bring your words to life. An appropriate gesture can liven up your conversation or help you reinforce an important point.

During a positive confrontation, it's especially important to be aware of how you gesture. It's easy to let your hands or arms fly around when you're nervous or upset. If you're not in control of your gestures, you might come off as being nervous. Or, you might lead someone to believe that he or she is physically threatened. Your gestures need to be consistent with your words. You need to know what you are doing with them. And people so often don't! Watch your videotape.

Aggressive Gestures

The following gestures can send the wrong message:

1. **Pointing Finger.** Men and women have a tendency to use the

pointed finger out of habit. And again, don't tell me you don't do this until you get feedback that you don't. I have had people come up to me and say that they don't point their fingers and they are doing it in my face!

So what? Big deal, you may be thinking.

I happen to know a sales representative with a nationally-known corporation who lost his job because he pointed his finger at a VP during a meeting. He said, as he was thrusting his finger forward, "But I need that information now!"

The VP apparently did not agree.

A woman said her little boy told her he knew how to count. He showed one finger and said "one." He showed two fingers and said "two." And then with a moving pointing finger he said, "No, No, No."

Bill Clinton used to point like crazy. He was obviously schooled not to. He now usually uses a pointed knuckle to punctuate his points. That's better because it's not perceived as aggressive.

Even a pen can become a tool of aggression if you're pointing it or it's too close to someone else's face.

2. Pounding Fist. When some people—usually men, I have found—are trying to make a point, they pound the table. This is an aggressive gesture and can make even the most carefully prepared WAC'em words seem aggressive too.

3. Crossed Arms. A crossed-arms position is not necessarily aggressive. Yet it can be seen as offensive or closed. Sometimes people cross their arms because they are cold—literally. Sometimes they simply don't know what to do with their arms.

Again, it always comes back to perception. If you stand with your arms crossed because you're cold but the person you're WACing sees you as defensive, what is the reality? Perception is reality. That person will respond to you as if you are defensive.

Passive Gestures

If you're using nervous gestures, you will be perceived that way—and maybe less likely to be taken seriously as a result. Nervous gestures distract!

1. Playing with your hands. People clasp their hands together and then rub them up and down. They crack or rub their knuckles. Who can listen to you when you're being so distracting?

Visualize saying this statement as you're wringing your hands: "Boss, I'd like to take the lead on the next project." You're going to look like a nervous wreck. Will your boss really think you're capable?

2. Playing with paper clips, pens, rubber bands, etc. I coached a CEO of a very large manufacturing company on his presentation skills. I asked him after his presentation why he was nervous. He said, "How did you know? I thought I was hiding it well?" I said, "You twirled a rubber band constantly!" He said that he didn't even realize he was doing it.

In one of my presentation skills classes, a man was using a pointer. During the presentation, he opened up the pointer and proceeded to beat his leg with it. The class had a hard time listening to him. He didn't know he was doing it until we told him.

3. Covering your mouth. This is a common gesture where the hand is used to partly cover the mouth when talking. It is as if you don't want the words to come out! It's impossible to look powerful if you're doing this.

Eye Contact

Like gestures, eye contact is an important body language concern, especially in American culture. We don't trust people who don't look at us. Susan told me this story:

"I went to this doctor who was highly recommended to me. He seemed very knowledgeable and smart, except when I asked him a question. He looked away when answering me. He looked at the floor, the ceiling, his hands, his instruments. Everywhere except at me! I didn't care how good he was, I couldn't trust him and didn't want him as my doctor."

You want to look people in the eye when you're speaking or listening to them. This is especially important during a difficult conversation. It's both Polite and Powerful behavior. Don't stare the other person down though; this is perceived as aggressive. You occasionally look away, but not too much. That will be perceived as passive behavior or create the impression that you are not listening.

When people don't look us in the eye, we make assumptions about them—often inviting conflict as a result. Yet, people look away for a number of reasons—shyness, cultural variables—and don't even realize that they may be causing a problem.

Women in particular have trouble with this. I used to do this myself. A number of years ago I was one of the first women elected to an international training group. Some of the men had vocalized that they didn't want me there. I was so nervous that my stomach felt like it was on a flying trapeze! I tried not to show it. I thought I did a good job of hiding my feelings. Yet after the meeting one of my friends on the committee came up to me and asked why I was nervous. "How could you tell?" I asked. He said, "You didn't look at the men when talking!" I also lowered my volume! I didn't realize I was doing this. I have noticed this in my classes. When some women offer their suggestions or ask questions they will look away.

In some cultures it is a sign of respect to look away (see section on cultural differences and conflict). But in American culture, you must train yourself to look others in the eye.

Seeing Eye-to-Eye

During a confrontation, you should be eye level with the person you're WACing. If you're not seeing eye-to-eye, it can appear that the person who is lower, due to height or seating position, is like a child looking up to the authority figure. If you're trying to be Polite and Powerful, it won't work. I walk over to participants in my workshops when they are seated. I stand next to him or her and look down on them. I ask them, "Do you feel powerful?" No. They tell me they feel very small and powerless.

Psychological Advantages Are Not Polite nor Powerful

But don't you want this psychological advantage over the person you're in conflict with? Doesn't it make you more powerful, to have to be looked up to?

Nope. Not in the context we're discussing, which is resolving difficult conversation with positive confrontation.

One of the aspects which we'll discuss more in the next chapter is entering into a difficult conversation under the best circumstances. Making the other person comfortable and at ease is truly what a Polite and Powerful person does. Powerful people do not have to intimidate or artificially inflate themselves in order to get their way or have a successful confrontation.

Often, there's a gender component at work here. Many men are naturally taller than many women. They therefore have a tendency to look down at women. It gives them a psychological power over them. It can give the appearance of aggression. You may grumble and say, "It's not my fault I'm taller!" You're right. It's not your fault and this is not a feminist issue. It's an etiquette issue. If you want to be a Polite and Powerful person having a positive confrontation, it is your responsibility to be aware of your height differentiation. It's on you to correct it. You may want to sit down during a difficult conversation.

A man was 6'2"; his wife was 4'9". Whenever they would argue, she would take him into the hallway and stand on the second step. She didn't know why she did it. It just felt better.

Facial Expressions

Your facial expression is an extremely important nonverbal. There are two big issues you need to be aware of.

Your facial expression must be consistent with your message. If not, people will believe your face before they believe your words. We have all seen newscasters who are smiling when they are telling us about disasters. It's not that they think it's funny, it's that they are probably so conditioned to smile that they do it even at inappropriate moments. But it looks just awful, doesn't it?

And there is a gender component to this aspect of body language as well. Women have a tendency to over-smile. We are taught from our earliest moments to please, be nice, don't offend. A man told me about the woman who smiled when she told him that he didn't get the requested transfer. She was sending him a confusing and mixed message.

Men usually need to smile a little bit more. I had a boss once who scowled while giving me an award. I left his office wondering, "Does he not really think I deserve it?" Once I got to know him better, I discovered that this scowl was his semi-permanent expression. He was a scowler by habit.

What Is Your Standard Facial Expression?

You mean I have one?

Yes you do. Your "standard facial expression" is my term for "What do people see when you're listening to them?"

One woman said she didn't know she had a stern standard facial expression, yet friends and neighbors would come up to her all the time and say things like, "Is everything all right?" She'd respond, "Yes. Why are you asking?" They'd say, "Because you look upset." She would say, "No I don't."

She didn't believe the feedback until she saw her wedding video. She said: *"It was the happiest day of my life and I looked miserable."*

Now she believes the feedback.

I've had people sitting in the front row of my seminars and based on their facial expressions I am saying to myself, "These people hate me and they hate everything I'm saying." Yet they are the people who come up to me at break and tell me they love the seminar. They should tell their faces!

One man in the front of my seminar e-mailed me after the seminar to tell me that he "very much enjoyed" the seminar and did I have any feedback for him on his nonverbals. He had not gotten a promotion and was concerned. I remember him because he had volunteered to do a demonstration with me in the front of the class. I had been surprised that his hand had gone up at all. He had looked so stern during the class I was surprised that he had wanted to participate.

Dressing For Confrontation Success

Your dress needs to enhance your professional presence so people look at and listen to you. It can be a key area that determines whether you—and what you have to say—are taken seriously or not!

If one of your employees comes to you and says, "Boss, I feel like I'm not taken seriously in this department," and this person is wearing totally inappropriate clothing, you may not be taking him or her seriously.

The image you project with your clothes might negate your W—What's bothering you. (I'm bothered because I'm not getting promoted.) I know! I know! It shouldn't matter what the person is wearing. What is important is the inside. I agree. But you don't want your outside appearance to stop people from listening to you.

There was a Ph.D. researcher who came up to me after class and told me she was upset that she was not getting promoted. She asked me to help her with her WAC'em words so she could confront her boss. She looked like she belonged in a nightclub and not in a laboratory conducting serious cancer research! If I thought that about her clothing, imagine what her boss in her department was thinking!

I told her "The first person who needs to be WAC'ed is you!"

Later she wrote me and told me how much of a difference her change in dress made for her professionally. She was promoted and felt that people were taking her seriously for the first time.

I went into an aerospace corporation to meet with their Human Resource department heads right after their promotion meeting. They were discussing the engineer who again was turned down for a management position. I asked why. The engineer was not promoted because he dressed like a slob and senior management was afraid that he would not represent the company well. I also asked if anyone has said anything to him. They said, "No." He keeps applying for higher-level positions and is getting turned down. I told them, "You need to WAC this man and tell him what you expect from him if he wants to get promoted."

I advise people: If you are going to WAC someone you need to be perceived as a credible person. Your clothing and your grooming (see box on p. 118 for tips) can enhance your credibility and confidence.

Dressing for Conversations with Your Neighbors

Of course, it might not matter so much what you're wearing when you're WAC'ing your neighbor. I don't advise doing it in your bathrobe or in a bathing suit. A man told me he was outside mowing his lawn when he saw his neighbor. He stopped and decided to WAC the neighbor about his hedges, which were growing uncontrollably and spilling into the first man's yard.

"I knew my words were right," he said, "but I sure regretted doing it that moment. I was sweating like crazy and had my shirt off. I just didn't feel confident."

The way you dress adds a lot to your overall confidence level. I tell people that before they WAC friends and neighbors, put on an outfit they feel especially good in.

Dressing For Difficult Conversations At Work

If you are WAC'ing at work, how you dress and look always matter. Here are three general guidelines for dressing for difficult conversations at work:

Clothing needs to fit properly. Your clothing needs to fit without overemphasizing your body. Nothing should fit too tightly, and there shouldn't be any pulling or bulging of fabric. Men need to be able to button their jackets and make sure their pants are long enough. Women need to be able to move their arms and must not expose cleavage or wear inappropriately short skirts.

Must be good quality and in good condition. Buy the most expensive clothing you can afford. You spend most of your time at work, so spend most of your clothing budget on work clothes. Less really is more when it comes to clothing. You want to buy good-quality, classic clothing—nothing too trendy. It usually is made better, lasts longer, wears better, and doesn't go out of style as quickly.

Know the message you're sending. What is your clothing saying about you? Does it project the image of a serious professional? If a man shows up at a meeting in business-casual clothing, but every other man in the room is wearing a professional suit—what message is he sending? If a woman wears a sexy, tight, seductive dress to a company party, what message is she sending? You want to be viewed as someone who pays attention to the details and is ready for work.

Guidelines for Powerful Professional Dress

1. **Business suit**. The business suit is still the most powerful look for both men and women. Darker colors convey more authority than lighter colors, but big men need to be cautious with black. It can be intimidating. If a woman wears very bright colors, she may draw too much attention to herself for the wrong reason.

2. **Shoes matter**. I have had numerous recruiters tell me that one of the first things they notice about a candidate is his or her shoes. They should be polished and in good condition. Thinner-soled shoes are more elegant for men. Women need to avoid very high heels — a 2" to 2 1/2" heel is appropriate.

3. **Don't skimp on accessories.** A good-quality leather briefcase, umbrella, and leather gloves are all a must. Buy the best watch you can afford.

4. **Don't ignore your grooming**. Make sure you have a neatly cut hairstyle that flatters your face, fresh breath, teeth in good shape, no runs in stockings.

Say It Loudly and Clearly

Voice is a significant issue for Polite and Powerful people. It's especially critical during a confrontation.

If you are going to get your point across to the other person he or she must hear you. Sometimes, if you're not listened to, it may be because the other person is a legitimate jerk. But sometimes it is because the person's voice was easy not to listen to — either too soft, too high pitched or too loud.

The Power of Voice

A woman was trying to sell me her organizing skills over the phone. She wanted to come in and rearrange my office. Believe me, I would love to have my filing cabinets reorganized, but her voice was so weak that I didn't believe that she would be strong enough to be able to tell me what to do. I didn't hire her based on her voice.

A couple of key areas to remember about your voice for difficult conversations include:

- **Volume**. Are you speaking loudly enough to be heard? Many people don't—both men and women, but especially women. The first thing I say in my women's seminars is: SPEAK UP. I teach presentation skills and after men and women get the feedback they are speaking too softly, when they raise their voices, they all feel as if they are shouting. They are not shouting. We can finally hear them.

A young woman was in one of my four-day seminars—positive confrontation plus women's issues. I talked about voice on the first day. She was a very quiet woman and did not volunteer information during the class. We start each day with going around and sharing what you did after class and whether you applied the knowledge learned that day. You can always say. "I have nothing to share." This woman had done that for the first two days.

On the third day though, she did share a story.

Before class, this woman stopped at her office. She saw her boss. He gave her an assignment to do that morning. She had no trouble WAC'ing him. She responded, "I can't do that. I'm in a seminar." He responded by giving her additional work to do. She said again, "Don't you remember? I'm in the seminar and can't do the work." He then remembered something else she should pick up on the way back from the assignment.

She was about to become upset that she would miss the seminar. Then it dawned on her that perhaps her boss was not hearing her. She remembered my seminar and what we had talked about concerning voice. She stood up, dropped her chin and said loudly and clearly, "I'm going to the seminar now." He said, "Okay, I forgot. I'll get someone else."

He had finally heard her!

- **Rate.** If you're nervous about having a confrontation, you might increase your talking speed without knowing. This will make it hard for someone to follow your WAC'em words. Don't try to increase your rate to get more information across. If you don't have time to say what you want to say, arrange to pick up on the conversation at another time.

On-Your-Own Assignment

You need to understand your voice image. Though you can hear your voice on videotape, you can be influenced by the visual. In this last chapter, I encouraged you to use your own voice mail system to get feedback on just the impact of your voice. It's a good idea to always listen to your voice mail before you send a message. And re-do it if necessary. If you do this regularly, you will quickly gain better control over your volume and rate. I give this as a homework assignment in my seminars and of all the assignments I give, I get the most positive feedback on this one. People really learn from this exercise. Try it.

The Bubble Man

Space is something you need to be very aware of during a confrontation. In the United States, when two people are communicating the average distance between them is three feet. You want to be at arm's length.

Do you stand too close? People can feel intimidated or uncomfortable if you do. Some people stand closer than the average three feet. One woman told me, "I know I shouldn't get so close to people, but I like them. And if they back up, I just go forward." I had to

WAC her on that one. She thought she was being friendly but she was actually being rude.

The Bubble Man is a real person I met. He told me he had a five-foot bubble—much wider than most Americans. He said he wasn't comfortable if people came any closer. He admitted that he used to tell people "Get out of my space!" Obviously, this is unacceptable behavior! He was being aggressive.

The other people in the seminar WAC'ed him. Kindly but firmly they told him he needed to stop doing this. They helped him come up with his WAC'em line for maintaining his space. It was, "I'd like to stand here while we talk so I can see you clearly."

Look, but Don't Touch

Touch is a touchy subject in our culture. In today's world of sexual harassment awareness, people need to be cautious with touch. But it's not always a harassment issue. Some people are touchy, some aren't. Those who are use touch as a way to connect with others; those who aren't, don't. One healthcare professional told me that she simply touched a man's hand when he started crying and he told the rest of the office she was coming on to him.

Though relationships vary, my advice is don't touch people when you WAC them.

What if, however, your confrontation goes splendidly? It often happens that both parties are happy that the proverbial air has been cleared. Is it okay to hug or touch the person then? I've heard people tell me it's happened spontaneously—erupting out of their relief.

At work, you will have to use your judgment. It simply might not be appropriate. When in doubt, I advise you simply to shake hands. Men will often pat each other on the back. That seems fine to me, but again in some corporate cultures or to some people, it may not be.

Most healthcare representatives suggest asking someone "Do you mind if I give you a hug?" before doing anything involving touch. That may work but consider what happened to Dave, a Website and technology developer for an advertising company:

"I had to reprimand an employee for not doing a job up to standard. I was dreading it because he had a reputation for getting dramatic. Whenever I had given him feedback in the past he became upset. I prepared my WAC'em words to ensure that I was being Polite and Powerful but not harsh.

"Well it worked! He took my comments very well. We both felt better. But as he stood to leave, he asked me, 'Can you hug me?' I didn't know what to say. I felt so put on the spot that I had to hug him and I hated it! Now I have to WAC him about that."

Power Has to Be Earned

During a confrontation you can use your nonverbals for good or for bad purposes.

I know a man who is 6'7" tall. That's tall! He admitted that during difficult conversations, he used to purposefully move in close to others in order to intimidate or distract them. It worked, but he realized that it was causing problems in his personal and work relationships. He's now a Polite and Powerful guy who sits down a lot to have difficult conversations.

I don't encourage you to try to gain power through your nonverbals either. If you're bigger, stronger, or taller than the person you're confronting, don't use it to try to intimidate others or to get your way. You don't want to succeed in a confrontation because you intimidated someone—that's not true success. Your nonverbals should support your Polite and Powerful behavior.

Power is something you earn—often through Polite and Powerful behavior. Good control over your nonverbals, voice, and visual appearance are important components to successful confrontations. But you have to give it time. Try keeping a log of all the aspects of nonverbal behavior that we covered here. Tune into how you stand, your eye contact, gestures, aspects of your voice, etc. Once you are confident you are doing one area correctly, move on to the next. Remember habits are hard to break. But stick with it. You'll be rewarded with good control over your nonverbal communication.

CHAPTER 9

THE OTHER PERSON

So far, we've talked a great deal about you. What's bothering *you*. How you can put *your* thoughts into WAC'em words. How *your* verbal and *your* nonverbal skills can affect *your* success during a confrontation.

Now we need to talk about the other person—the person on the receiving end of your WAC'em words. You've told the person What's bothering you. You've Asked them what you would like him or her to do in the future. You've Checked in. Each letter of your WAC'em is complete. Good job . . . but . . . just because you asked for something, doesn't mean the other person will give it.

Just because you acted Politely and Powerfully doesn't mean the other person will too.

Just because you are not on the offensive doesn't mean the other person won't be.

Welcome to the other side of WAC'em—the mysterious, unknowable, unpredictable, and exciting world of the other person.

No matter how much we think we know how someone will react to being WAC'ed—we can't really know. Even a loved one, a friend you have known since the beginning of time, can surprise you during a confrontation. As we discussed in the last chapter, you can't WAC'em and run. It doesn't work that way. The other person gets to have his or her say—whether we like what they're saying or not.

Though I don't know for sure how someone will, or will not, react, I can make some generalizations to guide you. There are six things that can usually happen:

1. The person agrees to what you suggested or asked for.

We love when this happens! And guess what? It does happen. While there are no guarantees for successful outcomes, it happens more than you might think. I hear it again and again—people tell me that they are often pleasantly surprised—that what they thought was going to be a wrenching, horrible conversation isn't actually that bad. Sometimes WAC'ing the other person is so easy, you can't believe it. You may end up getting what you want, simply because you have opened your mouth and asked for it. People often don't do this! But once you've had one positive confrontation, you'll be encouraged to try it more.

Quick and easy conflict resolution can often happen for the simple reason that the other person is not aware of how his/her actions affected you. And when you approach the person Politely and Powerfully, you can get surprising results.

A woman who had taken my seminar told me how she agonized for weeks about telling the man in the apartment upstairs that his loud music bothered her. She practiced her WAC'em and finally got her courage up to talk to him. His reaction stunned her. He apologized! He didn't know that it was bothering her and said that it wouldn't happen again—and it didn't. She was very pleased, yet sorry it took her so long to WAC him.

The other person, or people, may give you what you want because they recognize that it's the right thing to do. An administrative assistant said that this happened to her. She finally WAC'ed the others in her department about not cleaning up after themselves during their weekly meetings. It wasn't her job but she had been doing it. Once she pointed it out to them, they started cleaning up after themselves right away.

When the other person gives you what you want, make sure you thank him or her. And again, I can't emphasize this enough—stop talking about it. Move on to other things.

2. WAC'em Leads to a Discussion

Maybe the other person disagrees or has a different opinion. In fact, the other person may have information that you didn't know about. He or she may have other suggestions or ideas—good ones—that you haven't thought about.

Sometimes when we can't get exactly what we want, the next best thing is to work out a mutually acceptable solution.

A friend of mine pointed out that being married often requires a constant give and take. I find I do a lot of negotiating with my son, too. We often compromise with our partners and the people close to us to work out the differences. (This is not the same thing as being taken advantage of or acting like a doormat.) But other people have "wants" that need to be respected too.

A group of friends meets every two months or so for dinner. One of the members—Paul—doesn't like Asian food. When deciding which restaurant to go to, they would vote and the others would out-vote him and they'd all end up going to a favorite Thai or Chinese restaurant. Paul didn't like this so he WAC'ed his friends. He told them that he wanted to participate and he wanted them to accommodate him, at least some of the time. They discussed it and agreed to try a new non-Asian restaurant every third time the group met.

It's vitally important to create an environment in which the other person, or in this case, people, will express his or her thoughts and an honest discussion can occur. You need to understand their viewpoint and work towards a mutually agreed upon solution. If Paul had stormed away from his friends, it would have been aggressive. If he had stopped calling, it would have been passive. He didn't do these things. Instead, he Politely and Powerfully told them what was important to him. He gave his friends a chance to discuss it. He also didn't demand that they never go to another Asian restaurant—that wouldn't have been fair to the others. What he got was his preference, at least some of the time, and that made him happy.

Here are some suggestions for handling a discussion:

- **Be patient.** The person may have been caught off guard or may have difficulty wording his or her ideas.
- **Listen** (see box).
- **Ask questions.** Get more information whenever you can. Don't just throw question after question at the person. Listen to the answer and respond if appropriate. Ask follow-up questions if you're unclear about anything: "I don't understand what you mean when you say . . ."
- **Restate what you have heard the other person say.** You can use phrases like: "Are you saying . . . ." or "You're suggesting that . . ." or "If I understand you correctly, you're . . ." This is good for clarifying what is being said and to express that you understood what the other person said.
- **Explain what you can or cannot do and why.**
- **Offer additional options, if you have them.**
- **Don't focus on one little thing to judge or ridicule the person about.**
- **Agree to a solution.** This is great, but don't make commitments you can't keep.
- **Agree to think it over and meet again.**
- **Agree to disagree.** There may be times when that is the best or only resolution. Suppose you WAC your sister because she takes your elderly mother out for ice cream, which she isn't supposed to have. You say: "It's bad for Mom." She says: "It's not going to hurt her once in a while." You both believe you are right. What do you do? As long as your mother's health isn't in immediate danger from eating the ice cream, there isn't much you can do except acknowledge that you have different viewpoints. You and your sister both have your own ways of looking at the situation.

How to Listen

"Edith, the reason that you don't understand is that I'm talking in English and you're listening in dingbat."
— ARCHIE BUNKER

Listen up! One of the things that's consistently near the top on the list of what annoys people the most is other people who don't listen. Listening is very important to have a discussion and for any of the other WAC'em responses you may get. Here are some suggestions for listening.

- You can't listen and talk. It's been attempted. There are people who swear it can be done. It can't! Stop talking. Let the other person talk!
- You also can't listen when you're interrupting.
- Give the person your undivided attention. Do not answer the phone, work on your computer, or look away.
- Pay attention to your body language. Use it to show the person that you are paying attention. Make eye contact. Sit up straight. Don't fold your arms over your chest.
- Concentrate on what the other person is saying. Do not let your mind wander. Do not think about what you want to say while that other person is talking.
- Do not change the subject as soon as the other person has finished talking.)

But I Really Want It My Way!

If only the real world worked so that you could really have "your way," all the time, whatever you wanted. Clearly, it doesn't.

There are, of course, some issues about which you have such a strong position that there is no room for discussion. A woman had to tell another relative that she didn't want her teasing her daughter about her weight. She was not going to compromise. She felt her daughter's welfare was at stake.

Pick these "no further discussion" confrontations wisely. For all the others, I encourage you to be open to the discussion. You can learn a lot.

3. The Other Person Gets Defensive

This is the person who feels put on the spot and who clearly doesn't like it. He or she may want to deny the problem. Sometimes this person will try to make you feel bad about bringing it up. They will often make comments like:

"Boy, you sure are sensitive."
"Nobody else minds."
"I thought you wouldn't care about a little thing like that."

Don't get defensive back. It will be tempting! But don't do it. You have to remind yourself that *you* are the Polite and Powerful person. This defensive individual may not have the skills or the same ability to treat and consider others respectfully that you now have. Don't apologize or justify your feelings. Your goal is to try to engage the person in a discussion.

Sometimes a simple statement like: "I'm surprised by your response. I believe that this discussion would be helpful to both of us," is often all that is needed to encourage the person to become responsive and open to a discussion.

Some people may be more resistant. Don't let the person change the focus of the discussion. You want to acknowledge their point and then bring him or her back to the main issue.

Katrina works as an office manager. One of the executives, a woman, persistently called Katrina nicknames, like Kit Kat, in front of others—even clients—and that embarrassed Katrina. Armed with her WAC'em tools, she approached the executive and said, "I'm sure you don't mean any harm, but you often call me nicknames. Please just call me Katrina. I'd appreciate it. Okay?"

Well, the other woman was not happy to be told this. She said something like, "Oh don't be ridiculous. Nicknames are cute. Don't make such a big deal out of it. It's not that important."

But Katrina, knowing this woman's difficult personality, was prepared. She stood her ground and repeated her A: "This is important to me and I would like you to call me Katrina."

This last part wasn't easy for Katrina, but she took a lot of time beforehand to boost herself up. One of the ways she did this was to be mentally prepared. She didn't make excuses or discount herself. She calmly repeated what she wanted. She was Polite and Powerful to the last word.

Here are three ways you can handle yourself in this kind of sticky situation and others:

1. Ask for Clarification: Sometimes people say things and they don't really mean them as harshly as they come out. When you ask them to clarify, they have to explain their point in a clearer and often better way.

I asked a friend once after he had made a really offensive comment, "Why did you say that?" He simply said, "I guess because I'm being a jerk." And that was the end of that.

Asking for clarification can also stop you from quickly and aggressively responding to the other person's comment. It helps distance you from the words.

Clarification statements include:

"Why are you saying that?
"What is it about my request that's not working for you?
"I understand that you think this is a dumb idea. Please explain what specifically is bothering you about it?"
"What exactly am I doing that is causing this response?"
"Help me to understand what you mean by 'ridiculous.'"
"What exactly about this suggestion is so silly?"

2. Use a Defusing Statement: If the situation is getting stickier, using a defusing statement lets the person know you have heard him or her—without necessarily agreeing with him or her. You don't want to argue about who is "right." You want to find a better way for both of you.

Defusing statements include:

"That may be true. Still, I'm unable to meet the deadline by Friday."

"Perhaps, I did, though that was not my intent."

"There may be some truth to that, yet we have to follow company guidelines."

"That's an interesting point."

"That's probably true. My concern right now though is to clear this up."

But . . .

Notice that none of the above statements contain the word "but." This little word can pack a big punch—it can negate the positive statement that precedes it, such as, "You did a great job, but . . ." Now you're waiting for the next shoe to drop. People tend to go on the defensive and brace themselves for the worst when they hear this word.

Use "and" whenever possible. It's a much more neutral word. "You did a nice job and it would be even better if . . ."

Other words that can work include "yet," "however," and "although."

These defusing statements are then followed with a statement rephrasing your point. Here are some examples:

A colleague says, "You said that I would have the report by 3 P.M." You have no recollection of saying that. Do you really want to argue that? It will become "I said" vs. "you said." Don't get distracted by trying to prove what can't be proven. Often you can resolve it by using a defusing statement: "That may be true *and* I can give you the report by 3:30 P.M."

A friend went to a store to get a new pair of glasses. He had lost his. The owner of the eye glass store looked for his records and couldn't find them. He told my friend, "You didn't get your glasses here." My friend said, "I did get my glasses here." They each repeated their line about four times, before my friend in total frustration just left in disgust.

To stop the arguing, the owner could have used a defusing line: "That's curious that I don't have your record. Let me see how we can get you new glasses quickly anyway."

Two hours later the owner called my friend to tell him he had found the record—but it was too late. My friend took his business elsewhere.

3. Acknowledge the comment. This is when you acknowledge or agree with the comment the person has made. Often the comment is used to convey criticism, yet if you acknowledge it, there's no sting. It can even stop the conversation cold. This is a great technique.

A man told me that a woman screamed at him one day, "You're just too sensitive about this!" He looked at her and said, "Yes, I am sensitive about this." Her response was: "Oh, okay."

A brother said to his sister who lent him money: "You're so preoccupied about money. That's all you think about." She acknowledged the comment by saying: "Yes, I am concerned about money."

I saw a father run out of his seat to scream at the umpire for a lousy call he made against his son. The umpire said: "You're right, I blew it.'" The father couldn't say anything else—he practically crawled back into his seat.

Don't make excuses or try to justify your feelings, such as "If you were in my shoes you would feel the same way." Just acknowledge the comment.

On Your Own

Think about a situation in your life. Often you encounter someone saying similar comments about you again and again. What's the comment you have difficulty with? What could you say that is both Polite and Powerful?

---

4. The Other Person Gets Aggressive

This is often the bully or the shouter. But anyone can respond aggressively without thinking. What can you do?

1. Stay calm. Take a deep breath. Tell yourself you can handle it.

2. Don't attack back. Someone else's bad behavior is never an excuse for your own. This can be a hard concept for you to swallow. If someone is yelling at you, don't you want to yell back? No! As we discussed in Chapter 4, you will gain nothing by this. When you meet someone's aggression with your own aggression, you're giving that person power over you. The power to get you upset. It usually doesn't lead to resolution either. In fact, it can get you arrested or sued. I read about an argument that erupted between the dean of a business school and one of his professors. One of them shouted, "Shut up." The other hit him in the head with his briefcase! Their argument ended up in municipal court!

3. Remain Polite and Powerful. Sometimes you want to let the person blow off steam or come to his or her senses. Often, if you don't respond with aggression, you will defuse the other person. The person may just be having a bad day and will often realize it if you're calm. In fact, if you stay Polite and Powerful you may defuse the other person's aggression. One woman told me she uses this statement with her customers and kids: "Screaming at me will not help me help you. It will only make us more unproductive." She says it works every time.

A woman did this to me one day (even I "lose it" sometimes too). I went to a department store to pick up a suit that I had left to be altered. It wasn't ready. I was tired and hungry and I needed that suit in the morning.

I kept saying, (in a raised voice) "But you promised me . . ." The woman I was talking to obviously had taken my course! She stayed Polite and Powerful. She told me, "I understand you're upset. I regret that it happened. Here's what I can do to help you." She defused me. She also offered to rush the job through but couldn't guarantee the quality since she only had fifteen minutes before the store closed.

4. Use an Exit Line If Necessary. If the confrontation continues to stay aggressive, get out of Dodge and fast. You tell people, sometimes by your actions, what behavior you will or will not accept from them. You establish your boundaries and you are the only person in charge of drawing your lines. Sometimes you establish a boundary by leaving. (If you're on the telephone, you would hang up.) But if you do leave the room—don't storm out and slam the door. Use a Polite and Powerful line when you leave or hang up. I call this an exit line or lines:

> "That's not an appropriate way to talk to me. When you can talk to me calmly, call me back." This is exactly what a sales manager said to one of her representatives who had started shouting at her. He called back a half-hour later and apologized.
>
> or
>
> "I cannot talk to you when you're screaming at me. I'd be happy to continue this discussion when you can talk to me normally." (Pause to see if the person calms down). If they are still upset tell them, "I'm going to leave now. Good-bye."

And then leave! Don't linger by their door or in the hallway. Walk away. You'll lose your credibility if you hang around.

5. Decide if the relationship is worth continuing. If the person continues to deal with you in an aggressive manner, you need to ask yourself, "Is it worth it?" "Do the benefits outweigh the drawbacks?" I had a boss once—a virtual terror on two legs—who used to scream bloody murder at me. His temper was legendary. I stayed with the company for a while to gain some valuable skills and experience, but as soon as I had them and a good career opportunity appeared, I was out of there.

If you're having a problem like this, I'm not telling to quit your job tomorrow; you may want, or need, to stick it out for a while, but be aware of the negative consequences of maintaining the relationship.

WAC'ing Strangers

A fear of aggression holds many people back from WAC'ing strangers. In this day, an age full of easy gun access and violence, I can't say to anyone—"Go WAC someone you don't know." I can't say this because I don't know what will happen either.

What I can tell you is what many people in my seminars tell me: It's easier to WAC strangers than people they know. This makes sense. They don't worry about hurting a stranger's feelings as much as they do a loved one. The repercussions of WAC'ing strangers is temporary—it's not an ongoing relationship.

Is It a Safe or Unsafe Environment?

Before WAC'ing a stranger, however, you should consider the environment. Always use your judgement. If you're in the grocery store, bank, or crowded public place, chances are you don't have to worry too much about your safety.

Ed was in an excruciatingly long line in the bank when he noticed that a person was whisked out of the line by one of the bank employees. He didn't think anything of it, until it happened again. When it was his turn for service, he asked the teller why they had been pulled from the line. Her response was "They are regular customers."

Well, so was Ed. Before learning WAC'em, Ed admitted that he might have "lost his cool." But he did learn Polite and Powerful behavior so he used it. He asked to speak with the bank manager. He calmly asked the manager to explain the bank's policy on "special treatment for regular customers." The manager said there was no policy. When Ed explained the situation, calmly, the manager was apologetic. He said it wouldn't happen again.

Ed felt better. He had no guarantee that it wouldn't happen again, but at least he didn't feel "walked on." He had expressed his opinion and that alone made him feel better.

In this situation, Ed was reasonably certain that the manager was not going to get aggressive. And he didn't. Ed was Polite and Powerful and the manager responded to him with his own positive behavior.

Again, use your judgement and your Polite and Powerful skills. If you're in the express line at the grocery store and the woman's cart in front of yours is jammed with food, you can Politely and Powerfully remind her that she's in the wrong line. Maybe she didn't realize it. Then again, maybe she did. There are jerks out there. But at least if you say something, you'll have the satisfaction of having spoken up. And, if you don't lose your temper, you are going to look better. Let the other person look like the jerk.

There will be times when you should WAC a stranger, as this story illustrates:

A financial consultant took a group of prospective clients to hear a famous speaker. The event was a dinner held in a hotel ballroom sponsored by a financial association. Soon after they sat down and the speaker began his keynote speech, the table next to them became quite loud and disruptive. It interfered with their ability to hear the speaker. As the host, it was the consultant's responsibility to make sure his guests were comfortable. He did not control the situation. The prospective clients thought less of him.

The host should have asked the people to quiet down. If the group didn't respond by quieting down, he could have gone to someone in charge of the association's gathering. Chances are, it wouldn't have come to that. The rowdy group probably would have quieted down if someone had simply WAC'ed them.

If It Isn't Safe—Let It Go

If you encounter someone you don't know—on a street at night or in a sparsely populated area—or the person simply seems strange, having a confrontation may not be a good idea. The only thing I can tell you is to follow your gut. If you feel unsafe or even just have the "willies," let the confrontation go—and then get yourself out of there.

Margie and Ben went to retrieve their car from a parking lot after a late dinner. When they went to the booth to pay, the attendant was on the phone and stayed on the phone. He barely acknowledged them as he took their money. He didn't give them back their change. Ben called out that they were waiting for it. The attendant cursed, responded aggressively, saying among other things: "Can't you see

I'm busy?" Both Ben and Margie got the feeling that his fuse wasn't just short, something wasn't right about him. Though they were annoyed, they chose not to say anything. They left $.75 shorter, but safer.

Road Rage

Road rage can occur when you're on the highway and someone cuts you off. This act of rudeness is not a license to gesture rudely or shout out of your window. Both of these responses are in fact, dangerous behaviors—you can lose sight of the road or find yourself being tormented by the driver again. I know it's tempting. I get as frustrated as you do when a jerk cuts me off. But then again, maybe the person isn't a jerk. Maybe they made a mistake.

5. The Other Person Responds Passively

If someone gives you the silent treatment or is "blowing you off," you can't force him or her to talk to you. What you can do is let them know what you think about their unwillingness to talk. Stress that it's important to you that you are able to work out your differences.

- "I really need to hear your input if we're going to move forward on this."
- "It's important that I hear your point-of-view. What are your thoughts on this suggestion?"
- "I assume from your silence that you agree with me and unless I hear from you otherwise I assume that you will be home before dark . . ." (I said this to my thirteen-year old stepdaughter. Boy did she start talking fast!)

What if the other person doesn't say anything? What if he or she cries? Yikes! No one wants to be the cause of someone else's tears. What do you do then?

Maybe the person is really upset. Maybe the tears are a defense mechanism or a manipulation because the other person wants to avoid the discussion. It's usually best to acknowledge the emotion and focus back on the topic:

- "It seems like this discussion is really upsetting you. That's not my intention. Why don't you go to the rest room and get yourself together and then let's talk about it some more."
- "Why don't I leave for a few minutes so you can get yourself together. When I come back, we can talk about it some more. Here's some Kleenex."

6. The Person Says No (and Means It)

What if you are not going to get what you want—period? You have received a flat-out "No" from the other person. If this is your boss, you often can't force a discussion. "No" sometimes means "No further discussion."

Much earlier in this book, we talked about one of the reasons why people don't confront—they perceive it as too risky. They're afraid, for example, that they may ask for a raise and get a "No." Then what? Your boss knows you feel underpaid and are possibly unhappy. Maybe your boss is unhappy with you now. Before you curse yourself for speaking up, take a moment and think about it another way.

While there may be some risk involved in WAC'ing a higher up, getting a "no" doesn't always have to be a bad thing. The fact is you may end up with a different or new alternative that you never imagined you would—like Jane did.

Jane worked for a construction company as the office manager. She was asked by upper management to train the new controller for the parent company—a job she had been "filling in" until someone was hired.

At first, she was a pretender. She told herself, "This doesn't bother me." But it did. She evolved into a complainer. She told her friends and co-workers about how unfair the upper management was. "How could they ask me to train this guy? I'm doing the job now."

I suggested that she ask for the position. She hadn't thought of doing that. She prepared what she wanted to say, made an appointment with the head of human resources. They told her, "No," but impressed by her, they offered her another job with higher responsibilities and pay. She took it.

But Jerry had a different experience. When he Politely and Powerfully confronted his boss about the fact that he put him down in front of others and wanted to know why he was doing it, his boss admitted that he wanted Jerry to quit.

"At first I was really upset," Jerry told me. "I regretted opening my mouth. My wife and I had just bought a new house. It wasn't a great time to find myself unemployed. But the confrontation motivated me to find a new job and I did. I now have a boss who treats me with respect. I'm much happier now though it was a rough and uncertain time there for awhile."

So even though Jerry got a response from his boss that he wasn't counting on or didn't want, at least he found out where he really stood with him. As a result, he made a job change, and though it was difficult and scary at first, this change ultimately had a positive impact on his life.

Some people may say Jerry took a risk and got bitten for it. I say, in this context, the risk was worth it. In fact, the risk led to a higher pay-off for Jerry. "No" was the right answer. It got Jerry on the move. Who wants to work for someone who doesn't treat you with respect?

Even when "No" doesn't seem like a positive answer, I suggest that it's better to know where you honestly stand, than to stand in the old place feeling mistreated, misunderstood, or just plain unhappy.

Don't WAC Behind Someone's Back

If you ask someone else to WAC for you, you may avoid the confrontation but you may end up bringing a lot of negative consequences upon yourself. The home office of an insurance company had this problem:

Peter didn't like that his secretary, Betsy, was often too loud when she talked. It drove him crazy when she would shout him questions or answers rather than use her intercom. Peter complained to the office manager. He wanted her to say something to Betsy.

The office manager did discuss the problem with Peter's secretary. Betsy was upset that he didn't come directly to her. She didn't realize she was driving him crazy. It embarrassed her that the office manager was involved and that perhaps others in the office knew and felt the same way. Her attitude changed after that. Eventually she quit. She was a good and hard-to-replace worker.

This same office manager was approached by one of the secretaries on another issue: "Megan is using my printer. She's tying it up and I need it."

The office manager told her, "I think you need to discuss this calmly with Megan. Does she realize you're busy and need the printer?"

"I don't really know."

"Well," she said, "find out."

The office manager realized that if she could help the people in the office work their problems out directly, people would get along better in the long run. She gave the secretary a crash course on positive confrontation. The situation was quickly resolved. No one got upset.

Peter, in the above example, was being a wimp. He was afraid to say something to his secretary—and look what happened! I think in most situations it's better to be direct rather than use an emissary to confront for you.

I have heard countless tales of family feuds that begin this way: One sister tells another sister something about one of the sisters-in-law and when the sister-in-law gets a bad vibe, she tells her husband. The husband then tries to talk to his sister. Then she gets mad and tells the other sister about the brother. The other sister calls the other brother and now the whole family is in a fight!

The Focus Is Still on You

Though this chapter has focused on the other person and the many ways he or she can respond to your WAC, your main focus should always remain on you—your Polite and Powerful behavior. When you check in with the other person, you may find, they are only too happy to give you what you've asked.

However, the other person may get offended by your WAC words. He or she may act rudely. He or she may even shout at you. You can't control the other person. You can only control yourself and how you react. Polite and Powerful behavior, even if you're the only one using it, will still give you the best chance for positive conflict resolution.

CHAPTER 10

Eleven Simple Things You Can Do To Have A Positive Confrontation

We've talked a lot about how to prevent a negative confrontation. When a confrontation goes bad, there are many common reasons why—negative wording, accusatory statements, bad body language . . . When a confrontation goes well, there are common reasons why. You've gone into the conversation with a solid WAC'em worked out. You pay attention to your verbals and nonverbals. But there's more you can do to contribute to your success. Often, when I look at the confrontations that have gone well, the person initiating the WAC'em discussion took the time to do the following eleven simple things. They're simple all right. But they really matter!

1. Practice

I hate to be like your old piano teacher, but I have to tell you "Practice!" We talked about writing your WAC'em words down. It's also important to practice saying them. Read your words aloud. Ask yourself:

How do they sound. Are they harsh? Too soft?

How would you feel if someone said those words to you? This is vitally important. Listen to how the words would come across to someone else.

Repeat your words a number of times. You don't want to memorize your WAC'em words. You're not going to recite a script during your confrontation. But by practicing your WAC'em wording, you'll feel more comfortable and confident when it comes to say them to the other person. You're less likely to be too harsh or to discount yourself.

2. Handle Your Jitters

I'd like to give you a word of encouragement about the jitters. If you worry that you'll get so nervous that all your practice will go out the window, get in line; you're definitely not alone in having this fear. Many people feel very nervous when it comes to difficult conversation. They're afraid of making mistakes.

It's normal to be nervous. Your nervousness is really just energy. Energy isn't good or bad, it's how you handle it. Don't you think actors, athletes, and CEOs get nervous? Of course they do. But they're successful because they have moved ahead despite any fears they may have about making mistakes or "losing it in front of others." They've learned how to harness their nervous energy to create a positive experience. Many people say the energy helps them perform better.

A friend of mine is a successful writer. He told me that when he has to read in front of an audience he feels like not enough air is getting into his lungs. He's convinced he's going to pass out or hyperventilate. But he doesn't. "I take a few really deep breaths before I start. By the time I'm on the second paragraph, I'm calm and having a great time. I just have to sweat it out a little in the beginning."

3. Fake It Until You Feel It

It gets easier. It gets more rewarding. When you WAC instead of attack, the benefits you enjoy are numerous. You feel good about yourself for handling the bothersome situation, for one. Your relationship with the person usually improves because you're not harboring secret resentment toward him or her. The bothersome behavior will often stop. When you begin to experience these benefits, having those confrontations isn't nearly as hard. You've got lots of incentive.

But you have to start somewhere and the benefits don't come until after you've WAC'ed. So while you're getting some experience in this area, here's a trick that might help: People respond to your "outside" behavior. They don't know what you're thinking on the inside. They respond only to what you're telling them with words and non-words. Eventually, I promise, if you get the cues right on the outside, if you appear Polite and Powerful, the inside will catch up. You will start to feel more confident. You can use this to overcome the jitters. Tell yourself, you don't look nervous. And if you don't look nervous, will the other person know? Probably not—unless you tell them.

You know the old saying, "If you look like a duck, walk like a duck, quack like a duck, you're a duck."

People love this trick because it works. It's okay to fake it until you feel it.

A Tip for Handling the Jitters

It sounds obvious, but breathe. People tend to hold their breath or take shallow breaths when they're nervous. Before approaching someone for a difficult conversation, take a few deep breaths. Draw air through your nose, deeply into your abdominal cavity and keep drawing until your abdomen is fully expanded. Hold this breath for a slow count of seven. Then release your breath through your mouth, slowly as you count of eight. In two or three breaths you're going to feel better. It works.

I have reached a point in my life where I can pretty much WAC anybody Politely and Powerfully. That doesn't mean I don't still get nervous. I do sometimes get the jitters. But now I can look back and see my successful confrontations and that helps me move forward each time. Even when the outcome of a confrontation wasn't what I wanted, I still handled myself okay, and that's important.

---

4. Visualize Yourself Being Polite and Powerful

Part of your preparation for a confrontation will be mental. Visualization techniques are a powerful tool for many people. Some people swear that just by visualizing themselves playing flawless tennis they can improve their games. A woman I work with told me that to help herself stay on her diet she used to visualize herself in a pair of size six jeans.

Tom, a quality assurance engineer for an aerospace corporation, told me that he used to have dramatic fantasies of "telling off" the people in his department who were giving him a "hard time"—not getting papers to him on time.

"In my mind, I would confront these three specific people in my department. I would get very righteous, yell, and of course, have the perfect come-back," he said. "I could get my heart pumping and my blood pressure would go up."

These fantasies weren't helpful. Nothing changed. Tom didn't confront and only got more upset.

After he learned the power of positive confrontation, Tom decided to put his fantasy life to work for him in a positive way: "I would picture standing up straight, my face looking relaxed and calm. I would practice my WAC'em wording and say, 'When I don't get your papers on time, my part of the project gets sidetracked. I need to get them on time. Is there any reason why this can't happen?'

"When I finally did it, I was nervous, but I managed to say everything I wanted to say, Politely and Powerfully. They apologized. I get the papers on time. It was pretty easy."

When you get upset about someone's behavior, try to calm down.

Visualize yourself as the Polite and Powerful person you are. Like Tom, picture yourself confronting the person using your WAC words and being calm and self-assured.

5. Tell Yourself You're a Polite and Powerful Person

Before every seminar I tell myself, "You can do it."

This is an affirmation. I know it sounds corny but try it. It works! When you're about to have a confrontation remind yourself—"I can do it" or "I can handle it."

Your subconscious believes whatever you tell it. If you tell it you're a wimp, you're a wimp. Tell it positive things about your ability to handle conflict. These are affirmations that you want to get into your mental loop—that string of statements we whisper to ourselves on an ongoing basis. You'll be surprised to find out what you're thinking when you don't even know you were thinking anything!

People think this stuff—because it sounds too simple to be that powerful—doesn't work. I tell them, try it for a few weeks and then tell me it doesn't work.

One very bright software engineer told me he used to stand at the bus stop going to a job he didn't like and say to himself, "But I can't get another job. I'm stuck. I would have to get a new degree. That would take too long. No one will hire me."

These negative statements were in his loop. He tuned in, decided he didn't like what he was telling himself and decided that to try something new: "I stood there and told myself, 'I can get another job that I like better. I can do it. I'll get the skills.' "

He did it. You can too. Check in and listen to what you're saying to yourself. If necessary, reprogram that loop with a positive statement. Keep it simple—a short "I" statement will do. Use present tense—"I can, I will, I know . . ." Keep it positive—"I won't flunk the test" is not positive. "I will do well on the test" is positive. But you still have to study!

Come up with your one-line affirmation that you will use:

MY AFFIRMATION.

---

6. Find a Polite and Powerful Role Model

As I mentioned in the beginning of this book, my role model for handling conflict was Ann Davis. I used to watch how she handled herself in tough situations and learned from her. If you can, choose as your mentor someone that you see on a regular basis. Notice their words and their body language. Notice how he or she handles difficult situations. You don't want to copy the person word for word or gesture for gesture. Let them inspire you instead.

7. Build Your Confidence

Again, let me caution you—don't stop reading this book and immediately go out and WAC the "big one." The big one being your boss with the bad temper, your mother-in-law, or someone else whose reaction to being confronted can have a big effect on your relationship. I'm not saying that you shouldn't confront this person. I think it's wise to work up to the confrontations that will have the biggest impact on your life and well-being.

Not to oversimplify, but it's true that many aspects of positive confrontation are like habits. Like learning to drive a car safely. For most of us, it's awkward and even scary in the beginning. Yet after lessons and practice and experience, you don't think about. It's a skill that has become a habit. Positive confrontation is the same way. You get used to it.

Before you WAC anybody for the first time, role-play it with someone else, if possible. Play both roles. Practice saying your W and your A—what's bothering me and what do I want to ask the person to do—to a live person. Try to think of all the obstacles you might encounter during a difficult conversation. The more you practice, even if you're just role-playing alone, the more comfortable and confident you will be later in real-life.

8. Pick the Right Approach and Time

You've prepared. You've practiced. You've visualized and affirmed—you're ready to go. It's time to hunt the other person down and do this WAC'em thing! Ready or not here I come!

Please don't do this—this hit-them-over-the-head approach.

In your excitement or desire to "get it over with," don't force a confrontation to happen at the wrong time. Let etiquette be your guide in determining when you're going to confront. You need to approach the person. You're the person with something to say, so you can't wait for them to come looking for you. They might not even know you're bothered by something.

Right after a meeting while other people are lingering about is not a good time to confront someone. It may be a good time to ask the person if he or she is available to talk later. You should wait to WAC until you are alone with the person. If you don't have that opportunity, make it happen. Arrange a meeting with the person. At the very least, ask "Is this a good time for you to talk?" "Do you have a few minutes? There's something I'd like to talk to you about."

Above all, the rule of thumb is: If you're not calm it's easy to lose control. If you're not calm, postpone it.

Exceptions to the Privacy Rule

If for some reason, you don't want to be alone with the person because they may have a reputation for losing their temper or for some other reason, arrange to meet in a public place. Most office buildings have a coffee shop in the building or nearby. Meet during working hours when you are certain others will be around.

Don't Confront at Happy Hour

I caution you about meeting and having difficult conversations in bars. Having a drink may help you relax but it's also an opportunity for confrontations to get out of hand or sidetracked.

With a few drinks in your system, you may talk too much and you might say something you regret. You may end up hugging but chances are the next day, you both might feel embarrassed. You may not have a clear understanding of what was said or agreed to. You probably won't have accomplished anything.

9. Keep It Short and Simple

This is how you want the delivery of your WAC'em words to be. There's a tendency—especially on the part of women—to talk too much. Women tend to explain and explain and explain some more. Nervousness also causes you to keep going and going with words. Relief can cause you to talk too much too.

Also, keep it to one issue at a time. This will help you keep it short and simple and you won't get sidetracked by other issues.

Don't undo what you have done with your positive WAC'em words. Once you have done your C and have checked in with the other person—and you must do this—and are satisfied with the outcome, congratulate yourself in silence, shut your mouth and move on to other things:

"I appreciate your time. I have a meeting to get to now."

"Thanks for listening. I'll talk to you later."

"I have a phone call to make, so let's leave it at that."

10. Follow Up with the Other Person

The person you confronted might have wonderful intentions. When you did your C—checked in—and said "Is that okay?" they may have said, "Sure, no problem." But people don't change overnight. Sometimes what you are dealing with are other people's bad habits. It may be necessary to reinforce your point. It may be necessary to give the person a little time and space in which to make the changes you asked for. Some follow-up check-ins may sound something like this:

"Remember yesterday, when I mentioned that your music was too loud . . ."

"This is what I meant by that discussion we had."

"You wanted me to point out when you were doing that . . . Well you're doing that!"

It would be wonderful if you could WAC'em once and be done with any difficulty—but that doesn't always happen. Schedule a follow up meeting if necessary. Review any agreements that were decided upon. Make adjustments if needed. At work you may want to follow up in writing.

Even if you were right and the other person was wrong—Polite and Powerful people don't gloat over their victory. They don't need to be right. Powerful people aren't powerful because they get their way. They are powerful because they have the confidence to be gracious. If the person you confronted does make the changes, thank him or her:

"I appreciate that you signed me up for the class. The training was very helpful."

"Thank you for getting the report to me on time. It really helped."

11. Follow Up with Yourself

First, feel good about yourself. No matter what the outcome, you tried to have a positive confrontation. Next, evaluate the experience. Ask yourself these questions:

•What did I learn from the experience?
•How can I improve next time?

If you're not successful the first time, don't beat yourself up. It doesn't help. You are practicing new skills and mastering them will take time. It's okay not to like how you handled a situation and still like yourself. If you keep saying, "I'm stupid" that's not good. And, if you stay on "stupid," that's where you'll be—in a negative, destructive place.

Think about a person you confronted recently. What was the issue and how did you resolve it? Would you do it differently now? How so?

Keep A WAC'em Diary

Many people find it helpful to keep a WAC'em diary. It can help you in the beginning. Start by recording the following:

- Describe the reason for the encounter.
- What was your WAC'em?
- Where were you?
- Who was there?
- How was your body language?
- What did the other person say?
- Did you give the other person a chance to talk?
- How was it resolved?
- If you choose to confront the other person again, what will you say?

After four or five encounters look back over the pages. This is an easy way to quickly discover any similarities or problems you may be having:

- Are you having difficulty with the same person?
- Are you having the same or related kinds of conflicts again and again?
- Is it occurring at a particular time or place?
- Do you have the most conflict at home or work?
- What skills do you need to practice?

You will only need to do this as you get used to confronting. Soon, if you keep at it, the benefits I talked about earlier will be yours. You will feel better about yourself and the other person. You won't have to put up with the person's bothersome behavior anymore. You will feel less stressed out and happier.

CHAPTER 11

WAC'ing
in Writing

So far, we've talked about how to deliver your WAC'em but only within the context of face-to-face discussion. I have encouraged you to write down your W and your A, but only to help you clarify your thoughts and come up with positive wording. But what about writing down your WAC'em words in a letter or an e-mail with the intent that the person will read them? Can this be an effective way to resolve a conflict—especially if you're terribly nervous about having the difficult conversation?

The answer is sometimes it's not effective and sometimes it can be. First let's examine why it's not always an effective way to approach difficult conversations.

Dear John/Dear Judy Letters

I'm so sorry. I don't want to hurt you, but I'm must be honest. This relationship isn't working out. At all! I can't see you anymore . . .

■

Play along with me for a moment and imagine you're John or Judy. You realize your love affair is over. What will John's face look like as he gets the news—you don't want to see him anymore? What if Judy cries? You'll feel bad, lousy even, just awful.

Bottom line: If you write a letter, you're not there to see the smile torn from John's face. You don't have to be there when Judy's dam of tears bursts and gets your shoes wet.

It's tempting. But think about it more carefully. How do you know John got your letter? Maybe Judy didn't have a chance to read it yet or misplaced it. What if she still thinks you're going to see *Cats* with her? What if John calls and says, "I agree. We have some problems, but we can work it out." You're on the other end thinking, "Doesn't he get it?"

Maybe. Maybe not. The *Maybe* is one of the biggest reasons I caution people against WAC'ing someone in writing. You could be giving up your power—power in the sense of knowledge. Did they get the letter? Do they understand what's bothering you or what you're asking for? You simply don't know. You have given up any control you had as soon as that mailbox door slammed shut.

You have no control over, if and when, the person will read it. Even if the letter is delivered, letters do get lost in offices, go unopened, and fall behind the dishwasher. A friend said that she had written her boyfriend who was overseas in the Gulf War this great letter in which she WAC'ed him about his not writing her. However, he said he never got the letter!

How do you know if he got it or not?

You don't.

Here are five more reasons why WAC'ing in writing may not be a good choice:

- **There's no discussion at the time.** If the person reads your words and you're not there, there can be no talking about your concern or issue. You're missing the immediate benefit of the C. You can't check in and know where you stand. In some cases, this can be a good thing—it can give the person some time to think the issue over! It can be a bad thing too. How can you be sure you and the other person are on the same proverbial page in terms of understanding the situation? If Judy misinterprets your letter, you may have to end up WAC'ing her face-to-face anyway.

- **You could be viewed as a wimp who is unable to confront.** The person who is reading the letter can say to himself or herself: "This is ridiculous. Why didn't he just tell me? Why do I have to read about it?" (You'll further damage your image if you start your letter with an apology: "I'm sorry for writing this but I usually get so emotional when I try to talk about these kind of things. . . .")

    This is especially true for WAC'ing at work. A promotable person is one who is viewed as being able to handle difficult situations—confronting others Politely and Powerfully is part of that.

- **You may offend or confuse someone.** The other person may wonder: "Why didn't he just tell me?" Or, "Is he afraid of me? Do I seem unapproachable?" Or, "I thought Kyle respected me enough to talk to me man-to-man."

- **You may write too much.** When you WAC someone in person, you know it's important to keep it clear and concise. In a letter, it can be tempting to over-explain, explain a little more, and "Oh just one more little thing that's bothering me . . ." You lose your clarity if you're wordy.

- **You lose the nonverbal advantages.** If you're worried about how harsh your words may be or how well the person is going to take your WAC'em words, your nonverbals can help your delivery. You can express your concern for the person's feelings by the look on your face, by the openness of your body language and a gentle tone of voice. You can't do this in writing.

My belief is that if it's your concern, then you generally want to initiate the WAC'em conversation. Of course, of course, there will be exceptions to this—let's discuss what they are and why it's sometimes a good idea to do your WAC'ing in writing.

When It's Okay to WAC'em in Writing

There are some positives to WAC'ing a person in writing—you can express yourself carefully and thoroughly. If you're worried about losing your temper in person, you will have control in the letter. You can also avoid the other person's reaction, if you're sincerely worried about what that may be.

What About E-Mail?

I do advise you, however, to write a letter rather than an e-mail message. E-mail has become a very casual form of communication. People typically put less time and thought into e-mail writing. These communications are often dashed off—and you don't want to dash when you WAC. You need to think carefully about your W—what's bothering me and your A—what do I want to ask the person to do.

E-Mail Horror Stories

I know someone who WAC'ed someone via e-mail. The recipient didn't like being WAC'ed and to even the score, forwarded his message all over the company and beyond!

Plus, you can send it to the wrong person and not know it—until it's too late. I heard a story on National Public Radio that makes my point.

A journalist was upset, very upset, with his boss. He wrote a nasty e-mail about her to his co-worker. He said that as he went to hit the send button, he had the terrible realization that it was his boss's address on the screen. The worst part was he could see her in her office. He heard the little ding that indicated that she had mail. He saw her hear it and turn to her computer. He left the magazine that day.

As a general guideline—and we'll discuss more details about techno-conflict in Part Three—don't use your e-mail for sensitive communications of any sort.

Rather than e-mail, I do encourage you to write a letter to WAC—as long as it's appropriate to do so. Situations where WAC'ing someone in writing may include:

1. If you think the person will get defensive or aggressive and you won't be able to clearly express yourself. This doesn't mean the person will read your letter and still not react badly, but you have a better chance of getting your point across.

2. If it is a complex or serious issue between you and the other person, you may want to explain it in a letter. When you put it in writing, you can be sure of your words. As long as you edit yourself, nothing is going to slip out and cause a problem as it might in conversation.

A wife WAC'ed her husband through a letter. She explained all the ways his "flip" comments put her down. She discussed how it affected her self-esteem and how crucial it was to their marriage for the comments to stop. She had a lot to say and wanted to be clear about her wording so she wrote. He stopped. She's now able to WAC him in person.

When you write, the words are permanent. That is the good and bad news. It's good because it allows the person to read your words and then read it again if necessary. This can be helpful for clarifying complex situations. The person can take his or her time and really try to understand your position.

It's bad because your words are now permanent. You can't say you didn't say this or that. If it's down in writing, you can't take it back.

3. If the person uses humor to distract you and doesn't take the issue seriously. A letter will allow you to get your thoughts out without interruption. I have a friend who told me she couldn't WAC her father because he always made jokes. And, to make matters worse, he was funny. She would end up being cracked up by him—but still frustrated. She said she tried to bring him back to the issue by saying, "Dad, you're so funny, but when you make jokes out of the serious things I'm trying to tell you, I feel bad." That still didn't work. So she wrote him a letter.

4. If geography makes it impossible to say your WAC'em words in person, go ahead and put your thoughts to paper. A woman's father-in-law exploded at her during her family's annual holiday visit about her child breaking something in his house during the visit. She stormed out (husband and child, too) and went to a hotel. She returned home still upset. (Of course, because she had stormed out.) After my seminar, she decided to WAC him in a letter because he lived far away and the writing of her words would allow her to say exactly what she wanted to say. She wrote that it was important for him to remain in her life and yet she wouldn't allow him to explode at her. She wanted to hear his concerns but she didn't want him screaming them at her.

What About Reaching Out and WAC'ing Someone?

In any of the above situations, couldn't the person have telephoned the other person? Wouldn't that have been preferable?

Again, the answer is maybe/maybe not.

The woman described above who WAC'ed her father-in-law knew she had the telephone option but was still afraid of his temper. She was new to positive confrontation and was nervous. She was afraid she wouldn't be able to get her words out correctly. In this case, writing the letter was a good interim step. She may have laid the groundwork for future conversations on the telephone or in person.

Sometimes it just happens. You're on the telephone with your friend when the issue you're bothered by comes up. You've been thinking about saying something. You've been preparing your WAC'em words. Why wait? Perfect opportunity. I agree. Don't wait.

Other times, you'll want to have a discussion on the telephone because you know you won't be seeing that person for awhile.

Many of the same advantages and disadvantages to WAC'em in writing apply to WAC'em over the telephone. On the plus side, it is more direct and personal because you are speaking with the person. A discussion can occur.

On the down side:

- You don't have the chance to use your nonverbals in a positive or softening way.
- You can't be sure you're reaching someone at a favorable time. Also, the person can make up excuses or even have legitimate ones ("I have company") for getting off the telephone.
- He or she can hang up on you.

If you're very nervous or unsure about the person's reaction or temper—you may want to speak to him or her via the telephone. It does work for some people while they're building their confidence.

Here's some advice for WAC'ing successfully over the telephone:

- Try to set up your talk in advance or let the person know you'll be calling. This will help ensure you're reaching someone at a good time.
- Watch your tone of voice and volume. The only nonverbal that you can use to help make the conversation Polite and Powerful will be your tone of voice—make sure you have good control over it.
- Don't leave a WAC'em message on someone's machine or voice mail. This is rude. You don't know who might be able to hear it. Also, if you say something you regret, the other person can keep a copy of it. Second, don't leave a message like: "Kate, you're really in trouble this time. I need to talk to you ASAP." Kate will be looking forward to calling you back like she's looking forward to getting a cavity filled.

How to Write a Good WAC'em Letter

If you do write to someone about a bothersome situation or concern, the quality of your writing becomes important. I teach business writing and collect student samples before each seminar. I am continually stunned to discover how much conflict occurs because people write things and don't realize how the other person or people would read those words.

I went into a bank to teach business writing right after a vice-president sent a memo to all employees trying to reassure them that the company would work with them during an upcoming transit strike. His suggestions were good ones. Unfortunately, his wording was negative. Among other things, he wrote, "We will work with you but we don't want any of you abusing the system."

Not only did the employees begrudge him, they begrudged the company as well.

Read on for Polite and Powerful writing guidelines:

1. WAC'em applies. In writing, your W is the same. You tell the person what's bothering you. The A is the same. You tell the person what you want. The C will be slightly different. You need to ask the person to get back to you. At work, you can make a request—"I need your response by the end of the week." Or, depending upon the situation: "Please give this some thought. I'll be back in town next week and we can talk." Or, indicate that you'll give the person a call and let him or her know when that will be.

2. Choose your words carefully. Go back to chapter 7 and review the various verbal vices covered there. Make sure none of them, nor any like them you think up on your own, appear in your letter. Positive wording is critical even if you're WAC'ing someone on the moon.

If you write, "Any reasonable person would conclude . . ." You imply that the reader is *not* a reasonable person. "You failed to . . ." blames the other person. These statements would be harsh in person, but are deadly written down. There are no nonverbals at work to soften things. You can't smile, have a pleasant facial expression or nice sound to your voice when the other person reads your letter.

3. Don't try to intimidate or try to seem superior with your words. Why use "annihilate" when "eliminate" will do? Look at the box below for more suggestions:

Simple words are best:

INSTEAD OF . . .	USE . . .
Ameliorate	improve
Solicit	ask
Endeavor	try
Peruse	read or review
Terminate	end
Supercedes	replaces
Purports	claims
Utilize	use

4. Don't repeat yourself. Needless repetition is one of the most common writing mistakes. Your writing should be as clear and concise as possible. Redundant words take up space and diminish the impact of your WAC'em words. After teaching my Business Writing Skills seminar for many years, I've identified the twelve most commonly used redundancies. Check your writing against the following list:

INSTEAD OF:	USE:
qualified expert	expert
unresolved problem	problem
merged together	merged
fewer in number	fewer
file away	file
disregard altogether	disregard
final conclusion	conclusion
refer back	refer
meet together	meet

ask a question	ask
revert back	revert
new innovation	innovation

5. Write the way you speak. People have a tendency to become formal in writing. You want to create a conversational tone. You want to connect with the person, especially when you're not face-to-face. You don't use words like "herewith or "heretofore," so why write that way? Besides, most people don't know what these words mean. (One participant joked and said heretofore meant, "We're here in your class till four.")

How many times have you ever said, "Pursuant to our conversation" or "It has become necessary to reiterate excessive tardiness." You would never say this, so why write it?

6. Grammar counts. Even if you're writing to a friend, your grammar should be correct. If you're unsure about your grammar, consult a guide, run your document through your wordprocessor's spelling and grammar checker. Ask someone (preferably someone who doesn't know the person you're WAC'ing) whose grammar you know is good to proofread for you. However, you may not want anyone else to see your letter. It may not be fair to the other person.

7. Appearance matters. You want your document to be visually appealing so it will be read and, in some cases, won't add to the conflict.

- If you write by hand make it legible. If you hand someone an eight-page, handwritten letter with words crossed out and scribbled in the margins, not only will the person not want to read it, you will probably give him or her a scare.
- Create short paragraphs and wide-enough margins.
- Keep the bold and underline to a minimum. Convey your WAC through your words. **IF YOU USE EMPHASIS TECHNIQUES, LIKE THIS ONE, IT'S AS IF YOU'RE SHOUTING!** People are insulted by this—who can blame them?
- Use punctuation to punctuate, not to create an effect. Again, let the clarity of your points be made by your words,

not by a trick. One exclamation mark and one question mark only. Do not do this!!!!!!!!!! One woman once wrote to her employees: "The meeting is Monday. Everyone must attend!!!!!!!!!!!!" (Her group was insulted. As if they didn't understand what *everyone, must,* and *attend* meant.)

- Use decent paper. No cocktail napkins, no Post-it note collages, and no scraps of paper. Don't tear pages out of a notebook and leave the fringe on. Plain white paper or personal stationery is fine.

- **Read it aloud.** Reading silently isn't a good acid test for how it sounds. You must hear how the words sound by speaking them. If your letter sounds harsh to you, chances are, it will sound harsh to the other person. Go back and make it positive.

8. Write a first draft. If you're very frustrated or very upset with the other person, grab your pen. Go wild, spill your guts, blow off steam. Then throw that one away. You've gotten your frustrations out, now take a deep breath and write another letter. Even if you're not emotional, it's still a good idea to write a draft. Most effective writers—whether business or prose—understand that it often takes a few drafts before you've captured what you really want to say.

9. Be polite. Use please and thank you. No name calling, no cursing.

10. Use the correct salutation. Don't use nicknames unless you have permission to do so. I don't like when people call me Barb. I know a man named Charles who will stop reading a letter if it's addressed "Dear Chuck."

Be more formal if appropriate, especially in work situations. Don't address someone as "Dear Paul" if you always have called him "Mr. Bennett."

11. Provide complete information. It's tempting to take shortcuts in writing because it requires more time and effort than speaking. Don't make assumptions about what the other person does or does not know. You know what you want to say, but the words don't always convey it. I read about a law in Kansas:

"When two trains approach each other at a crossing, they shall both come to a full stop and neither shall start up until the other has gone."

I read that and was glad, at that moment, not to be on a train in Kansas. I'm sure the writer of this law knew what he wanted to convey. But did the conductors?

Be careful not to over-explain. Say what you need to say and then stop writing.

12. Proofread. It shows you took the time to be careful. Typos or missing words can also contribute to misunderstandings. A financial management firm was trying to assure their customers that they were in compliance for Y2K in a letter to all customers, yet there were typos in the document. If they can't get a letter right, how are they going to get a complicated computer issue resolved? Their clients weren't reassured.

A customer service representative wrote to a customer in response to a billing dispute: "Unfortunately we are going to credit you $700." However, she forgot to put in the "not." He meant to write, "We are not going to credit you $700." But they had to pay her . . . she had it in writing.

13. Sign your letter. The person needs to know that you were really the person who sent the letter. In a business or professional situation, "Sincerely" is the most appropriate word before your signature. If it's someone you know well, however, you can skip the formal closing. Simply use your C as your closing: "I'm looking forward to speaking with you" or "I look forward to continuing this discussion with you" or "Let me know when it's a good time to talk." Then simply sign—don't type—your name.

14. Finish it and then put it aside for *at least one day*. Never take a paper that's still warm from your hands or the printer and then run out and mail it. Reread it first with a fresh attitude and ear. If it still sounds good to you, then mail it. The benefit of this "cooling off" period is why I don't encourage people to WAC via e-mail. It is too easy to dash it off and too easy to send! One click and it's gone forever. At least with a letter, you have to print it out, get a stamp, address the envelope and then find a mail drop. If your letter is not Polite and Powerful, hopefully by that time, you'll have realized it.

Here are some excerpts from real-life WAC'em letters:

Situation: Cynthia is a student in a creative writing program. She became upset with her writing professor for using what she considered harsh language in her critiques. Since they primarily communicated in writing, Cynthia felt comfortable WAC'ing her in writing. She wrote:

Dear Marie,

The writing workshop has been such a great experience. I believe I can truly improve my creative writing by working with you. Please understand however, that when you use words such as silly, ridiculous, new agey, and boring to critique my work, it makes it difficult for me to hear and apply your otherwise constructive criticism. I would appreciate it if you would bear this in my mind in our future work together. Please let me know your thoughts on this.

Result: Cynthia's professor wrote back: "I'm so glad you told me about this. I had no idea I was being so negative . . ."

Situation: This is the letter from the woman who WAC'ed her father-in-law that we mentioned earlier.

Dear Wallace,

I'm writing to you because I need to discuss what happened during our last visit. When you started screaming at me after Trevor broke the vase, I felt insulted and humiliated. It's important for us to maintain a relationship and I need to know that the next time if something is bothering you, you will please talk to me calmly about it. And I'll do my best to accommodate you. If you can't assure me of this then I won't be able to stay at your house. Please let me know your thoughts on this.

Result: Her father-in-law wrote her after receiving the

letter. He said he didn't mean to offend her, yet "It's my house, and I will do what I want in my own house." They maintained a cordial, though much cooler, relationship after that. She never stayed at his house again.

Complaint Letters

Now let's talk about a common type of WAC'em letter—the complaint letter.

Do not confuse a person who writes a complaint letter with our notorious verbal complainer. The "in-writing" complainer doesn't wear everyone near him or her out with an endless tale of woe. This kind of letter writer is doing something to solve a problem.

Something you've purchased is not working or doing what you were promised it would do. You certainly have the right to complain about it. You'll want to write a slightly different kind of WAC'em letter to register a complaint about a product or service that you have purchased or received. The complaint can be registered in person, on the telephone, or in writing. Often, it's better to complain in writing. It establishes a paper trail; proof that you may need later, depending upon your situation.

Here's what you need to know:

- **Follow the guidelines for good writing.** All the writing guidelines are the same as I have previously described for WAC'em letters. Your choice of words becomes very important. Eliminate the negative words. Eliminate the extra words. Write the way you speak, and proofread. Give yourself a cooling-off period before mailing.
- **Be polite.** This is especially important in a complaint letter. You want the person who is reading your letter to help you. I have taught writing to customer service departments and the letters they have shown me that they have received from their customers are shocking. One letter told the representative to "go to hell." Others wished that harm would come

to the customer service representative and his family. The worst was the letter I saw in which the writer told the representative to go to a concentration camp. You get the picture—and it's bad.

You want the person to help you, not hate you! Do people who write letters like this really think that the person they have just cursed out will go out of their way to help them? Maybe they do, but they're dead wrong.

Customer service representatives tell me this all the time—"I may have to do something with the person, but it will be as little as I can get away with."

- **Write as high up as you can.** Complaint letters filter down. They rarely filter up. Use last names. I once took the time to track down the name and address of the president of an airline company and sent a complaint letter directly to him. I got a response in a few days. I didn't do that with a major department store. I just sent the letter to their customer service departments. I didn't even get a response.
- **Use the correct salutation.** Try to identify the person you're writing to. This is an important feature of your complaint letter. You want your letter to be opened. And if you offend the recipient in the first line, he or she may not continue to read your letter. Follow these guidelines for selecting successful salutations:

  1. **Use the person's correct name and title whenever possible.** Use last names if you don't know the person or have spoken to them once or twice. It's always better to err on the side of formality. "Ms." is the preferred term in business today for women.
  2. **Gender benders.** When you can't tell the person's sex, drop the honorary title and use the whole name: "Dear Pat Smith."
  3. **Use non-gender-specific wording.** When it's impos-

sible to include the recipient's name, use "Dear Customer Service Representative." Avoid "To Whom It May Concern." Most letters addressed this way can be thrown away or can take weeks to find the right person.

- **Explain what happened—but keep it simple.** This is your W. The other person usually wasn't there, so you need to let the reader know what happened. Provide enough detail that the reader understands but not so much that the letter becomes a major report. Also, enclose copies of any warranties, receipts, or guarantees.

Sounds simple doesn't it? It is until you're the one staring at the blank page dismayed about your last car rental. I do an exercise in one of my classes in which the participants write a complaint letter and then share it with another participant to find out if that person understands what the other wrote. Many times, I hear the comment "But, I don't understand what happened . . ." and then the other says, "Well, what I meant to say is . . ."

Someone wrote this:

"Due to the recent complications I have been experiencing with my PC regarding the lack of memory available to complete critical departmental spread sheets statistic and market analysis, it has been recommended . . ."

I said, "What? Try it again." They came up with a much better explanation of the problem:

"I was told the unit I bought would have enough memory for me to complete specific jobs which are critical to our work. It doesn't have enough memory."

15. Your A—what you want to ask for follows the explanation. Acknowledge what you want and ask for it directly. The worst they can do is say "No." Do you want your money back or a new item?

Be specific. Don't leave it up to the person on the other end to figure out what you want.

One customer service representative told me, "We never give money back unless someone asks for it and then there are no questions asked. We give them their money."

A number of companies instruct their representatives to respond to what is written, so if you don't ask for what you want, chances are you aren't going to get it. If you do ask for what you want there are no guarantees, but you have a better chance of getting something.

Again, when it comes to asking for your A in person, ask for what is reasonable. You can use the same WAC'em wording we've already discussed, such as: "I would like . . ." "I want . . ." "I need . . ."

Make your A clear. Again, don't overwrite:

"I am not the type of person that makes such a big deal out of things but considering the past experiences with my payments and the last several weeks being frustrated with my calls to him and now once again the check appears I really cannot understand what the big issue is as my not getting reimbursed my $15.00 stop payment fee."

More simply stated:

"I want to be reimbursed for the $15.00 stop payment fee."

- **Include a short conclusion.** Indicate when you would like or expect to hear from someone. Also, thank your reader for his or her time.
- **Sign it properly.** For letters of complaint, use a more formal closing, such as "Sincerely," or "Very truly yours." Sign your full name.
- **Make a copy of your letter and any other items you're sending.** Don't send your original warranty or guarantee. Complaint letters can be lost and misplaced too.

To WAC'em in Writing or Not?

Based on all of the information I've just given you in this chapter, you're going to have to judge each situation on its own and decide whether or not writing a letter is an effective way to approach the other person. For the most part my advice is to WAC the other person in person whenever possible. The advantages outweigh the disadvantages—most importantly the issue of giving up control that happens when you write a WAC'em letter.

If you do decide to WAC someone in writing, even if you're writing a complaint letter to a person you don't know, the rules of writing apply.

CHAPTER 12

HOW TO HANDLE
OTHER DIFFICULT CONVERSATIONS

You've learned how you can successfully handle and conduct yourself when you encounter one type of difficult communication — the confrontation.

You know what to do when someone's behavior is bothering you. You know how to handle yourself Politely and Powerfully. You know the words and body language to use and not to use. The skills you've learned so far in this book will empower you in new and surprising ways. Practice and adopt them and your life will be less stressful and you'll feel better about yourself. A lot better.

But you're not out of the well yet. There are more kinds of conversations that fall into the category of "difficult communication." Life's full of the kinds of conversations that make you nervous or uncomfortable. The kinds of conversations you'd love to get out of having, but you can't.

For instance, how do you tell someone . . .

You're quitting?
His fly is undone?
She's just been downsized?
Their favorite uncle is in the hospital?

It's not easy telling others these kinds of things. But there are times when not speaking up wouldn't be appropriate or fair to the other person. You shouldn't for example, let a co-worker walk around all day with broccoli in his teeth from lunch. This may sound silly, but it does happen all the time.

And on a more serious note, you have to have a conversation if you're planning on leaving your job.

Though different from a confrontation, the kinds of difficult conversations I cover in this chapter do have one important thing in common—how you handle yourself will have a big impact on the outcome.

The skills you've learned thus far for Polite and Powerful confrontations, including the WAC'em model, your verbals and nonverbals, can all be adapted and applied to many more of life's difficult conversations and sticky situations. So too, is the power you can harness by handling yourself well. You'll feel empowered. And you will feel this way because you won't be as weighted down by dread when you have to tell somebody something they're probably not going to like hearing. It's less likely you'll speak or act too harshly or too softly. You can neutralize difficult people simply by knowing how to handle yourself. It's so much easier going through life this way than the old way. People have the same reaction in learning how to handle different types of difficult conversations as they do when they learn how to have Polite and Powerful confrontations. You have turned a corner. You never go back. You won't want to go back.

While the natural by-product of Polite and Powerful behavior in positive confrontations is sometimes the newfound freedom to "let it go," the opposite is true for other kinds of difficult conversations. You learn how to stop avoiding and dreading them. You can meet them head on. You won't have to worry about them as much. You can be more direct. This is not to say that you'll always enjoy them. But when having them is the right or required thing to do you'll feel better about yourself knowing that you were direct and polite. You will then be in a better position to accept them as part of life.

When You Have a Choice and When You Don't

In some situations, you will have to speak up. "I have to tell Mark that his father is in the hospital." And you do have to tell him. Clearly, Mark needs to have this important information. Sometimes you will have a choice about whether or not you should speak up: You believe your friend Caroline dresses inappropriately. She thinks she dresses just fine. You think this could be why she's not getting promoted. Should you say something?

This is the kind of situation in which you have a choice.

We'll get to the specifics of these kinds of conversation shortly.

What you always have is a choice about *how* you tell Caroline and Mark what you want or need to tell them. This is how everything you've just read and learned in this book can help you. You now have a guide, a significant reservoir of skills you can use to handle just about any of life's ordinary difficult conversations with tact and honesty.

I have broken down the most difficult conversations into the four main areas that people typically dread, avoid, or feel embarrassed or worry about having:

1. Giving feedback
2. Giving bad news or unpleasant information
3. Making a complaint in person
4. Expressing sympathy

"*Sorry Sam,* You're Just Not Cutting It Here in Sales."

1. Giving feedback. Telling someone about what he or she is not doing well, correctly, or appropriately is considered "feedback." So is telling someone something good, but that's not hard—it's usually fun, so we're not going to deal with that in this chapter.

What we're talking about here is feedback that may be difficult for another person to hear.

Sometimes you are required to give feedback. If you're a manager or a parent it's part of your job. Sometimes you choose to give feedback because you believe it will help the person. There are four main areas we'll discuss:

a. Giving feedback when the person is not performing to a standard. This usually occurs at work, but it can also occur with children;
b. Giving your unsolicited opinion;
c. Saving the person from further embarrassment;
d. Speaking up about "unfair" or "unjust" behavior.

How you will give feedback to the other person in each of the above scenarios will depend upon the situation. Let's look at each situation separately.

- **Performing to a Standard**

If you're giving someone feedback about performing to an established or implied standard, you must first determine two things:

1. Are you the appropriate person? If you're the person's manager or the committee chairperson then it's your job to give feedback. If you're the parent it is your job to provide feedback to your child. "Ben, please use your fork when you eat."

If you're not the appropriate person, giving feedback can be a risk. And you know what happens to risk-takers—historically we know they are either promoted, fired or simply disliked.

A man asked for my help because he was not being promoted. He didn't know why. I soon discovered in talking with him that he frequently gave feedback to his co-workers about their job performance. His feedback was not welcomed by them. It wasn't his job to do this and they didn't like hearing it from him! This habit of his was holding him back from being perceived as a person capable of dealing well with others.

Sticky situations arise routinely between parents of children who play or go to school together. There was an occasion when two boys in my son's class got into a fight. One of the kid's moms happened to be nearby. She yelled at her son and she yelled at the other boy.

The other boy got very upset at some of the things the mother had threatened—like telling the principal about the incident. His mother then told the woman that in the future, if she had a problem with her son, to please tell her about it and she would address the issue with him.

2. In business, what are your organization's guidelines for giving employees or team members critical feedback? Are you basing your discussion on company's guidelines or individual objectives that have been established? If someone is not performing to a standard, you may be required to document each conversation you've had with the person.

When You Are the Appropriate Person, How Do You Proceed?

No, it's not always easy to tell people things they probably don't want to hear. But there are ways to do it that will make it a lot easier, both on the other person and yourself. Back in the beginning of this book we discussed one of the biggest obstacles to positive confrontation: Figuring out your words. What do you really want to say? The same is true for the "feedback" conversations. This brings us back to Don't Attack'em, WAC'em.

Adapt Your WAC

WAC'em can easily be adapted as a model for giving people feedback. You can use it, or at least adapt it, to help you figure out what you want to say and possibly suggest how the person should be handling him or herself in the future.

Define the Problem Using Your "W"

What's wrong with the person's performance? Be specific. Don't expect anyone to understand what you mean by "lousy," "sloppy," or "not up to par." You're not giving the person enough information.

You must specifically explain what in the person's performance or behavior isn't working. Your W may be something like:

"Jason, you haven't attended the last three meetings."

"Your latest report had half a dozen spelling errors."

"Every committee member is expected to work on one event a year. You haven't signed up for an event yet."

Your A: "Here's What I Need You to Do . . ."

You're asking someone to change or modify his or her behavior to meet a standard. Following the above examples, your A would be something like:

"Your attendance at all of our meetings is mandatory."

"You need to use your spellchecker on a regular basis and find someone to proof your documents also."

"We'd like you to contribute too. Can you coordinate the bake sale?"

Give the person a specified amount of time in which you expect to see improvement. In business, this may be dictated by company policy as well. The person may have thirty days in which to improve. But this can apply to family members as well. If your daughter has been coming home past her curfew, you can expect her compliance to be immediate. If your babysitter has been leaving the house a mess, give her another chance after speaking with her to correct the situation.

Your C: "Do I Have Your Agreement?"

Even if you have authority over the person, you still need to check in with him or her. The other person needs to have an opportunity to explain their behavior or to offer their thoughts. You may not be offering an option, but there may be extenuating circumstances in the person's life that you're simply not aware of. They may be caring for a sick parent or child or going through a personal crisis. You can be supportive and still be firm. If your company or organization offers resources such as counseling, encourage the person to take advantage of it.

"And If You Can't . . ."

Sometimes you need to explain what the consequences will be if the person cannot meet your expectations. Be clear. Be specific:

"You won't be ready to get the promotion."
"The monthly report will be assigned to someone else."
"We'll have to ask you to resign your position on the committee."

Some other guidelines for giving your feedback:

Do it in private. It's not appropriate to give people feedback in front of others. A group of six graduate students were having lunch with their professor. The professor said to the group, "You've all become more confident in your lectures and that's great." But then he turned to Jackie and said, "Well, Jackie, you still have some problems with this." Not appropriate! While it was his job to give his students critical feedback, he should have made this kind of comment to Jackie in private.

Balance the negative with the positive. Try to balance your criticism with some positive feedback if you can. "You have errors in your report which detract from your terrific observations."

- **Giving Your Unsolicited Opinion.**

Here's another kind of feedback situation. And talk about sticky!

Let's go back to the example of the friend who dresses inappropriately. You want to give her feedback. You haven't been asked to do so and you're not required to do it. However, you think it might help her get promoted.

Be careful, this is touchy stuff.

The other person may not be receptive to feedback. After all, he or she hasn't asked you for it. Before you say a word, you need to ask yourself, "Why am I doing it? Am I really concerned about this person? Am I really just putting him or her down?" You must consider the person; will he or she be open to your comments? You may harm your relationship.

A friend had a mole on her face. It was unattractive and perhaps unhealthy. I risked it and told her that I had had a mole removed for health reasons. That opened the door for me to suggest she get hers looked at. She did and had it removed.

A woman mentioned to me that her friend has an unattractive hairstyle. Other than this one blip in her appearance, she is attractive. Should she tell her?

If she chooses to say something, she has several ways to do so.

- She can be direct: "Mary, I like your hair better the other way," if she believed her friend is open to hearing criticism like that.
- She could be indirect. She can ask a question to inquire why the person changed her hairstyle, to get the conversation going.
- She can wait until asked for her opinion and then be honest—but Politely and Powerfully.

Ellen's friend Matthew wore thick glasses. She thought he'd look better in contact lenses. But when she told him her opinion, he told her, "My eye doctor told me I can't wear contacts. Do you really think I look that bad?" Oops.

This "donation" of one's opinions causes a lot of conflict in families, where members are often more free in offering their criticism. Three sisters finally had to put a moratorium on this behavior because they realized they were constantly fighting over comments like, "I liked your hair better before you changed it."

Another set of sisters, my own, are more direct. I once got in the car and one of them turned to me and said, "Phew you stink," because I had too much perfume on. I laughed. This is just how we are and it works for us.

You will have to evaluate whether or not to engage the conversation on a case by case basis. But follow two important guidelines:

Express concern for the person. "I care about you doing well," or "I thought you would want to know this . . . ."

If the person isn't receptive to your comments, drop it. Don't react back in a way that is insulting to the other person. You wouldn't for example say, "I thought you could handle the truth," or "I forgot how sensitive you are."

Then let it go . . .

But what if the other person asks for your opinion? Give it to him or her, but remember that this isn't a license to forget polite behavior. So you wouldn't say to your friend, "I'm so glad you asked me that because I've been dying to tell you that you dress too provocatively." You're going to make her feel worse.

Better wording would be, "Women in management in this company dress pretty conservatively. I would lower my skirts and not show any cleavage."

- **Embarrassing Situations.**

"Pssst . . . I thought I should tell you, your barn door is open!"

When you don't live on a farm, what does this mean?

The physician who was told this in front of a group of interns didn't know either. He kept asking, "What's a barn door?" He discovered later his fly was undone.

Here's the first rule of dealing with embarrassing situations: Be direct. Don't use innuendo or hand signals to deliver your message. If the person's fly is undone, simply describe the situation: "Tom, your fly is undone."

Sometimes, that's all it takes. But keep these points in mind:

Speak up. Generally, it's better to let the person know if he has a big piece of spinach in her front tooth or the dreaded toilet paper tail on her high heel. It's especially true if the person can do something about it right then and here. You will be saving the person further embarrassment.

A friend said that when he was in law school a professor walked into the auditorium to lecture from the stage. He had his fly undone. I asked if anybody said anything. He said "No."

I was horrified. "You let him lecture that way for two hours?"

He said "Yep! We didn't like him!"

Be discreet. Don't shout your comments out or say it so others can hear. Yes, we can all just crack up when it happens, but it's mean. A Polite and Powerful person would never do this. A motivational speaker was giving a great talk to his audience, walking person to person, interacting with them, but his fly was undone. No one said anything for ten minutes. A woman when he went up to her gave him a note that told him. He didn't blink an eye and fixed the fly without missing a beat with his talk. She later was rewarded by her organization for how she handled the situation.

If the person responds negatively be Polite and Powerful back. If you tell someone his fly is down and he says, "What are you looking down there for?"

Don't go there! Simply say, "I'm surprised by your response. I thought you would have wanted to know."

Simply describe the situation. "Mary, your slip is showing." This is really the W, and nothing else needs to be said. Also, don't touch without permission. If a woman has her back zipper undone, don't just fix it for her without asking permission to do so. A woman once went to remove a hair from a woman's chin and it was attached! There's another awful oops!

Send an emissary. If you're embarrassed because of gender, ask someone else to do it for you. My significant other and I were at a party. A woman's bra strap was showing. Marty said to me, "Why don't you go tell her." He asked me because he thought it would be less embarrassing for the woman. I did it. The woman was grateful.

Drop the subject quickly. Don't dwell on whatever it was. Just let it go.

- **Speaking Up About "Unfair" or "Unjust" Behavior.**

Back in Chapter 6, I advised you to "let it go if it's not your issue."

The way to determine what is or isn't your issue is by the direct effect another person's behavior has on you. If it doesn't have a direct effect, then it's not really your issue and you wouldn't WAC the person about that issue.

But what happens when you repeatedly see your co-worker arriving late and leaving early when the boss is out of the office? If he was asking you to "cover" for him and you feel uncomfortable doing so, you would have a pretty clear WAC: "Jason, I don't feel comfortable covering for you so you can leave early." (Your W). "Please don't ask me to do this anymore." (Your A)

But suppose he doesn't ask you to cover for him. Suppose his comings and goings may not affect your workload directly but it may really bother you that he's doing this and getting away with it.

Or suppose there's a handicapped parking space in your condo development. You have a neighbor who ignores the sign and parks there anyway. You're not entitled to park in this spot either, so it's not like she's taking your spot. But her behavior is driving you crazy! You believe she has no right to park there!

In both of these scenarios, the effect on you is not direct—you don't have more work and you still have your parking spot—but you still feel affected. You perceive the person's behavior as unfair or unjust. You're annoyed. What can you do about it? Should you speak up?

Before you speak up, make sure:

You have *all* of the information. Don't be so quick to label the person as a jerk until you know for sure that your co-worker hasn't received permission to leave early. Maybe he's working at home or has a sick relative. Maybe the woman parking in the spot has recently had an operation. If you don't have all the facts, you can't assess whether or not it's worth it to say something.

It's really worth it. I understand that you may feel outraged when you see another person do something that you think is unfair. But I also know that if you let yourself be frequently affected by what you perceive as unjust behavior, you are going to spend a good deal of your time feeling indignant and outraged. This is not a positive, energizing way to go through life. I have also found that people who grumble about "injustice" may sometimes be transferring their frustrations about one thing into another. Watch out for this behavior, it's draining.

Make sure you approach the person in a respectful manner. What you can do is talk to the person and ask for clarification about the behavior. Make sure you keep it simple: "Are you aware that this is handicapped parking?" or "How come you park in the handicapped spot?" You can also just describe the behavior or the perceived injustice, such as, "I've noticed that when the boss isn't here you come in late and leave early." You may learn something you didn't know or that may be all it takes for the person to stop parking in the spot.

But watch your nonverbals, especially your tone of voice. Keep your tone neutral. You don't want to pick a fight.

Use common sense. If you are concerned about the person's reaction, I wouldn't approach the person directly.

Decide whether you want to go over the person's head. You can go to the boss and say, "I believe that it is important for you to know that Jason comes in late and leaves early when you're not here."

I can't tell you to go out and do this. Each person must make up his or her mind according to the situation and people involved. I do suggest that you consider the repercussions to your own professional image and office relationships. Will you be perceived as a tattle-tale? A busybody? A hero? Will your co-worker find out that you said something and then hold it against you?

However, in the case of the handicapped parking violator, you can report this person to your condo association and let them handle it. In some cases, you could even call the police and report it. But I think you should call the police as a last resort. It's usually best to approach people directly when and if possible.

"I Hate to Have to Be the One to Tell You This, But . . ."

2. Giving bad news or unpleasant information. Our next area of difficult conversation—you're the one who has to tell someone something you know they don't want to hear.

No wonder we dread it or try to get out of it. Is there a nice way to say, "You didn't get the job?" or "You know how we promised you that shipment would be on time, well . . . ?" or "I know you've been looking forward to this trip for weeks but . . ."

On his late night television show, David Letterman used to have a segment in which he would call a person and break some news to him or her on behalf of one of his audience members who couldn't bring themselves to do it.

It was often a funny segment, yet I couldn't help wonder what would be the consequences to both parties off-air. After all, the person on the receiving end was ambushed—not to mention on national television.

While I think it's a terrible idea to deliver news like this, it does illustrate a great point—the length people will go to get out of having an unpleasant conversation. People avoid or delay these conversations because they don't know what to say or how to say it. But by doing this, you usually make things worse. If you don't tell the person, someone else might. Or he or she may find out anyway. Then you have to deal with "Why didn't you tell me?"

Every summer for five years in a row, Karen and Don vacationed at the beach with their close friends, Vicky and Jim. Karen and Don were ready for a change of scene and wanted to vacation alone. It wasn't that the couple didn't like their friends anymore—they just wanted to make this change.

Karen agonized about how to tell Vicky. "I was afraid of hurting her feelings." She agonized so much that finally Don couldn't stand it anymore. The next time the two couples were together he said, "I think you know how much we love hanging out with you guys. The thing is we've made a decision to take a different vacation this summer. We want to go away alone together."

As it turned out, Vicky and Jim were thinking of doing something different too. Karen could have saved herself a lot of trouble by being up front sooner.

By using many of the skills you've learned in this book, you'll be able to make this kind of conversation easier on the other person and yourself. Keep these points in mind during one of those "breaking it gently" conversations:

1. **Talk in private.** You don't announce in a meeting that one of your team members who was a finalist for employee of the year award—didn't make it. You need to let him know first.
2. **Avoid starting off with an ominous sentence like, "I don't know how to tell you this . . ."** You do know, and you're doing it. It's better to be direct and say, "I have some bad news . . ." or "There's been a change of plans . . ." and then just tell them quickly.
3. **Explain.** Offer the reasons, if appropriate. This doesn't mean you should make excuses or over-apologize. "We want to take a private vacation because, well, we're having some marital problems . . ." Too much information! Keep it simple. "We want to go away by ourselves this year." If you have to tell someone they didn't get the promotion or the raise, you need to tell him or her why, even if that may be tough to hear. A woman was told that she didn't get the promotion to sales representative because she was too soft-spoken. She appreciated knowing.
4. **Offer to help or give the person alternatives, if possible.** A woman I know had been dreaming of visiting the town in Italy where her mother was born. Her husband had promised her that he would take her on their tenth wedding anniversary. But when the time came, he was having some business problems and didn't have the money. While he dreaded telling his wife, he did something smart. He pulled out an account book and said, "I've just opened this vacation account. I am going to put $25 dollars a week into it and extra when I can. In two years we'll have the money."

"Your Uncle Is in the Hospital"

I do think it's okay to say, "I'm so sorry. Your uncle Vince is in the hospital." I don't think it's okay to build it up and make the news worse. Don't be dramatic and say things like "I'd like you to sit down before I tell you this . . ." or "I know you're going to be very upset when you hear this . . ." You should never keep people in suspense. It is usually clear from your body language and tone of voice that something is terribly wrong. Just tell the person what has happened.

Soften Bad News with Better or Positive News When You Can

A friend whose husband had a serious car accident appreciated the way her sister told her what had happened. "Beth," she said, "everything's okay now. Your husband is going to be fine, except he was in a car accident."

If she had said, "Your husband's had an accident," Beth said she would have fainted on the spot. I probably would too.

"I quit!"

You're moving on to another job or company. Or, you're making a lifestyle change that doesn't include full-time employment. This isn't bad news for you, but it's often difficult news to give to your boss.

Laurie had been working for three years as the marketing director of a publishing company. She had a long commute—two hours each way. She wanted to start working part-time and closer to home.

This normally self-assured woman was a walking nerve ending about telling her boss. She had no idea what she was going to say.

"Can't you just tell him that you've decided to leave the company? I suggested.

"Yes," she said. "But I feel bad."

"Why?" I asked. "Did you sign a contract or break a promise?"

"No."

"Did you work hard for three years?"

"Of course."

"You're not bound to this job, or obligated to your boss for life."

"I didn't think of it that way," she said.

This seems to be a common problem. We feel obligated or afraid of the other person's reaction.

As long as you're not obligated by contract to stay and as long as you're giving proper notice, simply tell your boss, Politely and Powerfully, that you're leaving.

Going into it originally, Laurie was full of ideas about what she would say. I said "Pretend I'm your boss. Practice on me."

Good thing we did this because the first thing out of her mouth was a nervous laugh. Her body language conveyed nervousness. Then she said, "Gee, I feel so bad about this, but I have to tell you how sorry I am, but I need to quit."

Talk about self-discounting language and behavior! I stopped her right there and gave her these guidelines:

1. Plan what you're going to say. Write the words down.
2. Practice. You're going to be nervous. Get a friend to role-play with you.
3. Don't apologize if you haven't done anything wrong. You can say, "I'm sad to be leaving this great group of people, I'll miss everyone. But it's time for me to move on." This is not saying, "I'm sorry, you're going to hate me, I know you're really busy and this is the last thing you need . . ." Don't apologize with your nonverbals. If you knot yourself up in your chair or play with your hair, you're not going to look like a person who has just made an important decision. You're going to look unsure and nervous.
4. Keep it simple. "I have another opportunity that I've decided to take," is fine. Don't give someone your life story and make excuses. You're not obligated to fill your boss in on all the details. How much you choose to share will depend upon your relationship. But for your initial conversation, keep it simple and short.
5. If you think the person may try to argue with you or try to talk you out of it, go in with a line prepared. Your line expresses your Polite and Powerful position, like this one does, "I appreciate your concern, but I've made my deci-

sion." No matter what argument the person may pose, just keep repeating your line. "I understand that you want me to stay and I'm grateful for the counter offer, but I've made my decision." Stick to your line. Unless of course they make you an offer that you can't refuse.

6. Don't burn your bridges. If you've had long, complex and satisfying fantasies about "telling your boss off" or clueing him in to how lazy your co-workers really are—forget it. I've heard story after story of bridge burners who now regret their actions. Telling someone off doesn't make you feel better for more than ten adrenaline packed minutes. Then you usually feel crummy. Nothing changes except now you've lost a reference.

After I had talked about this issue, a man approached me and told me this story:

"I was looking forward to quitting my job. I had gotten to the point where I hated my boss. He was a terrible manager and didn't treat everyone fairly. I told him off pretty good. I could tell he was pretty shocked. He said 'I always thought we had a good relationship. Why didn't you speak up sooner.' He seemed so sincere. I felt like a jerk."

"I Want to See the Manager. Now!"

3. Making a complaint in person. Here's a third area of common difficult conversations. We've discussed how to complain about a faulty product or service in writing, yet you can also do this in person. Simply taking a toaster back to the store where you purchased it or discussing your service at a restaurant is an example of complaining in person.

At least you'll probably never have to see the person you're complaining to again. This isn't license to be rude. I overheard a man berate a waitress about his food. I was appalled by his behavior. I felt the need to say something to her because the waitress seemed so upset.

Remember, the way your handle yourself during this difficult conversation can make all the difference in the outcome. This is the person who is going to help you get your toaster working or get your food cooked correctly.

Again—Adapt Your WAC

Here's how you adapt the first part of WAC'em. When you speak to the customer service person you need to explain what is wrong—that the cord is falling out. A complaint I often hear from customer service people is that people give their life stories. They babble on and on. "I'm actually not the sort of person to ever take anything back. . . ." Do yourself and the person you're complaining to a favor, get to your W quickly: "The cord isn't connected correctly."

Be Specific about What You Want Done

And then the A. What do you want done? Do you want a new toaster or the cord replaced? The A here is vitally important. As in writing, you must ask for what you want and you must be specific about it. If not, you may simply get what they give you. You may want a new toaster. Make sure you say that. If you don't ask for it, you may only get a new cord!

Be direct. "I want . . ." or "I would prefer . . ." Don't be unreasonable, ask for what is possible and fair. A waitress told me that when she offers people a free round of drinks or a complimentary dessert to compensate for a problem, and they insist upon getting an whole meal for free because their steak was undercooked, she immediately puts her guard up. "The staff goes on red alert because we know we have 'one of those kinds' of customers—the ones out to make us all miserable."

In situations like this, you probably won't need your C. The person will tell you—"I can take care of that," or "It's company policy . . ."

Of course, you may not like the company's policy on returns or exchanges, but at least you'll know where you stand. Then you can ask, politely of course, to see a manager.

You can also use your W and A for a work-related service problem. Suppose your customer service representative has come to your office to discuss your computer service and some of the difficulty you have been experiencing. Again you use the W to explain what is wrong and the A to ask for what you would like done.

In this case, you will probably use a C—"When can you have this toaster fixed?" or "I need to know if this problem can be resolved by Thursday." In a work situation, these people, in effect, work for you and you have the right to know when and if your C is going to be met.

"People who fight fire with fire usually end up with ashes."
—ABIGAIL VAN BUREN

It's not true that if you yell, act tough, or really give the people behind a counter a hard time, you'll get what you want. You can be firm and convincing without causing a scene. You will feel better about yourself and people will want to help you more.

I was in a computer store's service center, where they do repairs and make exchanges. A woman at the counter was so upset, I thought I was going to see steam come out of the top of her head. She cursed at the two people trying to help her. She repeatedly threw her hands up in the air, shook her head in disgust, demanded to speak to the store's manager, who was not yet on duty.

She made a big-time scene. WAC'em was not on her radar screen. Her verbals and nonverbals were aggressive and negative. She made everyone uncomfortable—even the other customers. When I see people behaving this way, I immediately feel sorry not only for the people who have to deal with complainer gone berserk, but for the complainer.

"Is this the way they go through life?" I wonder. If it is, they must have an enormous amount of stress and dissatisfaction plaguing them. (Aren't you glad this isn't you!)

When she finally left and it was my turn, I overheard the one representative say to the other: "Oops, I think her job ticket just got put in the 'take your good old time' box." The other representative laughed one of those knowing "inside" laughs.

I can't say I blame them for slowing up the woman's job!

Remember that the goal is to get your problem resolved! For any in-person complaints, make sure you follow these twelve guidelines.

1. Be polite. Say, "Hello," or "Good morning. You can also add: "I need some help." You want the person to help you and solve your problem. Always remember that.

2. Approach the situation with the right attitude. Yes, it can be annoying to have to say something, but you want your toaster fixed or replaced. The person you are complaining to probably didn't cause the problem. Expect things to work out.

3. Be cautious with your voice. Monitor your volume. No screaming. Speak loud enough to be heard.

4. Be cautious with your words. No cursing!

5. Pay attention to your body language. Look the person in the eye; no pointing fingers. Don't huff and puff and throw your arms about. Have a pleasant facial expression. Dress appropriately for the situation. You will be taken more seriously if you're not wearing a dirty t-shirt and jeans.

6. Give enough information on your W. Explain what happened but don't tell him or her your life's story.

7. Be reasonable. If you had the twenty-dollar model, you can't expect the store to replace it with a fifty-dollar model.

8. Make sure you have all the required paperwork—receipts, warranties, service records, etc.

9. Don't involve other customers in your complaint who may be in line near or beside you, even just by saying, "Can you believe this?"

10. If you're not satisfied with the response or action you get, ask the person for more information. Ask to see the manager. If the manager isn't available, ask for her name and telephone number.

11. You can express your frustration; "I'm frustrated. I've spoken to people three or four times and haven't gotten any results." This is not the same as attacking the person.

12. Be open to suggestions. If you can't get what you want, what can you get? Ask. You may be surprised.

"I'm Sorry for Your Loss, But Trust Me, It's Better This Way."

4. Expressing sympathy. Our last area of difficult conversation is one we all have to deal with sooner or later. Yes, this is hard! It's natural to feel awkward and tongue-tied in this kind of situation. Yet, it's a mistake to avoid saying something to a grieving person. It's understandable that people feel awkward and don't want to upset the person. I often hear, "I worry that I'll make them feel worse."

You probably won't. *It's important to say something.* It is incredibly helpful for the person who has experienced the loss to hear expressions of sympathy from other people. Often, people come to understand this when they're in the throes of loss themselves. They realize how much they appreciate hearing from people who will also miss their loved one or simply understand how difficult it is.

So what exactly do you say? It can be as simple as:

"I'm so sorry for your loss."

"I know this must be a difficult time for you and your family."

"You're in my thoughts."

I would caution you against saying: "It's better this way." Well, how do you know? Don't make this assumption; it may be hurtful to the other person.

People often say, "I know what you're going through." And they do. If you can, share some of your own experience. "I lost my dad, last year. The holidays were rough, but it does get easier."

This is one situation where I encourage you to write a note or send a sympathy card. If you add personal information about the person the grieving family can read the note again and again:

"She was a wonderful person and I know how much she will be missed."

"I know how your father felt about you. He told me often that you were a special person for him. He was so proud of you."

If you use a commercial sympathy card, that's fine, but make sure you add a handwritten note to it.

The Benefit of Having Difficult Conversations

As you can see, instead of avoiding or dreading difficult conversations, you can simply put your WAC'em, verbal, and nonverbal skills to work in helping you have other kinds of difficult conversations. Whether you need to put an employee on a performance improvement plan or tell your close friends you don't want to vacation with them this year, knowing how to handle and hold all types of difficult conversations is empowering. Time you used to spend in dread or avoiding and worrying is now free time you can use in a creative or constructive way.

CHAPTER 13

WHEN YOU
GET WAC'ED

By now, you should have a pretty clear idea of what it takes to handle yourself Politely and Powerfully during a confrontation or a difficult conversation. You also now understand how to handle the other person—no matter how he or she reacts. But one important thing we haven't talked about yet: What happens if you're the one getting WAC'ed?

Believe me, it's bound to happen—even Polite and Powerful people make mistakes and do bothersome things by accident. You are probably going to do something that someone else finds bothersome, unacceptable, and possibly even offensive. Maybe you'll have no idea. Maybe you'll be surprised. "What? Me?"

You may get WAC'ed by someone or someone may give you feedback, either about job performance or something personal. You may be the person whose blouse is unbuttoned or whose fly is down.

Relax. We all need feedback. You need it to grow. It isn't a negative thing. Have you ever met someone who can't handle criticism? Usually, these people are annoying because you can't tell them anything.

I personally would rather know if I was doing something bothersome than not know. If a client suddenly drops me, you bet I want to know why. It may be because their training needs or budget has changed, but if it's something I've done to lose the business, it's critical that I find out. I especially want to know if my blouse has accidentally come unbuttoned!

What You Need to Know if You Get WAC'ed

Everyone in the world makes mistakes.

You're not perfect. Start getting over that now if it's a problem for you.

IF YOUR FLY IS DOWN, PULL IT UP AND KEEP ON SMILING.

Who gets out of this life without making a fool of themselves? Even Polite and Powerful people will carry the banner of toilet paper on the heel of their shoes, have the icky things stuck in their teeth, trip over their own feet, and have other embarrassing things we haven't even thought up yet happen to them.

It's not what happens to you that matters. It's how you handle what happens to you that makes all the difference. The best story to illustrate this is what happened to me during a big seminar I was giving. I was wearing a cordless mike. At the first break, I forgot about it and went to the ladies' room. I was going to the bathroom! With the mike on! One of the women ran in and told me, but not until it was too late.

I had to go back. But how do you go back into a room with sixty people who have all just heard you go to the bathroom? You just do it. What choice did I have? I had only one real choice—I had to laugh at myself. I went back in, and with a totally serious expression on my face, I said, "There's a theory that states that you have to have a significant emotional experience in order to change your behavior," I paused and then said. "Well ladies and gentlemen, I just had quite a significant emotional experience. I will never, as long as I live, forget to turn off my microphone!"

The whole room broke out laughing.

Of course I wanted to flush myself right down that commode and never resurface when I realized what had happened. It was an embarrassing situation yet since I handled it with humor and grace, it helped build the rapport with my audience. It would have been worse to have pretended it never happened.

You Need Feedback in Order to Improve

We get job reviews to find out how we're doing. Even though we may not want to hear something that we're doing wrong, incorrectly, or inappropriately, wouldn't you rather hear what you're doing wrong so you can fix it?

These are general guidelines for handling yourself when you're on the receiving end of criticism, feedback or a WAC:

1. Don't Get Defensive. Going on the defensive when you meet with critical feedback or when you get WAC'ed is the least constructive thing you can do. I know this can be hard, but you've got to keep an open mind. Hear your critics. Listen to the comments. Accept that you may at times offend someone. If you don't "hear" and "accept" you let others have power over you. You twist in the wind of resentment, insecurity, and defensiveness. This is no way to live.

I try to be open. After every seminar, I give my participants feedback cards. Occasionally, I'll get a negative comment. At first, I would think, "Oh no, they hate me. Maybe the whole seminar was a bomb," etc. But that wasn't the case at all. Over time, I've learned not to hit the panic button, but to think about it and learn from it. I learned to consider the bad and the good. I always consider the feedback I get carefully. After all, if it can help make my future seminars better, I'm all for it.

2. Consider the source. If I have forty-nine feedback cards that say, "You're great," and one that says, "You stink," what am I supposed to think? If the one person doesn't give me a reason, I have to dismiss the comment. For all I know, maybe I look like his ex-wife or her ex-best friend. If the comment is specific, however, regarding the content of a seminar or my delivery, than I will consider the feedback carefully.

Before I will change my behavior, I ask myself, "Who is the person giving me the feedback. Is he or she an expert or a jerk? Does the person know what he or she is talking about? If the person is an expert, the feedback is a gift. And you are fortunate to get that kind of advice from that caliber of person." If an expert gives me feedback, I seriously weigh what that person had told me.

My speech coach, the one who told me she knew I was from the East Coast by the mistakes I made in my speech, provided feedback that was important for me to hear. I would have kept right on making those mistakes in my presentations. It may be a small thing, but the small things can bring your image and reputation down, too.

And what if the person is a jerk? If the person is a jerk and I mean a true jerk, be polite, thank the person, and put the feedback on the back burner in your mind.

3. Is This An Isolated Incident? One comment here or there usually means a lot more about the person who is giving you the comment than the validity of the comment. Once I received the following comment: "Barbara, you should never wear white stockings. They make your ankles look thick." In all the 1,300 seminars I have given, I only received that one once! Chances are that comment had a lot more to do with that person's perception of women in white stockings that the reality of my ankle size.

Yet, if you start getting feedback from a number of people and or situations that are very similar, chances are there is some validity to the comments and I would weigh very seriously the validity of the comment. If three people you know and respect tell you, "You talk too fast," you better sit back and consider that it may be true.

4. Consider How the Other Person Handles the Conversation/Confrontation. Chances are, you might not simply get WAC'ed, but you may get WAC'ed by someone who doesn't have the same skills that you do. In other words, you will be at the mercy of whatever confrontational skills, or style the other person has. But you're not helpless. Knowing the skills you've learned in this book, there are lots of ways you can save the situation and handle yourself Politely and Powerfully.

- **If the person is aggressive:** You don't expect someone to discuss an issue with you if you're shouting at him or her or shaking your fist at them. The same goes in reverse. Someone may have the right to WAC you, but they don't have the right to be aggressive or rude to you. If this happens, say, "I very much want to hear your thoughts, but I can't listen to you if you're yelling at me."
- **If the person is passive:** You need to tell the person there's no need to be sorry, if for example they are apologizing profusely. Tell the person: "You just need to tell me what's going on."
- **Is the person specific?** If you feel the person is being vague or not specific about what you're doing that's bothering him or her, ask for clarification. You need to know the person's W and A. Before you learned WAC'em you may have had a hard time clarifying your thoughts and understanding what was bothering you and what you wanted in its place. The other person may be having this difficulty too. Rephrase what they're saying, and repeat it back to him or her. Ask, "Let me be clear. You're saying that when I made that comment about your boyfriend, you thought I was saying he was a jerk." Or "I understand that you want me to stop leaving my laundry in the washing machine."

Your Response

You will usually have to respond to the person, whether or not you agree with what they've told you or how they've told you. Here are some guidelines to help you handle your response:

1. **If you're wrong, apologize.** You love it when you WAC the other person and he or she realizes you're right. So again, in reverse, you need to be the person who recognizes a mistake. "You're right," can go a long way to resolving conflict and mending wounded relationships. But don't over-apologize or make excuses. If you've made a mistake, one hearty

and sincere, "I'm sorry about that," is enough. Don't make excuses for your behavior if you're wrong. "Well, you see boss, I haven't been sleeping well and my brother is in the hospital and the holidays are coming up . . ." You're going to sound like a jerk if you make excuses. I remember reading about a journalist who had been caught taking too much creative license by fabricating an interview. He gave a statement in the publication that was full of excuses: "A loved one is sick and I've been under pressure . . ." I read that and I thought, I would have had respect for you if you had just said, "I made a mistake. I was wrong."

2. **Why not give the person his or her A?** If what the person is asking for is no sweat to you to do it or give it, than why not? Often, this is part of the bargains that couples work out between themselves. If it makes your husband crazy that you leave dishes in the sink, why not put them in the dishwasher? Sometimes, even simple gestures go a surprisingly long way.

3. **If you disagree, discuss the issue.** If you really don't like the person's A, then suggest another one. Explain how you feel or what you think is a workable compromise.

4. **You can ask the person to handle it differently in the future.** If the person didn't WAC you in an appropriate way, ask him or her to change this behavior in the future. "From now on, if you have a problem with me, can you come to me right away? I'd rather clear it up then let it get to this point. Okay?"

5. **If the person has power over you, you may not be able to discuss the issue.** If the person's your boss, you may have no choice but to agree. I'm not talking about ethical issues, such as someone asking you to do something you don't think is right or legal, just the practical ones. If your boss wants the report formatted a certain way, he's the boss. You may have to do it his way.

6. **Maintain good nonverbals.** Try to keep your arms open. It's a natural defense mechanism to cross our arms when we feel under threat. But you're not under threat, so unfold them.

Open body language will show that you are open to hearing the other person's thoughts. It will make you look Polite and Powerful. Try to tune into your facial expression too. Don't scowl. Try to keep a neutral expression on your face.

7. **Listen!** One of the most important things you can do when you get WAC'ed is to listen. When you WAC someone you want them to listen to you and take you seriously. It's only right that you do the same in return. Review the box on page 127 for reminders on how to be a good listener.

8. **If you get upset, try to pull yourself together.** You may be caught off guard and you may get emotional. It happens. If you feel like you might cry or you're getting very upset and are afraid of blowing your lid, ask to leave for a moment or two. Go somewhere quiet and pull yourself together. Tell yourself you can handle it Politely and Powerfully and then get back in there. Or reschedule a time to meet.

WAC'em Helps You Receive Criticism

People tell me they love WAC'em because it helps them both give feedback to others, and to receive it themselves. The best advice I can give you if you get feedback or WAC'ed is to try to be open-minded. Don't be afraid to see your own rough spots. We all have them, it's how we deal with them that counts. People who get defensive, the ones "you can't say anything to" are often annoying to others.

Conclusion to Part II

You've come a long way and you've taken in a lot of important information. Let's take a breath and recap for a minute. In Part II of this book you have learned how to:

- WAC instead of attack. You now have a fast and effective way for getting your words for a confrontation or difficult conversation together. You know to specifically define

What's bothering me? And what do I want to ask the other person to do? You can use your WAC'em card included on the dust jacket of this book until you can get your words together more quickly on your own.

- How to interact with the other person during a confrontation. You check in with the other person to see if what you've asked for is possible. You should have a discussion if you disagree. Try to work out a mutually acceptable alternative. You know what to do if the other person is not Polite and Powerful—you stay on Polite and Powerful behavior no matter how tempted you are to do otherwise.

- Use your verbals and nonverbals to help you have a positive confrontation. You know how self-discounting language, negative words, and bad diction are some of the verbal influences that can affect the impact of your WAC. On the nonverbal side, good control over your body language, your tone of voice, and your eye contact are all important to your success as well.

- WAC someone in-person, in writing, or over the phone. While it's usually best to WAC someone in person, you can also do it in writing (but avoid e-mails) and over the phone, but remember you can lose your control of the WAC and you also don't have your nonverbals to assist you in a positive delivery of your WAC'em words.

- Handle yourself during other difficult kinds of conversations—giving feedback, including unsolicited advice, giving bad or unpleasant news, making a complaint in person, and expressing sympathy. The important thing is not to avoid and worry about having these conversations. Having them now is much easier, especially when you adapt your WAC and employ the verbal and nonverbal skills you've learned.

What's Next?

It's time for us to talk about avoiding conflict.

But wait a minute! Isn't this a book about confrontation and about not avoiding difficult conversations?

Yes it certainly is, but as you will soon discover, part of the "power" of positive confrontations is not having to have them at all. Not because you're choosing to let them go, but because you're living your life in such a way that you reduce the likelihood that a conflict or a problem will arise. I like to think of this as "conflict free" living. It's a great way to go through life, as you'll soon discover.

PART III

CONFLICT-FREE LIVING

CHAPTER 14

THE SECRET TO AVOIDING CONFLICT IN LIFE

In Part II of this book, you've learned many useful tools to help you handle conflict successfully. You'll soon, if you haven't already, discover how much better you feel knowing that you can approach any difficult situation or difficult conversation with poise and confidence. When it comes to conflict, there's only one thing better—not to be in the difficult situation or need to have the difficult conversation in the first place.

Of course, no one can have zero conflict in his or her lives. You'd be living under a rug or inside a very big bubble if you had a totally conflict-free life. But you can move towards having less and less conflict in your day-to-day life. I've seen many people do it. You can do it too. Actually, you've already started moving towards zero. You took your first step to a more positive way of life when you learned (and continued to practice) WAC'ing people instead of attacking them.

Another step you took is learning (and practicing) effective verbal and nonverbal communication.

Yet another is learning how to handle difficult conversations.

You're pretty close. But you can get even closer by doing one more thing: Learn how to avoid *causing* conflict. A significant way to do this is by learning how to be the kind of person who treats others with respect, kindness and understanding. If you use these positive behaviors, you will be able to establish rapport and make a connection with others.

Like so many changes I prescribe in this book for less stressful living (like using my WAC'em model and paying attention to your verbal and nonverbal communication) learning how to establish rapport is pretty simple. Yet make no mistake; the positive effect upon your life can be profound. When you are able to connect with others in a positive way you feel good about the people around you and you feel good about yourself. Others in turn will feel good about interacting with you.

What "Rapport" Means for You

So what exactly, within the context of this discussion, does "establishing rapport" mean? The *American Heritage Dictionary* defines the word "rapport" as: "A relationship, esp. one of mutual trust and harmony." Sounds good. For our purposes though, we need a little more information. I therefore add the following—" . . . achieved, in part, through common courtesy and practicing good etiquette."

I'd also like to make the distinction between minor and major rapport. Saying "Hello" to and conversing with the clerk who checks out your groceries is an example of minor rapport. You may not want to establish a long-term relationship with him or her—in fact you might not ever see this person again, but why not be friendly?

An example of major rapport would be having a conversation with, and getting to know, a neighbor or someone you meet at a trade show or convention. This is a person with whom you may want to have an on-going relationship.

Keep in mind that establishing *both* major and minor rapport with others is important. Both will impact the quality of your life and reduce the amount of conflict in your life. When you are friendly to clerks in grocery stores and friendly with your neighbors, it's much more likely that these people, will in turn, be friendly to you.

Beyond Minding Your Manners

Because good rapport means you need good etiquette skills, this chapter and the next two are mostly about etiquette, but within what will probably be a new context for you. Yes, minding your manners involves saying, "Please," "Thank you," and "Have a nice day." That's not new. What is new is learning and using polite language and many other etiquette skill areas to:

- Handle yourself with grace, poise, and good humor in a world where these things often seem rare.
- Get along with your co-workers, neighbors, and new people you happen to meet.
- Get along with people you don't know.
- Establish better rapport with the people you already have long-lasting relationships with.

The Benefits of Good Rapport

Knowing how to establish and build rapport with others will help you to avoid conflict in many areas of your life. Reduced conflict is the main benefit you'll experience. There are others. You'll meet other people more easily. You'll feel confident in what used to be awkward situations, like making an introduction. You can make small talk with anyone. People will welcome your presence.

I know, I know, it sounds too simple to be true—how can good rapport achieved through good etiquette skills bring all these terrific things to your life? But it is true—etiquette skills can be invaluable to you. So many of us just don't know the rules of etiquette. And to make things even muddier on the white carpet, many of us don't know the rules have changed. This lack of knowledge causes problems—conflict, misunderstandings, even serious misunderstandings.

I'm going to talk about the etiquette areas essential to establishing and maintaining good rapport. If you learn these skills, your life will be, in general, a lot less full of conflict than it currently may be. You'll even have those days where your conflict thermometer is at zero.

The reason is simple—You get back what you put in. People respond to what you put out in the world. It's hard to be nasty to people who are nice to you.

Eleven Simple Ways to Establish Rapport

To brush up on your rapport-building skills there are eleven life-enhancing, relationship-building skills that you'll need to learn and practice. The eleven things I discuss here may seem like little things and each one taken on its own can be. But taken as a whole, these eleven things can make a huge difference in how we connect, or fail to connect, with others. The best part is, they're easy to learn. They're simple to put into practice. You can read this chapter, put this book down, go out into the world and start.

All you have to do is remember them and put them in practice.

1. GREET AND ACKNOWLEDGE OTHERS

This first one is the most simple and most powerful: Greet and acknowledge people. Say, "Hello," "Good morning," "How are you?" and "Good-bye."

Many people are astonished that is number one on the list. It's too simple or silly they say. But it is number one for a reason. This is a big source of conflict for people. People don't like to be ignored.

When you see people you know or even those you don't know, you should look them in the eye and say something—"Hello," "Good morning," "How are you?" This establishes a human connection between you and the other person. It's as if you are saying, "I see you. You have become part of my day. You are on my radar screen . . ."

Now you don't have to walk around all day being a parrot saying "Hello," "hello," but when your path crosses with someone else's, you should acknowledge the person.

■

How Do You Feel about People Who Don't Say "Hello" to You?

Recently I had a stress test. The doctor had me talking during the test. He asked what I do for living. I said I teach etiquette and assertiveness in corporations. He said, "Please teach my technician that when I say, 'Good morning' to him, he needs to respond back. It drives me crazy that he doesn't!"

People really dislike it when others fail to greet them and it happens all the time.

You probably don't like people who don't greet you. In fact, you are probably pretty quick to make a negative assumption about the person. They are rude, unfriendly, or think too well of themselves. Then it becomes tempting not to be nice to them!

I'm truly amazed sometimes that I need to tell people to say hello to others. And my exact wording is "If someone says hello to you, you *have* to say 'hello' back.' "

Now, I'm not talking about meeting someone in a dark alley; in that case, you don't even say "good-bye," you just run. The rest of the time, when you're safe and comfortable, say, "Hello."

I hear complaints that people walk the halls of corporate America or academia, avoiding looking at others and when someone says "Hello" or "Good morning" to them, they often do not give any verbal or nonverbal reply.

The Impact of a Greeting

The whole atmosphere of any organization, be it a major corporation or a book group meeting, can be changed when people say, "Good morning," "Have a nice day," or "How are you?"

And, you don't need to know someone personally to express a simple, pleasant "Good morning." As I mentioned earlier, minor rapport is important to establish too. If you move into a new neighborhood and you see a new neighbor across the street, what do you do? Do you say hello? There are people who tell me they don't greet their neighbors because they don't want to get too involved.

Saying "hello" isn't getting "involved"; it's being polite. It doesn't mean you have to invite your new neighbor over to dinner (though you certainly can do so). It just means you are aware of others around you and are a pleasant person. How can this be bad?

Greeting Neighbors . . .

Greet your neighbors—when you see them. I hear unfriendly neighbor stories a lot. People hate when their neighbors pretend they don't exist. And it happens all the time!

When I moved into a new townhouse I made sure I greeted my neighbors when I saw them. By doing this, I established a connection between us. It was a minor connection, but a connection still.

A friend of mine who lived in a different building didn't talk to any of his neighbors. We both put our trash out early, but he got a letter and fine from the condo association. One of his neighbors complained about the trash. My trash went out at the same time. None of my neighbors said or did anything!

My point here is not about how to get away with sneaking your trash out early. Rather, it's how people react to you and feel about you, even if they don't know you well. To my neighbors, I was a part of the neighborhood. My friend wasn't a part of his neighborhood— all because he failed to greet and acknowledge his neighbors.

Greeting Co-Workers . . .

Here's a story to show you what can happen if you ignore your co-workers.

I was brought into an organization to teach their salespeople assertive skills. During the day, a number of the administrative people complained to me that when the salespeople (who had come from the field and were unknown to them) walked into the coffee room, they did not acknowledge them. Yet, as soon as the head sales manager walked into the room, the salespeople all said "hello" to him. The administrative people were insulted and furious—"Aren't we worth a 'hello?' " And when one of the salespeople needed some work done . . . well, you know the rest of the story.

I don't blame them for being insulted and not wanting to do his work.

Say Hello—It's a Catchy Habit

Why should you take the initiative and say hello if the other person won't do it? You should because you can get other people in the habit of saying hello, simply by saying it yourself.

Clare took the initiative with saying hello to her boss. Initially, she thought he was "stuck-up, unfriendly, and an old grouch bucket." The reason—he never said "Hello" to her when he walked into his office in the morning. He rarely said "Good night," either. I asked Clare if she tried saying "hello" to him?

"Well, maybe I used to but I don't anymore. Why should I?"

"Try it," I said. "You may not feel it's your responsibility to always be the one to offer a greeting, but just try it anyway."

She did try and as it turns out, the "old buzzard" isn't so bad after all. It took some time. Eventually he caught on. He now says "Hello" to her and will even stop and ask her how she's doing. He even seems more cheerful when he comes in to work. I think it's possible he just got out of the habit of using greetings. Now he's back in the habit and seems better for it.

The payback here is clear: Less stress and conflict for Clare. She and her boss now have created a more pleasant environment at work.

Establishing Rapport with Strangers

You can establish rapport with strangers simply by offering a greeting in public places. Again I am not talking about a dark alley, but why not say hello in line at the bank or the grocery store? I go to the post office fairly regularly in my town. Recently, there was a new clerk and I said, "Good morning," to him. He looked at me with shock and surprise. "Oh, good morning to you!" he said back, clearly pleased that I had greeted him. While I may not be looking to establish a close personal friendship with him, I'm a regular customer; he's a part of my day. He knows my son and me now. He always goes out of his way to be pleasant and when I mess up my shipping forms, he is a lot more understanding and helpful.

Don't tell me this strategy of niceness doesn't work until you put this into practice. You'll see. It does work. Try planting a pleasant expression on your face. Smile and say hello. Give it a try. What a difference it makes in creating a pleasant mood.

2. INTRODUCE OTHERS

Along with the greeting another important ingredient to establishing rapport and avoiding conflict at the same time is to make introductions. Again, this seems simple. But it's amazing how much this one gets botched up. What a lot of awkward, unnecessary tension this causes when people enter rooms or join conversations. People don't make introductions and yet get upset when they in turn, aren't introduced.

As I see it, people don't make introductions for three reasons:

- They don't realize it's their responsibility;
- They don't know how to do it properly;
- They forget the person's name.

But no matter what the reason, you need to make an introduction. In many ways, a poor introduction is better than no introduction.

The correct way to introduce a person in a professional or business setting is to mention the name of the person of importance or higher rank first, regardless of gender. It used to be that women's names were said first, but in business this rule no longer applies. And if you don't know who is most important, then choose the person who you want to make a good impression upon and mention that person's name first.

If you forget someone's name, just admit it. It happens to us all. In this embarrassing situation, lessen your own and the other person's discomfort by having a Polite and Powerful statement on the tip of your tongue. If you have just one line to remember, you are more apt to remember it and be more comfortable because you have something to say. Sample lines can be:

"I'm sorry. I've forgotten your name."
"Please excuse me; I can't recall your name."
"I know your face, but my mind's gone blank."
"I know I know your name, but please remind me."

Don't explain your lapse to death — "I can't remember your name because I'm so preoccupied and I was up sooo late last night . . ." It happens to everyone. People understand that.

When you make introductions properly, you make others comfortable and that's a great step to make in establishing rapport and reducing conflict.

If Necessary, Introduce Yourself

Patrick and his co-worker walked into a meeting. His co-worker took the empty seat next to the VP. A few minutes later, Patrick saw the co-worker greet the VP and shake his hand. The two men appeared to connect.

Patrick later approached the co-worker and said, "I thought you didn't know the VP."

"I didn't," he said, "But I decided to introduce myself."

As a result, he made a connection with an important person in his company.

3. Everyone Needs to Shake Hands

Yet another greeting area that causes misunderstanding and interferes with establishing rapport has to do with the good old American handshake. We judge people based on the quality of their handshake and we make assumptions about them — often inviting conflict as a result.

Joanne made an assumption about her future brother-in-law. When she met him for the first time, he did not extend his hand to her. "Right away," she said. "I assumed he was a male chauvinistic pig."

He wasn't a male chauvinist pig. Later the two became friends. But what if this had been their only meeting? She would have made her assumption about him and it would have stuck. She would have walked away disgusted with him and meanwhile, he would have had no idea why she seemed to want to get away from him so quickly.

Women make assumptions about other women based on the way they shake hands. One woman said about another woman's limp handshake: "Right away I lost respect for her."

Men make assumptions too—I hear complaints from men who have gotten bone-crushing handshakes from other men, such as, "It's as if he's showing me how tough he is."

Women with limp handshakes and men with crushing handshakes aren't necessarily wimps and bullies. They may have never been taught the proper rules of handshaking etiquette or they're not aware that they're shaking too softly or too harshly. People also get confused because there are more than one set of rules that governs handshaking etiquette. There are rules for social behavior and rules for business behavior. Which rules apply for the handshake?

Social Etiquette Versus Business Etiquette

The handshake—or failing to shake hands—is the perfect example of how not understanding the new rules of business etiquette can cause conflict and have consequences for people. Here's an illustration to show you what I mean:

A senior VP walks into a meeting of three men and one woman. The three men stand up and shake hands with him. The woman does not stand up nor does she extend her hand. They may nod.

What assumption would you probably make about this woman? You would probably assume, as most people do, that the woman is not equal or part of the group.

Depending upon our point of view, we can blame the man or the woman for this. Yet, each is very possibly just doing what they were taught was correct social behavior. Many men, both younger men and older men, were taught to wait for the woman to extend her hand. Many women were taught that they don't need to stand. I was taught these rules myself. For years I did not rise upon introductions or extend my hand to men. I no longer agree with these rules. As you can see from the example above, conflict can easily occur when the social rules are carried over into the workplace.

In the olden days—unfortunately meaning my childhood—there were very few women in the business world. Men and women rarely interacted in the business world. Men and women interacted in the social world based on the social rules of etiquette. So when women first started appearing more and more in business, the only rules were the social rules and they spilled over into the workplace. Men continued to follow the social rules of greetings.

Today, women want to be treated equally in the business world. This means many of the rules of social etiquette don't apply in business and professional situations. We no longer make our business etiquette decisions based on gender. Instead we make them on rank and host/visitor status.

In a business situation therefore, everyone should rise when the CEO or special guests walk into the room. Every person should extend a hand for a shake.

If you are the host, it is up to you to greet and introduce your guest. You can't however, force your guest to shake hands but you can set the example by extending your hand.

But what about socially? Should a woman extend her hand and shake? This is a good question and not easily answered. Now, the social rules have also changed because more and more women are working and the new business ways are being carried over into the social world. Yet, there are still many women who are not in the working world and who don't know to shake hands or prefer to remain seated.

Often times, our greetings for social situations are more personal anyway. We often hug and kiss people we know well. I think in social situations when new people are meeting, women should rise and shake hands. But again, many women and men may prefer the old way, so my guideline is this: Take your cues from the situation and the people involved. Give someone the benefit of the doubt in social situations.

If this seems confusing that's because it is! Etiquette is like a dance, but it's not a waltz where every step is conveniently planned for you. It is much more the movement to a rock and roll song. You go with the flow and adjust as you go.

Women Need to Shake Hands!

Still, there are many people who don't know where the flow is flowing—especially women. Many women were *never* taught to shake hands. At least 35 percent of all women in my seminars don't shake hands correctly. 75 percent don't stand when I introduce myself to them. 90 percent of the men do stand. Women complain about being invisible in the business world, and sometimes it's because they're not initiating the greetings necessary to establish rapport. It's hard to ignore someone who walks into a room, looks you in the eye, and shakes hands with you.

Yet by the end of the day, the women shake hands correctly and tell me that in the future, they will stand upon greeting.

Many women were never taught how to shake hands. It is the absence of this know-how that can be very awkward for women. When men are shaking hands, a woman is often left to wonder, "What do I do? Should I put my hand out?"

And some women are comfortable with shaking hands with men, but not comfortable with shaking hands with women. Often times, women are surprised when I come up to them and extend my hand. They're often not prepared to respond to my greeting.

In the United States, the handshake is the proper business protocol greeting and if you want to be taken seriously in business you *must* shake hands. A number of women told they would not be taken seriously had they not shook hands. One told me she was told that one of those "deciding factors" that got her job was because she shook hands with the interviewer at the beginning of the interview and at the end.

Women Need a Firm Grip!

Men complain that women give them the limp handshake. Women complain that men give them the limp handshake. Women complain that other women give them limp handshakes. Sometimes a limp handshake is just a lame greeting but its impact can be lasting. As we've already discussed, some people will make assumptions about you. Chances are, in this country, they'll think you're a wimp.

So how do you shake hands in a way that's not too limp? You also don't want to break the bones in anyone's hand either.

Let me end the suspense by giving you the formula for the handshake that both men and women should use in business situations and that is now becoming accepted more in social situations as well: The higher-ranking person should extend his or her hand first. But because of the gender issues, it doesn't always happen. You should give the higher-ranking person a second or two and if he or she doesn't extend a hand, you should extend yours.

To shake hands correctly:

1. Say your name and extend your hand.
2. Go in with the thumb up, at a slight angle. Make sure thumb joints meet.
3. It should be firm but not bone breaking. Men: it's not a competition! In the United States two to three pumps is enough.

4. DON'T USE NICKNAMES WITHOUT PERMISSION

This is a short one compared with #3 above, but it's important. Many people are very particular about what you do to their names. Some people will take offense if you greet them by a name they don't want to be called. It may not bother you whether you are called Robert or Rob, Marjorie or Margie, but other people do care:

- One man said that to make sure people don't use his nickname, when he greets people, he extends his hand and says "My name is Richard; don't call me Dick."

- A mechanic told me that other men always called him "buddy" or "pal." This offends him.
- A friend of mine named Charles doesn't like when people call him "Chuck." He refers to it as an "unauthorized shortening of my name." He will not do business with people who do this.

Why risk offending someone by using a nickname? If the person has a name that is typically shortened, like Patty for Patricia or Bob for Robert, ask the person what he or she wants to be called.

5. KNOW THE "NEW" RULES OF HELPING ETIQUETTE.

Helping etiquette is another illustration of social etiquette causing conflict in the workplace. It used to be that men were expected to do the following "helping" things for women:

- Open the door
- Order for her, or let her order first.
- Pay the bill
- Carry packages
- Assist with coats
- Hold chairs

But like the rules of greetings, the rules of helping etiquette have also changed significantly in the workplace. If a man helps a woman on with her coat, pays her bill from a business lunch, pulls out her chair at a board meeting, etc., what image of a woman is created? It creates an image of a dependent woman who needs to be taken care of. In the workplace today, this is not the image women want if they want to be considered competent, credible, and powerful.

In business and professional situations, women should not expect men to do these things for them. But what about socially? When people ask me about the rules, again I tell them that what you choose to do socially is no longer guided by hard and fast dos and don'ts. And yes, it can be confusing. As I explained before, you can be in a social situation where the person is applying the rules of business etiquette.

Couples work out how much helping etiquette they are comfortable with in their relationships. I like when Marty opens the car door for me. He likes opening the door for me. So, this is what we do. It's our choice.

Yet, I do not expect men in business to open doors for me unless my arms are full. Which brings me to this point—helping etiquette, regardless of gender, should be guided by one simple principle— help anyone who needs help. If a man is having trouble negotiating his arm into his coat, what should a woman do—stand there and laugh or ignore him? Of course not. She should help him with his coat.

A candidate for a director's position was interviewing with a VP. He was a prized candidate. When the director went to leave, the VP helped him on with his heavy coat. The director said that gesture helped him decide in that company's favor.

Some women get upset with men when they try to "help" them. Instead of jumping to a conclusion, like "What a sexist!" I invite women to take the jerk test first. It really is possible the man waiting for you to exit the elevator is doing what he thinks is expected of him. Or the man holding the door for you is simply being nice. And yelling at him as many men have experienced is just wrong. Very wrong.

Should You WAC a Man Who Is Helping a Woman?

If you're a woman, what do you say to the man who wants you to exit the elevator first?

Well, you can simply say, "Thank you," and let it go at that. I personally feel I would be inviting more conflict into my life by challenging every man I have met in an elevator who wants me to exit first. Am I really bothered if a man I don't know at a corporation I'm visiting for a day holds the door for me? No, I'm not. But if a woman is in a situation with a colleague or co-worker who persistently insists upon helping her, she can choose to say something. All the roads of us this book lead us back to "Don't Attack'em, WAC'em."

Your W (What's bothering you): "I know you're just being nice, yet when you continually open doors for me, pull out my chair, and pay the bill at lunch, I feel that it creates the impression that I'm dependent on you or that I can't take care of myself."

Your A (What do you want to Ask the person to do): In the future, if I need help I'll ask you.

Your C (Check-in with the other person): Okay?

You can also adapt your WAC and keep it shorter: "Thanks, I appreciate the offer, but I can handle it myself."

"But I Insist!"

There are still some men who want to follow the social rules in business situations. This may be fine, a courtesy, or kindness here and there. But be aware of overdoing it. You may invite conflict by continually helping a woman who doesn't need help.

6. KNOW HOW TO MAKE SMALL TALK.

After you've said hello, the introductions have been made, and you shake hands, what do you do next? If you want to establish a relationship with a person you don't know, you've got to engage that person in conversation—even if you think you're "bad" at engaging in small talk.

You may be shy. The unfortunate truth is that sometimes in our society we judge the "shy" harshly. We think, "She's stuck-up," or "He thinks he's so important!" when in reality these people are sweating it out just as much as the next guy.

If you're shy or prone to get tongue-tied, you should challenge yourself to overcome this condition. The ability to make small talk is a crucial skill to develop in business and helpful in everyday life. It helps you establish and maintain rapport.

One friend of mine who has battled chronic shyness her entire life said that she realized she was contributing to the problem when at a reception a woman made a passing comment to her: "Oh, here's the ice queen again."

For those of us not endowed with the "gift of the gab" there are ways you can compensate. Believe me, I've been witness to the transformation of tongue-tied people who learn to become fluent in the language of small talk. They are skills that can be learned. Here are some suggestions:

1. Ask questions to draw out the other person and create a two-way conversation.
2. If appropriate, refer to the last time the two of you were together.
3. Try to find out what the other person's interests are.
4. Watch your use of buzzwords and expressions that others might not understand.
5. Avoid controversial subjects like politics, religion, ethics, and the like. This is not to advocate superficiality. It's advocating getting to know people better first before you start debating with them on sensitive issues. Good small-talk topics include: the weather, movies, books, sports (if all are interested), the environment you are in and so forth.
6. Know your nonverbals. While you're engaging in small talk, your nonverbals are important. Don't cross your arms, for example, this will indicate that you're "closed." Smile. Make eye contact. Show that you are listening. And do listen. Pay attention. People sense when someone is genuinely interested or not.

Put Yourself "Out There"

Say "Hello," make the introduction, extend your hand, and start the conversation. The key thing about the etiquette of rapport is that you must be willing to participate. You will meet many people in the world who simply aren't going to have the same understanding of etiquette issues as you now do. So take the lead, extend your hand, introduce yourself. If you decide that the person isn't interested in building a rapport with you, simply make a polite exit, like "It's been nice chatting with you, good-bye."

Small Talk, Big Results

Once you learn and practice the skills of small talk you become more comfortable. You'll start to see results. It gets easier, I promise.

One woman told me her success story. She was very shy and would not talk to people. But the new skills she learned gave her the confidence to try. She was on a plane and started making small talk to the woman next to her. This was a first. Well it turns out that this woman's husband is the key researcher on a project that the shy woman is working on and she can now get to meet him.

I believe that I was accepted into a graduate program on merit, but that my admission was speeded along because I had established rapport with the dean's secretary. After we had chatted a few times she had said to me, "I made sure your papers were seen by the dean."

7. PAY SINCERE ATTENTION TO OTHERS.

Talk all you want, shake hands all you want, but you can't connect and build relationships with people unless you give them your sincere attention. People want to feel like you're listening to them and interested in what he or she may be saying. I'm amazed that I have to tell people: "Don't answer the phone when someone's in your home or office." This is such rude behavior! Taking a call while you're already engaged in a conversation is a fast and sure way to let someone know that he or she isn't as important as the person who may be calling. This is why there are answering machines. I was told of a managing partner in a law firm who took phone calls when a client was meeting in his office. Until he read my etiquette book, he had no clue that he was being rude. And this man has a law degree and a Ph.D.

And if you must answer the telephone, you should explain why. "I've been expecting this call. It's important." Do your business and then get off the phone as quickly as possible.

A friend visited a sick friend who received a call from another friend and proceeded to talk to her for twenty minutes while she was there! I would have been upset with my friend too. It would have made me think, "What? Is her other friend (who isn't even here) more important than me?"

This problem of inattention doesn't just happen with the telephone. A man told me that he was interviewing with an executive who opened his mail during the interview. He ended up being offered the job, but not taking it, partly because "Who wants to report to a person who doesn't seem to care that I exist?" I wouldn't want to work for a person like that either.

Networking Abusers

"Networking" is another situation in which it's especially important for you to give people your attention. There's nothing worse at a business function than the person running around handing out a box of business cards. They're not really paying or giving attention — they're giving business cards. It's obvious that he or she has no interest in really meeting you or getting to know you.

Another sure sign that someone is not really interested in getting to know you is when you encounter the person who talks to you, yet is looking at everyone else or scanning the room. You know they're not establishing a rapport with anyone. And that's the very point of networking. I often wonder why people who do this bother to attend functions.

Eye Contact Is Key

To show someone that you're paying attention to him or her, you must make eye contact with him or her. We've talked about eye contact before, especially in Chapter 8 as part of paying attention to your nonverbal signals. We'll talk about it again. The issue of eye contact comes up again and again in this book because making eye contact is one of the simplest, yet most effective ways, to connect with others.

Some people have told me that they get a little uncomfortable making eye contact. If you're not used to it, it can be uncomfortable. I tell them, it's okay to look away now and then, you don't want to stare the other person down. But it is important to make eye contact. You'll get used to it.

If you're in a situation and you're making eye contact but the other person isn't (remember, the person may not have the same skills that you do) what can you do? First, don't assume the person is a jerk. The person may be uncomfortable or from a different culture. Second, you can stop talking and that often encourages the person to look at you. Other than that there really isn't a lot you can do.

8. DON'T INTERRUPT OTHERS

This was on our list in Chapter 1. Many people consider this to be one of the most annoying habits out of all the annoying habits we have. People don't know they are interrupting, and don't know what to say when it happens to them. As a result conflicts can occur. People will not want to have more conversations with you. They may avoid you. You can't build relationships if people see you and head the other way.

> "Don't interrupt me when I'm interrupting you."
> —WINSTON CHURCHILL

You may be an interrupter.
"You mean me?"
Yes, you! A lot of people don't know they're interrupting until it's pointed out. It's become an ingrained habit. Now, of course, people do occasionally interrupt one another, but when it becomes a regular pattern it is bothersome to others. This is the man that no one wants on their team because he keeps interrupting during meetings. He has no clue. If you catch yourself mouthing the words that you think the other person is going to say, then you may have this problem.

I heard about an energetic book discussion group that made a rule: You can't speak until at least five other people have given their opinion. This is a great rule. Practice it whenever you're in a group discussion.

How to Handle Being Interrupted

If someone interrupts you, you can express your displeasure about it, but don't act rudely. You will look unprofessional. In a meeting a woman didn't know how to handle interruptions. She exploded and screamed, "Well, if you want to explain, GO AHEAD."

The man who had interrupted her responded, "Well it's all yours, so talk!"

She lost her cool. It destroyed her credibility. Conflict arose between them after that. She asked me what to say the next time she is interrupted. I told her to come up with a Polite and Powerful line. Here are some possibilities:

"I'll be happy to address that as soon as I finish my thought."

"I'll discuss that as soon as I am finished."

"Hold that thought."

You can try to continue talking and give the person a hint that way, but there are people who don't get hints. That's why I recommend the direct, but Polite and Powerful approach—"Excuse me, I wasn't finished."

Gender Issues and Interrupting

Men interrupt women more. I've seen this in my classes. I've seen it in meetings. I've seen it happen in social situations. I pointed this out when I was teaching a communication skills class in Oman and one of the women in the class agreed with me. She said, "That's absolutely correct. You can see it on your American TV shows." I was startled yet realized she was probably right—a pervasive bad habit would certainly be apparent on our television programs.

On Your Own

What will you say when someone interrupts you? I encourage you to come up with a Polite and Powerful line. You'll get used to saying it and find that it works.

---

9. Use Humor Wisely

I don't want to get into a discussion of political correctness and humor. That's not what this book is about. It is about how to get along with others, how to deal with conflict when it arises. Therefore, when attempting to build rapport be cautious with humor. You're not going to get along with others if you go around telling jokes that others find offensive.

When I talk about this subject, people always groan. Then the storytelling starts, "My friend is always telling the grossest jokes . . ." They groan because the constant inappropriate joke teller annoys them.

Humor can be an effective communication tool or you can bomb badly with it. Humor can be difficult to pull off because what is funny to one person may not be to another. And sometimes what people believe is funny, hurts or puts down other people and invites conflict. I don't want to ban jokes, but I do think people would be wise to be judicious in how they unleash what they think is humorous.

It May Seem Like Just a Joke to You . . .

Telling inappropriate stories or comments, dirty, off-color jokes is not simply okay. There are loads of people out there who really don't understand the consequences, which is why I want to share this next story.

On the first day of a new semester, a man in my MBA class told a dirty joke during his presentation. I WAC'ed him for it. I told him it was inappropriate. He was furious with me. He accused me of being politically correct and no fun. Yet, by the following week, he said he had noticed that he was telling those types of stories more than he had thought. And he had been mad at his management for not considering him a viable candidate for promotion. By the end of the semester he had written me a letter:

"The first day of class made me realize that the way I presented myself was largely responsible for why I had not been considered a serious candidate [for promotion]. My behavior contributed to the way they [peers and supervisors] responded to me and in turn, contributed to my poor attitude in the plant.

"I began to make a conscious effort to change some of the things that were bogging me down. At first I really didn't want to believe that these things were the cause for my failure to get noticed in the company. But I realized quickly that they did.

"It was about three months after the first day of class that I was offered the position of Die Shop Superintendent."

Using Humor to Avoid Facing the Issue Is Not Okay

A customer service representative tried a humorous approach with a disgruntled customer. He said, "Why be upset that your shipment was late. The stock is going up!" The customer didn't laugh. He thought the representative wasn't taking his complaint seriously. The customer started getting upset with the representative and using aggressive language. The representative had no clue that what he said was inappropriate.

What he said was inappropriate because people want you to take their issues, their thoughts, and their WACs seriously. If you laugh someone off either because you're not taking that person seriously or because you use humor in uncomfortable situations, you may be harming your relationship with that person.

Humor Must Not Be Cruel

Have you ever met a person who was very funny but who always relied on making fun of others—their professions, religion, culture, personal quirks, ethnic background, etc? Besides the fact that it makes you look bad, it can make the other person feel bad. It just isn't nice!

A man went into a potential client's office and noticed that there was a picture of the man, his wife and their six kids. He said, "Good Catholic, eh?" The potential client did not do business with him based solely on that comment.

When Humor Works

Don't be humorous but have a sense of humor. Humor can be used to defuse difficult situations from developing. It can stop you from taking a situation too seriously.

One morning my mom was visiting during the coldest winter on record. It was about ten degrees outside and I was getting my son ready for preschool. She looked at me and said, "Barbara, don't forget to put on Jacob's jacket." I said to her, "Thanks mom, I am sure I was about to let him out of the house without it!" She laughed and got my point.

After someone asks a ridiculous personal question, you can respond with humor to get your point across without actually WAC'ing the person:

"I'll forgive you for asking if you forgive me for not answering."

A man asked me, "Are you still pregnant?" I said, "No, I am carrying this for a friend who is on vacation."

The most important etiquette guideline for humor is to remember that what you think is hilarious someone else might find offensive.

10. USE POLITE LANGUAGE

It is time to re-engineer kindness back into our everyday lives. One very simple way to do this is to use polite words. I remind people—because I have to—to use polite words in corporate America just as I do when I lecture in my son's elementary school!

Doing so in business, school and everyday life, will help you with new relationships and well-established ones.

These are simple words, such as "Thank you," "Please," "Excuse me," and when appropriate, "I'm sorry."

If you bump into someone and don't excuse yourself, the other person may become angry with you. You invite conflict into your life by not acknowledging the bump. If you say, "Thank you" to someone, he or she is more likely to help you in the future.

A job hunter asked a recruiter to call a company and put in a good word for him. She did. He got the job. He never called to thank her. She was insulted. She told me she would never help him again because of this.

The Power of Polite Language

The manager who uses polite language with his administrative person is more apt to accomplish what he or she wants. The customer who says "please" to the clerk is more likely to have a pleasant exchange than a nasty one. Though I say "thank you" to the ticket machine on the New Jersey turnpike—and it doesn't influence the outcome!

Using polite words also means no cursing and no sexist or racist language. You can instantly turn people off from wanting to get to know you. You may mean no harm but you can still do harm. You can offend people and appear as if you are aggressive.

11. BE CONSIDERATE WHEN SHARING SPACE WITH OTHERS

When I ask people, what's the kind of stuff that drives you nuts at work? I hear the word "inconsiderate" quite a lot. This is:

- The person who doesn't replace paper in the copy machine (or who doesn't let other people jump in line who only have one copy to make when the person has 300).
- The person who breaks office equipment and doesn't let anyone know it needs to be fixed.
- The person who leaves a teaspoon of coffee in the pot for the next person. Is it so hard to make a pot of coffee?
- The person who lets his or her uneaten food turn into a science experiment. Remove your old food from the refrigerator. Clean up after yourself.
- The person who leaves empty soda cans or coffee cups on the meeting room table for someone else to clean up.
- The person who doesn't respect the privacy of others. Don't

listen in on phone conversations or read things on other people's desks.

- The person who borrows things and doesn't return them. And don't borrow things from someone's desk when that person is not there.
- The person who plays music loudly or who makes loud distracting phone calls.

You spend a good portion of your day and your time with your co-workers. You should, therefore, make every effort to be considerate when sharing work space. If you are not considerate with others at work, people may avoid you. They may see you coming and think, "Oh no, here comes that Tony, he never makes a pot of coffee." Wouldn't you hate to be Tony?

Sharing Space at Home

Space sponging doesn't just occur at work. You need to be considerate when sharing space with the people in your personal life as well. Most of the conflicts I hear about between roommates and spouses has to do with space sharing: "My roommate borrows my clothes without asking." "My husband leaves big messes in the kitchen." "I'm always the one who cleans the bathroom." "She listens in when I'm arguing with my boyfriend." "I have to get up early and she stays up late with the light on."

Many of these common "space" conflicts can be avoided simply by applying some of the same rules of etiquette listed above—namely don't borrow other people's things without asking, don't leave messes for other people to clean up, respect the privacy of the people with whom you live, and don't make too much noise when the other person needs quiet.

Of course, on some issues, such as playing music or dividing up household chores, you may have to negotiate with the other person. All healthy relationships involve give and take.

Respect Your Neighbor's Space

You may only share a property line, and you should respect that line, but the space you share with your neighbors is in a sense much larger than a fence or driveway. You can reach into another person's space with loud music and loud voices too. I once lived near a family with teenagers. They were a nice family except the kids were often loud—they yelled a lot in the yard, they played loud music, and one of them played the drums at ten or eleven at night. At first I thought, well this will stop soon because it must be driving the parents crazy too. Apparently not! (This is a good example of why we often don't WAC people. We think "they must know this is bothersome behavior . . ." yet in reality, they often don't know.) I ended up WAC'ing them. They were surprised when I told them I could hear the drums as clearly as if they were being played next to me. They were apologetic and suggested different times for their son to practice.

Though I still heard the drums occasionally at night, at least it wasn't late at night. It could have been worse—much worse. I have heard horror stories about nightmare neighbors. I have heard stories about parents who don't properly supervise their kids, who walk their dog on everyone's property, who use the next door neighbor's garden as a short cut, and more. These are simply rude behaviors. Behaving rudely back doesn't usually help. It only makes things worse. Sometimes people don't realize that you're bothered by something. So speak up, just make sure you do it Politely and Powerfully.

Start Doing These 11 Simple Things Today

While I don't encourage you to put this book down and go out and WAC your boss your first time out of the positive confrontation gate, I do encourage you to start practicing these eleven behaviors—immediately. They're all easy to implement (though the handshake and small talk skills may take you a little time) and you can begin to reap the benefits right away.

And there are more benefits to avoiding conflict coming your way. In this chapter we've covered one aspect of good etiquette: Rapport building. But there are other etiquette areas that cause conflict because people don't understand the basic rules of etiquette and the new rules in today's workplace.

The next two chapters deal with two areas that are ridden with conflict—our use of technology and our global society.

CHAPTER 15

TECHNO-ETIQUETTE
FOR DUMMIES AND SMART PEOPLE

Now we head out of the simple world of firm handshakes and the etiquette of greetings and into the not-so-simple world of technology and etiquette. I call the rules of etiquette that govern the use of technology "techno-etiquette."

Techno-etiquette matters because we're in an age of technology galore—cell phones, lap tops, e-mail, voice mail, video conferencing, the Internet, news groups . . . I can send a fax from my computer while I read a message from my friend in Holland. And it's great. We can communicate with each other better, faster, and a heck of a lot cheaper than ever before.

How We Got to Be Technologically Rude

And it's not so great. Our use of technology, whether at work or at home, can quickly become a source of conflict. We can cause problems for other people—often unknowingly. Others can perceive us as annoying and rude. We are also on the receiving end of annoying behavior from others. Even normally not rude people are making techno-etiquette mistakes. Sometimes big ones!

It's understandable that we're making mistakes in how we use technology. First, our mothers couldn't have taught us how to be polite with e-mail and voice mail since they didn't exist when we were growing up. Second, new communications technologies hit the scene so fast that organizations haven't had time to establish guidelines for how to use them. Ten years ago I had to learn how to turn a computer on. Now, I'm training professionals over the Internet!

Finally, the technology is ever-changing. That means the rules and guidelines are ever-changing too. No wonder we're all a little bit out of breath.

Yes, It Is a Big Deal

Let me play devil's advocate for a moment. This new technology did happen quickly. Who can learn the rules, when many of us feel as if we're still playing catch up? "I'll worry about this later," you may tell yourself. "I just want to get online with the rest of the world." So what if you make a few mistakes—it's no big deal.

Only it can become a big deal over time.

When you catch your breath, think about the co-worker who leaves you fifteen-minute-long messages—with all the important information said in the last two sentences. Think about the friend who sends you chain letters via e-mail. These people are annoying! Maybe you're annoying too. Annoying behaviors add up and can become flat-out problems somewhere down the road.

Learning how to use technology Politely and Powerfully will allow you to lead a more conflict free life. Techno-blunderers bug you and probably bug other people too. A hassle here, a hassle there. Hassles add up too. This chapter will help you understand how *not* to be become a techno-blunderer. You'll also learn how to cope with a techno-blunderer if there's one in your life.

**Here are the top 10 techno-related errors that can drive
the people you deal with crazy and/or send
a negative message about you:**

1. Using your cellular phone to hold conversations in public places. The man who answered his phone in church is not an urban legend. He's real and people don't like him. I was coming back from Washington D.C. on the train and the man behind me was answering his personal ads on his cell phone. I tried not to listen!

2. Not letting a caller know who is in the room when the speakerphone is being used. It can be embarrassing. The same applies for teleconferences. I was told a story about a woman who was visiting her friend. He answered his phone and put his friend on speakerphone. It turned out he was her date from the night before and started telling his friend how bad the date was! This kind of thing happens a lot.

3. Using a speakerphone when you share office space with others. They hear your conversations and it's distracting. This one appeared within one of the twelve most common conflicts we discussed in the beginning of this book. Many people get WAC'ed about this one.

4. Using call waiting in business. The person responds to the second call and ignores the person who originally called. It's insulting. Call waiting annoys your friends too!

5. Answering the phone and talking to a caller when you have a visitor in your home or office. Many people do not know this is rude . . . and people get very upset with the person who is doing it. (This isn't new technology, but it really still occurs a lot and is really annoying.)

6. Not leaving your name and phone number at the

beginning *and* end of a voice mail message. Once is not enough! It's inconsiderate to make someone replay a message to get this information. And say the numbers slowly. This drives people crazy. A friend of mine left her number where she was staying for the weekend and wanted me to call her. She gave the numbers so quickly I couldn't get them. She was annoyed with me. I was annoyed with her.

7. Rambling on someone's voice mail. Does anyone really listen after fifteen seconds? Keep it short and simple. I hear complaints about friends and co-workers who send six minute long messages. People stop listening. The senders get annoyed when you don't do something they've asked, yet it was at the end of the message and many people never get there.

8. Spelling and grammar mistakes in e-mail messages. Remember when we discussed your word choice and delivery in Chapter 11. People will make assumptions about your competence!

9. Using all capital letters in an e-mail message. It's the written equivalent of getting yelled at—and it's difficult for the person to read.

10. Sending junk e-mail. Don't add people to your mailing list for jokes of the day or chain letters without having permission to do so. Also keep in mind that a joke you find hilarious might be offensive to someone else.

The Why and the How of Technology Use

There are two main issues to Polite and Powerful techno-communications. The first is why you're using one technology over another. What led you to that technology? What might be the consequences of making the choice?

Second, you need to think about how you are using the technology. Are you using it Politely and Powerfully? Are you making mistakes?

Why You Choose One Technology Over Another

Suppose you have a new client who needs information and she tells you she needs it fast.

Is it better to e-mail, fax, or Federal Express the new client information? This question *should be* at the heart of why you choose one technology over another. Which one is most effective and appropriate—or not—for your purpose? But too many people don't stop to question their choice. Often, they are thinking of convenience—their own.

Kenny didn't think it mattered how his new client received information—just that she got it quickly. He needed to let her know that the support materials she requested would be arriving at her office via express mail. His first meeting with her had been two days earlier. She had told him she wanted the information immediately.

Kenny should have stopped and asked himself, "Is it most correct to e-mail, telephone, or fax her the information?"

Only he didn't stop to ask himself this question. He dashed her off an e-mail—because it was most convenient for him. Because he didn't know her well, he didn't know that she disliked using e-mail except for in-house communications. Her e-mail address was on her business card, but she didn't check her in-box as frequently as he thought she would have. She didn't get the confirmation right away and she was steamed at him.

As Kenny put it: "What a way to annoy a new client. Now I know—because I asked—to always fax her important information."

Just Because You Like It . . .

Our reason for choosing one message system over another largely depends upon our personal perception of, and comfort level with, each of the various technologies—and that's a mistake. You need to consider the other person and not yourself. This is very important in business today. While you think e-mail is the fastest way to get your message to your potential client, she might perceive your message as too casual. She may think, as Kenny's customer did, that you dashed off a message to her rather than taking the time to fax her a more official communication.

An AT&T employee told me he told his Microsoft representative to stop e-mailing him. "If you want to talk to me, call me. I am the phone company!" I love this example; it really illustrates how people can get used to communicating one way and then forget to consider the consequences.

Your choice of technology isn't just a source of potential conflict in business. Meg and Gary, instead of sending out birth announcements, e-mailed the news of their son's birth. Gary's relatives however, did not all have computer access. They felt left out.

How You Use the Technology You Choose

There are many different ways to create an e-mail or voice message. I will give you the guidelines for how to create good ones in just a little bit. First, let's talk about the consequences of making techno-blunders. Here's an example of what can happen:

A boss e-mailed her employees with comments and instructions all the time. Yet they rarely did what she suggested. She was furious at them. Yet she was using all caps and her employees were annoyed with her. She didn't know that all caps are the computer equivalent to being shouted at.

How she used the technology she chose was problematic. She wasn't using it properly and she invited conflict.

The Ground Rules for *How* to Use Technology Successfully

"But I didn't know!" is not an excuse to get you off the hook for causing a techno-blunder. If you're using the technology, it's your responsibility to use it correctly. It's your responsibility not to offend others.

If you want to get along with your co-workers, relatives and friends and send a positive message to others, you've got to pay attention to the details. Your techno-etiquette skills matter! Sometimes they are huge errors, which can immediately cause conflict, and sometimes just minor infractions, yet they add up and can erupt into conflict over time.

There are some basic ground rules surrounding the appropriate use of each of today's technological mediums. The main areas for technologically based conflict are telephone, e-mail, voice mail, and cell phone. Here are some guidelines to help you create conflict free techno-communications:

E-mail—Dos and Don'ts

E-mail offers the opportunity to convey information to others quickly and inexpensively. It's a great way to keep up-to-date with relatives, friends, clients, vendors, and business associates.

Keep in mind however, that especially in business, how you use your e-mail communicates your degree of professionalism to others. In business, you should check your e-mail three to four times a day, and if possible, always respond to e-mail within twenty-four hours.

As we discussed previously, one of the reasons why you don't want to WAC someone via e-mail is because there are no nonverbals to soften your message. Even if you're not WAC'ing someone, you can still accidentally offend someone. Your voice and your facial expression really can soften what the receiver might view as a strong statement or criticism.

Remember the story about the journalist who accidentally sent his boss an e-mail about her to her? I heard a story the other day that's similar. One friend was complaining about another friend, and accidentally sent the friend she was complaining about the message! Think before you send.

Here are some additional guidelines so you use e-mail without offending others:

It's Appropriate to Use E-mail To:

- Reach hard-to-reach people. Most people answer their own e-mail, providing you with a fast way to contact people you may not be able to reach over the phone or via postal mail. This is not the same as pounding on someone's door, so it's not offensive as long as you don't send several messages in a day.

- Document or prove that a message was sent and received. Sometimes in a conflict, you need a record. This easily provides that.

- Be less intrusive. The recipient of your e-mail can respond when he or she has time. This is very polite.

- Communicate news of events, ask questions, share tips, delegate assignments, and/or announce upcoming meetings. This provides an easy way to make sure people have information and are kept informed so there is less conflict.

- Let large numbers of people know something quickly, maintain relationships with people, clarify ideas, or congratulate someone. Though I am not sure about e-mailing your future father-in-law for the hand of his daughter is the way you want to tell him your intentions. Though I know a young man who did!

But It's Not Appropriate to Use E-mail To:

- Convey confidential information. If you don't want people to know something, don't send it via e-mail. Talk about inviting conflict!

- Communicate with a potential client when the relationship is new—unless you are specifically asked to do so.

- Say thank you. E-mail does not replace situations that have always required a handwritten note, especially to thank someone. Stationery and your handwriting make your thank you personal. (A quick note of thanks through e-mail may be okay if a formal thank you isn't required.)

- WAC someone, reprimand someone, fire someone, or offer condolences. In these situations, you will need your softening nonverbals.

- Send chain letters via e-mail—they are as annoying as the ones that used to come with a stamp on it.

- Send out formal invitations. If you're having a quick get-together, then it's okay, but for parties you're planning in advance, do it the old-fashioned way.
- Communicate with family and friends if you're at work. (This is inviting conflict from your boss. You're wasting company time!)
- Send jokes to people you don't know well. Even if you think someone won't be offended, they still might be. I know a paralegal who was reprimanded for sending the entire office jokes, top ten lists, and quizzes. The office manager (who was on her distribution list) felt she was wasting everyone's time.
- Forward mail that was intended for "your eyes only." It's easy to trace it back to you.
- Blow off steam. Never send an e-mail when you are angry. It's too easy to send it and you can't take it back. It may be funny when it happens in the movies. It's not funny in real life.

Writing Rules for E-mail Etiquette

The same rules of writing that I told you about in Chapter 11—word choice, diction, grammar—apply to e-mail writing as well. Always remember that an e-mail message, though it may be more casual, still advertises your writing skills. You must use proper grammar. Just as in a report or business letter, mistakes are noticed.

I heard about a man who was well respected in his organization—until he started sending out e-mails. They were full of mistakes—grammar, spelling, you name it. Some of them were so bad; they were saved and sent around behind his back! This was terrible for his credibility as a manager.

One of my students forwarded me this e-mail that he received from a director in his organization. What would you think of the writer of this e-mail?

DEMANDS FOR SHIPMENT MONITORING, AND

THE STRATEGIC NEED TO DEVELOP OUR COMPA-
NY'S DIRECTION, CONTINUES TO GROW. COUPLED
WITH THIS, THE INDUSTRY QUALITY EFFORT CON-
TINUES TO MOVE FORWARD AS WELL.

IN ORDER TO DRIVE THE DEVELOPMENT OF
OUR CAPABILITY, IMPLEMENTATION OF OUR
PLANS, AND COORDINATE WITH THE SALES/SER-
VICE TEAMS THE NEEDS OF OUR CUSTOMERS, I AM
PLEASED TO ANNOUNCE THAT TOM JONES WILL
HEAD UP THIS EFFORT.

You would probably think that he needed to brush up on his e-
mail writing skills! And he does—both in terms of format and writing style. Not only is this message hard to read because it's done in
all caps, but it isn't until the last sentence that you understand what
it's about.

Here are some additional writing guidelines specifically for conflict-free e-mail communications:

1. Keep your messages short. This shows a respect for your
   reader's time.
2. In business, especially, eliminate extra words. For a paper
   memo, the guideline is one page. For e-mail, it's one
   screen, or about twenty-five lines.
3. Use short paragraphs. It's easier for people to read when you
   do. It's hard to concentrate on a long paragraph printed on
   a piece of paper, and on a computer screen it's even more
   difficult. You must always think of your reader!
4. Use a subject line. This will help your reader focus on your
   topic.
5. As I've already mentioned, don't use all capital letters. They
   shout and are difficult to read. Don't use all lower cased letters either, it looks sloppy. Even if your reader is a friend, he
   or she might think, "Can't she even take a minute to make
   this easier to read?"

6. Limit each message to one subject area.
7. Message only necessary people. Don't waste others' time by sending to the entire message list.
8. Proofread *every* message. Words must be spelled correctly. Be aware that it's more difficult to proof on a screen. Read out loud slowly from the screen to catch your mistakes.

Nothing Can Replace Face-to-Face Communication

Now that I've given you the guidelines for good e-mail writing, stop and think before you hit the "send" button. Do you have to e-mail this person? Maybe you should talk to the person face-to-face. I'm amazed that people e-mail each other from one cubicle to the other, back and forth all day long. Why not talk to the person?

Not talking to people directly, at least some of the time, can become a problem. I met with two teams that were working together from different divisions and locations. There was an incredible amount of conflict between them. At my suggestion, the director brought both teams together and in ten minutes the problems were resolved.

Keep Your E-mail Addresses to Yourself!

One last guideline I offer you on e-mail use—don't give out the addresses of your friends. Companies on the Web have a trick to build their mailing lists—they give you discounts if you give them the names of your friends and relatives who might be interested in them too. Before you give out anyone's e-mail information, you should check and make sure this is okay.

A friend sent me an e-mail floral bouquet. I clicked on the site and there was a picture of flowers and a card from her. It was cute, until I started getting barraged with messages by the company. It undid her nice deed.

Telephone Abusers

Unlike e-mail, the telephone isn't a new communication medium; but technology has changed the way we use the telephone. The new changes, combined with some old bad habits, mean more conflict in our lives.

In my classes, the participants rank the most annoying telephone courtesy violations. Telephone violations are a common source of annoyance for people. These six appear again and again and drive people crazy!

1. **The Rude Talker.** This violator ranks number one. It's the person who takes telephone calls while you're in his family room or office. He or she answers the phone and proceeds to have a conversation as if you weren't there!
2. **The Stalker.** This person paces back and forth like a hungry lion while you're on the phone. She wants to talk to you, so she hovers over you, shadows the door and makes you feel uncomfortable. Kids are notorious stalkers when a parent is on the phone.
3. **The Interrupter.** This person barges in on you while you're on the phone and just starts talking to you! He ignores the fact that you are on the telephone. Oh, it's not an emergency, either!
4. **The "Doesn't Wait for an Answer" Person.** This person asks, "Would you please hold?" when answering the telephone—but doesn't wait for an answer. And then he or she leaves you on hold for what often feels like an eternity.
5. **The Black Holer.** You want a person. What you get is a machine. When the phone is answered, a very nice voice presents you with a menu of items to choose from. You usually have to respond to three or four prompts before you get to the department or person you want. And unfortunately, at that point, you get a busy signal or the person has left a message stating that he is out of town—and you are unable to get back to the main menu to find someone

else to talk to! You, of course, have been calling long distance.

6. **The Call-Waiting Clown.** I have a friend who constantly answers her call waiting while she's on the phone with me. I understand that occasionally, she might be waiting for an important call, but this is a bad habit. Unless you have children, teenagers, or an elderly relative who needs to reach you in case of emergency, you should be cautious with your use of call-waiting. If you are expecting an important call, let the person you're talking to know up front that you may have to put him or her on hold for a minute—but don't leave them hanging on for too long. In business it's rude to use call-waiting. Invest in a system that will pick up your calls for you while you're on another call.

Voice Mail Technology and Answering Machines Dos and Don'ts

Twenty-five years ago, the only way the phone got answered was by a person. Now, it's rare to even get a receptionist. Whether you realize it or not, we often judge others, including the competence and courtesy of a business operation by the way someone uses the telephone or the quality of the voice mail greeting or system.

Just because it may be convenient doesn't mean that voice mail is always the appropriate technological tool for communicating with your friends, customers and clients. Don't use voice mail to:

- WAC someone.
- Introduce yourself to someone—it's usually better to do that in person or with a live telephone conversation.
- Offer condolences.
- Convey confidential or critical information.
- Negotiate.
- Criticize or fire someone.

Six Voice Mail (and Answering Machine) Habits
that Drive People Nuts

When it's appropriate to use voice mail or an answering machine, do so, but do so correctly. Here are the most common mistakes I hear about that drive the people who have to listen to messages left by others crazy:

1. Speaking too fast. The number one complaint people have about voice mail messages is that the caller speaks too quickly. The receiver will have to replay the message repeatedly in order to understand it.
2. Failing to leave your phone number. Don't assume the person you're calling has memorized your phone number or is listening to messages with a Rolodex handy. Always leave your phone number at the beginning of the message and repeat it at the end.
3. Expecting to get voice mail. You may get a live person, and you will probably come across as unprepared. Always assume the person will answer. I hear countless stories of people who are left hemming and hawing because they didn't expect to have a conversation, and yet, they're the caller! You set yourself up to look bad and to get embarrassed.
4. Overusing. Nothing is going to turn someone off faster than being called repeatedly and pestered over voice mail.
5. Not providing enough information. Let the person know what you are calling about. You may eliminate phone tag.
6. If you are using an answering machine, do not listen to your messages when other people are around. They may hear things they shouldn't.

What Does Your Telephone Message Say about You?

Even the quality of your greeting matters. It's often the first impression people have of you. I called someone who had called me about coaching him. He felt his professional image needed to be better. His message said, "This is Tim. Okay, speak now."

When we finally connected, I told him the first thing he needed to do to improve his professional image was change his message. Here is the advice I gave to Tim about that:

1. Say hello! You may think this is a no-brainer but it's amazing the number of voice mail messages that fail to incorporate this basic courtesy. After the greeting you should identify yourself by your full name.

2. Keep your message short. It's annoying to waste people's time by making them listen to music before leaving a message. It's even more annoying when they're calling long distance.

3. If you can, inform your callers of when you will return or will be checking in for messages so they'll know when to expect a return phone call. Be sure to keep your message up-to-date. It's frustrating for others to get a message that says, "Hi I'm out till June 2" and you are calling on June 5 and get that old outdated message.

4. Speak slowly and clearly. Make sure there is no distracting background noise when you record your message.

It may seem like a little thing—what your voice mail or answering machine greeting says—but it's the kind of little thing that people—often unknowingly—judge you on. Why risk having someone think you're not professional or sincere? Why risk creating confusion on the part of your caller by not giving them enough information?

Sharing "Message Space" with Others

You now know that "sharing" with others, whether it's a refrigerator or a voice messaging system, is a juicy conflict area. I've often wondered how many family fights were started because someone forgot to let the other person know they had a message or erased a message someone else needed by accident. (If my family is an indicator, probably a lot!). When you're sharing a messaging system or machine with others be considerate:

- Don't erase messages for others unless you ask first.
- Don't insist upon saving messages you really don't need. Your voice mail isn't a Rolodex.
- Set up individual mailboxes. This allows everyone to have their own message and their own box.
- You may want to have a silly or funny message. Only you might be the only person who enjoys it. Some people get turned off by goofy messages. It's also hard for your caller to know if he or she has the right phone number.

Cell Phone Users—The New Bad Guys

Cellular telephone technology is fairly new, but the problems it can cause are almost the stuff of legends. A whole new breed of bad guys (including women) has emerged—people with bad cell phone habits.

Stacia told me this story:

"I commute to work on the train. It's forty-five minutes each way, but I don't mind, it's my only 'quiet time' of the whole day. The train pulled out of the station and a man proceeded to speak on his cell phone. He was so loud; the whole car could hear every word he said. Everyone was rolling their eyes and making faces at him. He was on the phone for twenty minutes straight. I finally wrote him a note telling him that the whole car could hear his conversation and it was disruptive. I walked up and handed it to him. He got off the phone and everyone clapped."

There are also cases of more than just conflict but acts of out-and-out destruction. Accidents have occurred because people were dialing instead of looking when driving.

Yes, cell phones are a remarkable convenience—you're "in touch" at all times. They have also created a way to make downtime more productive. But using a cellular telephone can make you into one of the growing number of techno-blunderers, and using them improperly can be rude. Here are four simple things you can do to be one of the good cell phone guys:

1. There would be a lot less "road rage" if people didn't use their cell phones while driving. You are apt to make mistakes in your car while driving and talking. When using your telephone in the car—be careful! Pull over to the side of the road or into a parking lot. If you must use your telephone while in transit, never dial while you're driving. If you use the telephone a lot in your car, consider installing a speakerphone.

2. There would be less airplane, train, restaurant, and sidewalk rage if people would stop using their cell phones in crowded areas. Be aware that you may be disturbing others around you. If there are other people around and you receive a call, leave the room to talk. It's never good manners to broadcast your conversations. The number of people who complain about this is stunning. One reporter called me to find out the rules because she wanted to do an article about this after she was attending a conference and a man's phone went off. He talked and disturbed everyone around him!

3. The technology is good, but not perfect, so always let someone know if you're calling from your car or cellular phone in case you're suddenly cut off.

4. Never discuss sensitive or confidential information on your cellular telephone. Eavesdropping technology is also advanced.

Don't Attack Cell Phone Abusers—WAC'em

If someone is in a restaurant or other public place and using a cell phone disruptively—don't get rude. For some reason, people who normally don't act rudely act rudely when confronted with cell phone abusers. I have seen people walk up to cell phone users and say things like, "You think you're so cool; well you're not!"

Don't do this—walk up to someone and make a pronouncement—especially to strangers because you don't know how they might react. Instead use a simplified WAC. "Please lower your voice, we can hear you."

Fax Faux Pas

Do you remember when a fax machine was just about the most amazing thing you'd ever seen? Now, they're commonplace. Many people even have them in their homes and most people with computers have the capability to fax from them. An advantage of fax technology is that it allows you to communicate quickly while providing a close approximation of your original document.

Facsimile technology is certainly older than e-mail and cell phones—yet people are still making mistakes when sending faxes— probably because no one ever gave them guidelines. Don't send a fax to:

- Offer condolences if someone has passed away.
- Convey confidential information—the fax is the least secure of all the technological mediums. You don't know who might get it.
- Send long memos or reports unless you have permission to do so.
- WAC, criticize, or fire someone.
- Send unsolicited sales materials.

You might think, who would send condolences via a fax? But I assure you, all of the above happen and they all create conflict.

Create a Professional Cover Sheet

Like a voice mail greeting or message, a fax cover sheet provides someone within an instant impression of you and your degree of professionalism. Once it's out there, you can't take that impression back. Make sure that your fax cover sheet includes the following:

1. A professional look. In business, don't use cute cover sheets. Your cover sheet should be as professional as your letterhead.
2. Your company's name, address, telephone, and fax numbers.
3. The total number of pages.
4. The action you would like the person to take upon receiving your fax.

Do You Really Need to Fax?

Think before you send. Faxing may be extremely convenient for you. You don't even have to copy the paper you're faxing. But is it convenient for your recipient to receive information this way? Like e-mail, you must stop before you hit the send button. Would it be better for the other person to get your letter or documents in the mail? Yes, it takes longer for you—you have to make copies, type or write a label, put a stamp on it, and mail it. But if this is the best way for your recipient to have the information, especially in business, you should think of the other person's convenience and not your own.

If You're on the Receiving End of a Techno-Blunderer . . .

I've given you the guidelines for avoiding causing problems and conflicts with your use of technology but what about the other technology users out there? What should you do if you're on the receiving end of an annoying e-mail message or a rambling voice mail message? What else? Don't attack the person, WAC'em. It's important to keep in mind that ignorance of techno-etiquette is widespread. The person sending you the e-mail in all caps probably doesn't realize that he or she is bugging you. Remember to take the jerk test before you get really annoyed.

You probably won't have to make a big deal out of your W and A. In this case, I think it's fine to WAC the person right back in an e-mail. This is not giving you license to WAC via e-mail on other issues. Simply write back and tell the person, "I'm sure you're not aware of this, but it's very difficult to read your messages. Please don't use all caps. Thanks."

It would not be Polite and Powerful to write: "WHEN YOU E-MAIL ME IN ALL CAPS I HATE IT. DO YOU UNDERSTAND WHY?"

It's okay to voice mail about a simple voice mail annoyance too. "Kathy, I'm sure you don't realize this, but if you don't leave me all the information on your message, I can't do the work on my end. In the future, please give me all the report information."

Some voice mail issues may be more delicate. For example, if the person leaves messages that are really long, he or she may be offended. It's probably better to handle this one face to face. "Kathy, when you leave such long messages, my system gets full and I can't get other important messages. Please just leave the essential facts and we'll connect later. Okay?" In this case, your nonverbals will help Kathy not be offended.

Stop. Think. Then Send.

No question, technological advances such as e-mail, voice mail, cellular telephones, and fax machines promote much faster, easier, and cheaper communication in the world. It's critical to keep in mind, however that how you use them can affect your relationships with others and your professional image.

Before you send an e-mail or fax or leave a voice mail message stop and ask yourself two things:

1. Why am I communicating this way? Is this appropriate?
2. Am I using the technology correctly? Am I possibly offending someone or sending the wrong message.

The key thing is to remember is that none of the technologies we've discussed can, or should, replace the person-to-person contact. If you keep e-mailing Aunt Margie because it beats getting trapped on the phone with her, that's not going to replace an actual visit or telephone call.

CHAPTER 16

INTERNATIONAL ETIQUETTE

How to Avoid Cultural Conflict Even in Your Own Backyard

Back in Chapter 5, the "jerk" chapter, we discussed international differences that may cause conflict. You may be thinking, "I'm not going anywhere, I don't need to know these things."

But you do. You do because you may encounter an international visitor in the U.S. and think he or she is a "jerk" for many mistaken reasons. This is an area of major conflict. If we don't understand the cultural differences, we are quick to put a negative spin on the person's behavior.

Like techno-etiquette, never before has this been such a hot issue.

The reason? Forget the global village. What we've woken up to is a thriving global metropolis. It's hustling and bustling with people of different nationalities, religions, beliefs and customs—many of whom you're likely to meet either socially, through work, or just walking on the street. Our business and social landscapes are increasingly international. With that come new conflicts—a cultural kind.

In fact, you can be on your best American behavior and still offend people. Take corn, for instance. Who thinks about etiquette implications of corn? Most of us don't. In the U.S. we eat corn on the cob and love it—period. Yet one day I served corn to my new Polish friend when she came to dinner and I could tell she was offended by something. When I asked, she said that in her experience in her country, corn is for farm animals only!

Now I know.

This chapter will help you deal with both sides of the international issue—when you're the traveler *and* when you stay at home and encounter international etiquette conflicts. You'll probably be surprised to discover how ripe this area is for misunderstanding.

When You're the Traveler

When you're the traveler, ignorance of another country's protocols and business etiquette issues is simply not acceptable. To operate successfully in the global arena, whether you're traveling abroad for vacation or for a big meeting, you first need to be aware of cultural differences, and then to understand the impact those differences have on both personal and business relationships.

Americans especially need to be better educated about international etiquette dos and don'ts. Since the United States is physically isolated from most other countries, Americans often grow up without much international awareness training. Most of the blunders Americans make while traveling internationally can genuinely be attributed to ignorance rather than malice—but as I've said in the last chapter, it's up to you to know the rules. You may not mean any harm but the damage is still done. Relationships have been damaged. You look foolish. Friends get their feelings hurt. Clients take their business elsewhere.

An American vice-president of a pharmaceutical company was in Japan. When he received his counterpart's business card, he proceeded to pick his teeth with it. That's certainly rude in the U.S., but very offensive behavior in Japan. This executive made a bad impression.

I was returning from Paris and the man next to me on the plane, once he discovered that I teach international etiquette, asked to me to explain why this incident occurred: He and his wife were in a fine French restaurant and the food was served. After he started eating he gave the waiter the "okay" signal because the food was great. All of a sudden there were three waiters yelling at him in French and waving their hands. He had no idea why they had come to his table!

I told him he had given them the "worthless" sign in French.

"Oops," he said. "I offended them and didn't even know it."

The same gesture means "money" in Japan and in parts of South America it is considered vulgar.

When you know how to handle yourself in international situations, you'll be more confident on your travels. You'll avoid conflict. You'll project a positive impression about yourself, and in some cases, your country.

The Rules of International Travel

Etiquette varies from culture to culture. Of course, culture is just one of the many contributing factors to behavior. Others include personality style, gender, age, religion, education, and the organizational climate in which the person works. Therefore, there are no absolutes; every rule for international etiquette is likely to have an exception.

But there is one basic guideline that can help you successfully navigate the globe. *If you're the traveler, you must adapt.*

Just as we expect visitors to our country to adopt our customs, you are expected to figure out how to function in another country. After all, you are the one who is doing the touring if you're on vacation. You're the one selling or representing if you're traveling for work. This means you must read and study before you go. Many culture-specific guidebooks, Websites and travel agents are available to tell you about the particular customs of the country you are visiting.

A woman once told me that when she visits Japan she has no intention of bowing. She said she would never bow to anyone. She would not be submissive.

I told her I disagreed. "This is an etiquette issue, not a power issue," I said.

What You Should Know Before You Go

There are many ways to cause misunderstanding and conflict

when you're traveling internationally. Doing a little reading and asking some questions before you leave can prevent a lot of it.

Before arriving in a foreign country, to avoid causing a problem make sure you know:

Some key phrases of the language
Greeting rituals
Dress code
Religious beliefs and customs
Customs regarding punctuality
Gift-giving etiquette
Social structure, such as the role of women
Business culture, such as how decisions are made

Learn a Few Key Phrases of Your Host's Language

You don't necessarily have to learn a whole language in order to make a positive impact when traveling abroad. Speaking even a few key words of a language can be a sign of mutual respect. Learn the basic greetings, including "hello" and courtesy comments, such as "please," "thank you," and "you're welcome." Just as you want to establish rapport in your own country, you want to establish rapport with others, especially your host, when traveling.

Take some language tapes on the plane with you. The doorman or concierge at your hotel can also often be helpful in teaching you correct pronunciation.

Avoid Jargon and Buzzwords

When traveling internationally, there are plenty of opportunities for misunderstanding, so don't add more by using phrases such as "beef it up" and "I'm all ears." Many American expressions do not translate well across languages.

An American businessman said: "Wow. You really jumped through hoops to get that accomplished."

His Korean counterpart thought he was saying that he didn't do the job correctly.

Slang phrases and jargon can confuse or even unintentionally insult another person.

Know Your Global Greetings

The handshake is not the only greeting in the world, though you will often encounter it when you travel. Be aware, however, that it may have a different feel than in the U.S.

In the United States, we believe that the appropriate handshake is firm. A limp handshake in Japan, however, is customary, not a sign of weakness. In Japan, though, the traditional greeting is the bow. Bowing is a gracious way to say "hello" and acknowledge another person. Men bow with their hands at their side, palms down on their thighs. Women bow with their hands folded in front. You must return a bow; failure to return a bow is rude.

Another aspect of the greeting in Japan is the business card exchange. As part of the greeting in Japan you should expect to exchange business cards. This exchange is more elaborate than in the U.S. where we are casual about handing out our cards. We often give each other business cards upon leaving, sometimes as an afterthought. In Japan, however, you give the card with two hands to show that you are giving it with respect, care, and attention. When you receive a card, show respect for it. Don't quickly put in your pocket. Hold it in your hand and examine it.

You may also be hugged or kissed in Latin America, the Middle East, or Europe. If you are unsure if a greeting involves kissing or hugging, let the other person start and follow his or her lead.

Don't React Negatively to Unfamiliar Customs

Don't make negative comments about a custom you find different, disagree with, or may even find offensive. Be respectful of the differences you encounter. Sometimes I'll say, "That's very different from what we experience in the United States." And occasionally when I am teaching in the Middle East, if I'm pressed for more information or to give my opinion I will say: "It would be very difficult for me to live under this system. I'm used to another way."

An engineer told me that she went to Taiwan and the first night she was there she went out to dinner with her colleague and his wife. The second night she went out to dinner with the man and his mistress. That rotation continued the whole week while she was there. While uncomfortable, especially at first, she understood that she was the visitor and so she did the Polite and Powerful thing—she went along with it.

Also, don't compare or brag too much about your own culture and customs. This is considered rude. You should focus on the customs of the culture in which you are visiting.

When in Abu Dhabi . . .

When you encounter a custom that's unfamiliar to you be open-minded. If you find yourself in a restaurant and your host begins to eat with his or her fingers, don't ask for a fork. Try eating with your fingers. You just might enjoy yourself. I did. I was very surprised that when I was in Abu Dhabi and one of my students took me out to dinner that I enjoyed eating with my fingers. Some foods are eaten with three fingers, others with five.

When you are given a strange food to eat, the guideline I give people is: Don't ask. Swallow quickly. Some other surprises you may encounter while dining overseas:

In parts of Europe you will be surprised to see owners with their dogs lying patiently on the floor in the restaurants while the owners eat and the dogs are very well behaved.

A consultant for an American corporation told me that on a recent trip overseas he ate the spinal cord of a cow. He feels it's his responsibility to eat, or at least try, what his hosts are eating. His clients think well of him for eating unfamiliar foods. If you don't think you could pull off eating a spinal cord, at least take a bite, to show your openness.

Others have told me they've eaten baby bees and live fish in Japan.

When I was working in the Middle East, another American woman told me she was disgusted by the treatment of women in this part of the world. She told me she was doing her best to "enlighten" all of the women she met—even strangers on the street. I tried to "enlighten" her. There are age-old customs and religious beliefs that inform all cultures. It was not this woman's job to go around pontificating. She was there to represent her company. She had set herself on a course to possibly offend a great number of people and not be invited back.

But what if you really feel strongly about an issue? Fine. If you do and choose to take on a role of an activist, that's a different matter. Don't become a visitor spouting opinions. Become involved with organizations that support your causes.

Be Cautious with Humor

Earlier, in discussing how to establish rapport with others, I advised you to be cautious with humor. As a former English as a second language teacher, I can tell you it's even more important to be judicious in your use of humor when dealing with ESL speakers. One of the ways to tell if someone is truly fluent in the language is whether they are able to joke in the language. This is a nuance that takes time. A Korean friend said it took him six years to finally "get" our sense of humor.

An international corporation based in the United States sent a manager to Japan. While there, he committed such a faux pas in telling a joke that they lost the contract. He was not an uneducated man. He just didn't know. And it was costly. He had used inappropriate humor.

Every culture varies when it comes to humor. There are also differences in the type of humor that is appreciated—or not appreciated—such as slapstick or puns. Something in the United States that is considered fair game for a joke may not be elsewhere. You should not joke about the Queen in England, for example.

Telling a joke will not enhance trust or your business relationship if it is misunderstood or unintentionally insulting. It's not even a good idea to joke about your own country. The person you're speaking with may not be familiar with your culture or your humor and again, you don't want to cause confusion. I tell my clients not to be humorous, but to have a sense of humor—that's important.

I was in Kuwait and was invited home to my host's house for dinner. His wife had spent a lot of time preparing as evident by the dining room table. It was covered with food from one end to the other. The first thing out of my mouth was "Do you think there is enough?" She took me seriously. To her, this wasn't funny. I had some backpedaling to do on that one.

Don't Expect Things to Be Done the "American" Way

Another area that causes problems for American travelers is that they expect things to be done the "American" way. But if you're in China, England, or Argentina, why would things be done the American way? You're not in America!

Again, it's up to you to adapt. You may be used to a noon lunch meeting, but in some countries lunch is eaten later. You may be used to staying late at the office to finish a project, but don't automatically expect the same from international co-workers. Some cultures believe that when the workday is over, it really is over.

Sometimes, the misunderstandings can be more serious. A Cuban woman working in the United States doesn't use e-mail to communicate with her boss; she feels it's too impersonal. But when her boss e-mails her, he expects an e-mail from her back. He doesn't understand why she insists on speaking to him in person. Why, he wonders, is she wasting his time?

Understand the Importance of Relationships

In her mind, the woman in the above example is not wasting her boss's time. She's building a relationship with him. Failure to understand that relationship-building is an important part of doing business in other cultures is the source of many international misunderstandings.

Many cultures do not embrace the American philosophy of getting right down to business, nor do they place the same emphasis on the value of work, or have the same management styles. In many cultures, you must establish a personal relationship before you can do business. Don't be impatient with this "getting to know you" step—it builds trust. You may even spend a lot of time socializing, but again, it's a necessary part of establishing the needed relationship.

Many foreign business professionals want, and need, to have relationships with the people they are interacting with.

Small Talk . . . Big Problems

Overseas, small talk isn't just a polite prelude to business discussions; it's a part of doing business. What you say will be used to establish a sense of who you are. Be prepared to discuss the country you are visiting. Read about the country before you go and pick up a newspaper while you are there.

As I mentioned in Chapter 14, when I gave you advice for making small talk, it's often best to avoid debating religion or politics. You can express your curiosity and interest in another culture's politics and religious beliefs, but these topics have potential for conflict.

Dress for International Success

Clothing is a form of nonverbal communication everywhere though what is considered appropriate attire varies according to climate, religion, and culture. Follow these guidelines for international dress:

1. Never dress up in "native" clothing. You are not a native, so don't try to look like one—you might be laughed at or considered rude.
2. When traveling on business, wear good quality conservative clothing.
3. If you're unsure of what to wear, ask your host or travel agent before your trip.

While in the Middle East I asked my agent—a kind of cultural tour guide—what would be appropriate to wear. He was very pleased that I had asked him, as this causes many problems for international visitors.

When I was getting ready to go to South America, I'm glad I asked. I was told to bring "dressy" clothes for evenings out. My traditional business garb wouldn't have been appropriate.

Know the Nuances of Nonverbal Communication

It's common to misinterpret the nuances of nonverbal communication if you're not prepared in advance. Eye contact, gestures, and space are two areas where many Americans have difficulty. Not only do misunderstandings occur, but many Americans also find that differences in eye contact and space can become serious impediments to their ability to listen and understand during conversations.

The meaning of gestures vary greatly across cultures, too. Roger E. Axtell in his book, *Gestures: The Do's and Taboos of Body Language Around The World,* notes that "identical acquired gestures mean different things among different countries. Since we use these acquired gestures unconsciously, it behooves us to become more conscious of what we are signaling and those signals may be misinterpreted. Each society has its own rules for gestures."

We'll discuss eye contact and space a little later on in this chapter.

Know the Rules of Gift-Giving

This one surprises people. How can you go wrong by giving or not giving a gift or the right one? A gift is still a gift!

In business, gifts can either contribute significantly to the development of a long-term business relationship, as is often the case in Russia, or be discouraged, as is often the case in Germany. Success at gift-giving in the international business arena requires knowing your host country's gift-giving customs. Make sure you ask the following before giving any gift: Does it violate any cultural or religious beliefs? Does the color or the item itself have an unintended meaning? Is the gift appropriate to the occasion?

Here are a few gift suggestions that are appropriate for gift-giving: chocolates, liquor (except in Arab countries), flowers (as long as they are appropriate in that culture), items particular to your state or region, baseball caps of famous sports teams, or good quality stationery and pens. Flowers vary in meaning: Don't give white lilies in England. It's for death and red roses are for lovers only in Germany. Also if you have a hobby or are really talented at something, like pottery, woodworking, or glass blowing, you can give a sample of your work for a gift.

International Etiquette in Your Own Backyard

In the beginning of this chapter, I told you if you are the visitor you must adapt. Ideally, all of these guidelines apply in reverse to international travelers visiting the United States.

Note my choice of the word "ideally." The reality is that people all over the world need a better understanding of international etiquette. When it comes to cultural issues, things are slow to change. We are slow to change. Visitors to this country are slow to change.

The other issue is that cultural diversity makes life more interesting. I enjoy, as I think many people do, learning the culture and customs of others. There needs to be a give and take, a willingness to learn on both sides. This is how cultural conflict will be avoided.

We had new Chilean neighbors. I had extended to them a casual dinner invitation for Sunday night. When the day came I called to talk about what time they should come over. No one was home. Around 4:00 P.M., I knocked on their door but still, no one was home. I figured it was casual so they either forgot or just couldn't make it. No big deal. At 6:30 P.M. we sat down to dinner. At 7:00 P.M. the doorbell rang. It was my neighbor asking what time dinner was going to be.

As we discovered, Chileans traditionally eat very late, around 10:00 P.M. in the evening. We all laughed at this misunderstanding. These neighbors ended up becoming good friends. We compromised and usually had dinner around 8:00 P.M. Later for us and earlier for them.

Conflict will also be avoided by your willingness to be gracious as well as Polite and Powerful. I was teaching a Japanese family about American culture. They had just arrived in the U.S. When they entered my office they bowed to me. I bowed back. You should have seen the smiles on their faces. It made all the difference in our ability to establish rapport.

So What Are the Guidelines?

If you're at home, you're in your own culture. You aren't technically required to adapt or change your behavior. However, I encourage you to be open-minded when you encounter cultural differences. Your life will be more interesting and less stressful if you do.

All of the guidelines I gave you for when you're the traveler can apply even when you don't leave your own town. However, there are some common conflict areas Americans have when encountering internationals at home:

Don't React Negatively to Different Customs

A Brazilian woman who had just come to the U.S. kissed me good-bye after just meeting me. I was taken aback, but kissed her cheek back.

It's never a reason to act hostile or rudely to a foreign person because he or she doesn't know or follow our customs. He or she should make every effort to come here and adapt, true, but it may take time, the person may not have the same resources that you do, and he or she may not have the same desire to free themselves of conflict that you do.

Increased awareness on your part, however, about the rules of international etiquette can free you of one burden: Thinking the person is a jerk, out to get you, or just being flat out rude. When you understand that the person is probably operating out of ignorance, and not directing any behavior at you deliberately or personally, it's easier to "let it go."

But what if you're really bothered by a custom your international colleague or friend practices while visiting here? You can speak up and communicate your discomfort—but do it Politely and Powerfully:

- **Be discreet.** Don't correct someone publicly. Take him or her aside and discreetly WAC them: "I'm sure you have no idea (softening statement) that in this country men don't hug each other in business. (What's bothering you.) I don't mind because I know you, but it would be better if you made a habit of just shaking hands. (What you've asked him to do.) Okay?" (Check-in).

- **Don't insult.** You're not putting down their custom, you're simply informing him or her of ours. Don't say anything harsh, such as; "We wouldn't dare do such a thing here!" Be polite and sensitive about it. More positive wording for your W would be: "It is customary in the U.S. to wait in line . . ."

- **Follow up.** Check in with the person to see how he or she is managing. Make yourself available. Be helpful and supportive. Become a mentor. Answer any questions the person may have about American culture. If you are hosting an international visitor, it's your responsibility to help them adapt and be comfortable.

Nonverbal Differences Can Make a Difference

You know by now the importance of having good control over your nonverbal messages. It's important to understand nonverbal messages that vary from culture to culture. I know a head nurse at a U.S. hospital who was working with an Asian doctor on a project. They met weekly. The nurse was getting increasingly annoyed because when they would meet the doctor did not look at her. She thought the doctor didn't value her since she was the nurse. One day the nurse exploded at the doctor, "Who do you think you are? You think you are better than I am. The least you can do is show me some respect and look at me when we are talking."

The doctor looked up and said, "But I am showing you respect." (This nurse felt like a jerk. A big one!)

Eye Contact

In many Asian cultures it is a sign of respect to avert the eyes. Yet in the United States we don't trust people who don't look at us. We think they're sneaky, shifty, hiding something, or "that jerk is just plain not listening to me!"

Many cultures use direct eye contact to indicate sincerity, attention, and respect. In many other cultures, direct eye contact means the exact opposite. Americans in particular have difficulty with people who don't make eye contact since American culture says that such a person may be evasive, deceptive, or simply not listening. You need to be aware that eye contact says and means different things depending upon the person's culture you're dealing with.

Space

I hope the Bubble Man—the man who likes a wide bubble of space between him and the other person—never gets a visit from a Middle Eastern or Latin American person. People stand closer in these countries and they often do so when traveling.

We very quickly make negative assumptions about people based on space. I was at the home of a French business associate who had relocated to the United States. He sat down next to me on the couch to show me renovation pictures. He was so close to me I couldn't focus. This man wasn't "coming on to me" or "invading my space." The French are more comfortable with closeness. Once I remembered this, I was able to relax.

It's common for people to tell me about international colleagues who stand too close. They don't like it. But they do get used to it. Both sides must adjust. A physician told me that she could always tell the difference between the first- and second-year Arab interns. The second year students learned to adapt to our custom and stood further away.

When approaching someone from another country, whether you're here or there, always be aware of your proximity to that person. There is no international average distance that people should stand apart. In some cases, the American average of three feet will be too close, while in others it's too far away.

Generally people in the Middle East, Latin America, Italy, Russia, France, and Spain will stand closer together than Americans do. Arabs may stand as close as two to three inches and to back away from them is considered an insult. Asians will usually stand further away. It's important to know what your comfort level is with space. Be prepared at times to communicate in your discomfort zone.

Global Greetings

Don't make assumptions about international people based on their handshake. I hear about this one a lot from Americans who deal with people of different cultures for business. This is a common area of misunderstanding that can lead to conflict.

A pharmaceutical sales representative went to shake hands with an Asian physician and she received a limp handshake. The rep said: "I immediately lost respect for her."

Fortunately, she was able to remind herself that it was probably a cultural difference. Not only did she adjust her attitude, she loosened the grip on her handshake when meeting with her Asian customer in the future.

If you're meeting with an international person here, keep in mind they have the same issues we do. Often, their customs take over before they know it. An Argentinean man told me he had to learn not to hug his American counterparts. He knew the U.S. greeting but he was so accustomed to hugging, it was difficult.

If you receive an unexpected greeting from an international visitor, don't act rudely. Return the greeting. While it's the traveler's responsibility to adapt, it's also your responsibility to be gracious. People naturally want to share their culture with you. It's a wonderful opportunity to learn. But if you're uncomfortable being hugged by someone, follow the guideline I gave you for WAC'ing on cultural issues. You can tell him or her, "In this country, the traditional greeting is the handshake. Let's use that greeting from now on."

Be Sensitive about Language Differences

I have a Belgian friend who said that he was a slow learner. He didn't learn his fifth language until he was twenty-two!

While it's true that many people all over the world speak English, especially international business people who speak our language quite well, you need to appreciate that it's usually their second, or even third language. We are very critical of others who are not speaking English well. Yet those who are critical are usually only able to speak one language.

My Polish friend and I decided to help each other learn the other's language. I said to her one day, "Polish is so hard!" She looked at me in surprise and said, "English is so hard." I stopped complaining.

You often need to speak slower, not louder. It really isn't funny to watch Americans shout at others who are speaking English as a second language. They are showing their ignorance.

Differences in English

"Where's the ladies' room?"
"Take the lift to the loo."
"Thanks. What's a lift? And oh, what's a loo?"

And remember, even if the person you're speaking with does speak English as a first language, such as in England or Australia, you still need to be aware of differences in the meaning of words and phrases. For example, "I bombed on the presentation" means you performed poorly in the U.S., but in England means you did well.

A man from the United Arab Emirates told me that when he was living in the United States, he told his American girlfriend that she looked "like a deer." To him, this was a compliment because deer in Arabic is an attractive animal/term. She was offended and told him, "You look like a donkey." (Which was not Polite and Powerful on her part by the way.)

If you are unclear about the meaning of a word or phrase, don't be shy, ask. It will help your avoid misunderstanding if you do.

Polite and Powerful is an International Language

No matter where on Earth you travel, if you are Polite and Powerful within the context of each culture you travel to, you will be a happier and less stressed traveler.

Even if you meet an international traveler who is not adhering to our customs, give the person the benefit of the doubt. He is probably not a jerk. If you have a relationship with the person, try to help him or her adapt.

And don't forget . . . give yourself a chance. It may take time to learn new behaviors, and you may occasionally err, but if your effort is sincere, that will count in your favor. Effective global etiquette will ultimately say that you are a respectful, gracious, and Polite and Powerful person. You are the kind of person that I want to do business with or would be happy to meet on the street.

A Final 12-Step
Pep Talk

Congratulations! You're no longer a pretender, avoider, complainer, displacer, self-discounter, bully, or shouter. But you may be wondering how to get started as a Polite and Powerful person. We've covered a lot of ground together about positive confrontation and conflict avoidance! It's a lot to learn, yes. What should you do first?

First, take your time—you don't have to learn and implement everything in this book overnight. (All along, I've cautioned you against running out the door with your WAC'em arms flapping. Don't fly into work tomorrow, swoop down, and WAC your boss.) Work your way up to the big ones.

Here's a twelve-step plan to help you get organized:

1. Start where the book starts—with self-awareness. Take a few days and tune into who you are as a confronter and as a communicator. You don't have to do anything other than think and reflect. Keep a journal—even a small memo pad will do. Writing down things you realize about yourself for a few days will help you pinpoint your areas for improvement. Review the self-assessment exercise on page 29. Tell yourself: "I'm tired of being a bully (or a displac-

er, or a pretender . . .) it's time to change."

2. Believe that you have a right to tell someone else in an honest, direct, and polite manner how their behavior affects you. Believe that whatever obstacles may have been holding you back before *can* and *will* be removed.

3. Self awareness will allow you to move to the next step—focus on the areas of your confrontational style and communications skills that you feel you may need the most immediate help with—whether it be not shouting at others when you get upset or standing without crossing your feet or crossing your arms. Practice—you can break bad habits. I have seen people think, "I can't" and yet they do.

4. Before you decide to confront anyone—give the person the jerk test. Do they really mean you harm? Review all the reasons in Chapter 5 that may be the cause of the conflict. Is this one to let go?

5. If you decide to have a confrontation, prepare your WAC'em wording. Review all the steps in Chapter 6 that will help you figure out:
   W = What's Bothering Me? (Be specific)
   A = What Do I Want To Ask the Person To Do or Change? (Be specific)
   C = Your Check-In with the Other Person
   Once you have your WAC'em wording right, review the Eleven Simple Things You Can Do to make your confrontation positive. Role-play with a friend.

6. Believe that you can have a positive confrontation.

7. Come up with an exit line that you can use in case the confrontation starts to not go well so you can get out of the room. You can always WAC another day. "I can see this isn't a good time, let's talk again later," or "I'm getting myself a little worked up; I'll pick this up with you later."

8. Use your WAC'em card on the dust jacket of this book to help you review your W, A, and C before your difficult conversations start. Keep it in your wallet or purse so that you can pull it out in case of emergency.

9. Take inventory of how you did and what you would like to

do differently in the future. Do not expect perfection of yourself, in the beginning or ever. The power of positive confrontation is a skill you can learn. You can get better at it—and you will.

10. Follow up with the other person. You won't change overnight and the person you WAC won't either.

11. Once you feel comfortable in the world of positive confrontation, make an effort to reduce potential conflict in your life. Go back and review the etiquette skills you've learned in Part III of this book.

12. Enjoy the benefits of positive confrontation: You will be able to let things go. You will feel better about yourself. You will improve your relationships with others. You won't waste time avoiding or dreading difficult conversations. You will understand how to treat others Politely and Powerfully.

I Want to Hear From You

Send me your success stories so that I can share them with others. You'll also find additional information, tips, and advice on my Web site. Good luck, and don't forget—even if you don't get exactly what you want out of confrontation, if you handle yourself Politely and Powerfully, you can still feel good about yourself.

Like the many men and women I've taught Polite and Powerful behavior to over the last ten years, I hope you enjoy the benefits of living a less stressed out, conflict free life.

Good luck!

ABOUT THE AUTHORS

Barbara Pachter is a business communications consultant, speaker, and seminar leader who speaks nationally and internationally on topics including assertiveness, business etiquette, international communications, women's issues, and presentation skills. She has conducted over 1,300 skill-building seminars for clients including NASA, Merck & Co., IBM, Arthur Andersen, and Pfizer, Inc. She is an adjunct professor at Rutgers University and the co-author of four books on business etiquette and communication skills, including *The Prentice Hall Complete Business Etiquette Handbook*. She lives in Cherry Hill, New Jersey.

Susan Magee is an award-winning writer whose articles and stories have appeared in many magazines and newspapers around the country. She lives in Philadelphia.

Barbara Pachter can be reached at:
Pachter & Associates
P.O. Box 3680
Cherry Hill, NJ 08034
Telephone (856) 751-6141
Fax (856) 751-6857
E-mail: pachter@ix.netcom.com
www.pachter.com